COMMUNISM: A TARNISHED PROMISE

The Story of an Idea

James R. Ozinga

Oakland University

CHARLES E. MERRILL PUBLISHING COMPANY

A Bell & Howell Company

Columbus, Ohio

For Kurt and Karen

two excellent chips
from an aging block

Merrill Political Science Series

Under the editorship of

John C. Wahlke

Department of Political Science

The University of Iowa

Published by
Charles E. Merrill Publishing Company
A Bell & Howell Company
Columbus, Ohio 43216

This book was set in Times Roman.
The Production Editor was Linda Lowell.
The cover was designed by Will Chenoweth.

ISBN: 0-675-08697-3

Library of Congress Catalog Card Number: 74-31980

1 2 3 4 5 6 7 8—82 81 80 79 78 77 76 75

Printed in the United States of America

Preface

The word communism has had a long history. It has been used to characterize the society of early hunters and gatherers, Plato's philosopher-kings, and the early Christian community. In more recent history the word described the social attempts of sixteenth-century religious groups such as the Anabaptists, and the secular seventeenth-century English movement known as the Diggers, or True Levellers. The underlying meaning of the word in these examples was a sharing of whatever there was to share within the group.

By the mid-eighteenth century communism was a more general critique of society. It had become an indictment of private property as well as an optimistic statement about human character. It drew life from criticisms of civilization's progress or lack of it and became one of the ways of expressing discontent with the established society. Particularly in response to the enormous changes brought about by the industrial revolution, communism was nearly indistinguishable from socialism in its protest against the great disparities of wealth that were furthered by capitalist private property. These attacks were often expressed in the context of frustrated aspirations of the French Revolution, and revealed many different varieties and leaders of communism.

One such leader was Karl Marx. He easily eclipsed the influence of the others by the first quarter of the twentieth century, however, not because he so coherently blended Hegelianism, French revolutionary frustrations, and an analysis of economics in Britain; but because his particular interpretation, expanded on by Engels, became the ideological vehicle for Lenin's successful seizure of power in Russia in 1917. From that point on,

Marxian communism as adapted by the Russians had the power of a large state behind it. Subsequent to the Second World War other nations and parts of nations were drawn into this ideological framework, for example, Eastern Europe through Soviet conquest, and China as a result of a prolonged, indigenous guerrilla war. Very large and powerful nations now advanced adapted Marxist ideas and implemented them in various ways.

Although most people hearing the word communism would now equate it with Russia or China, or perhaps Cuba, the word still retains its larger meaning. A kibbutz in Israel emphasizes social sharing without reference to these nations or even to Marx. Some coal miners in Britain advocate a communism that is equally distinct. *Within* so-called socialist countries Marxian communism itself can be a method of protest against governmental communist practices, demanding a return to the humanistic spirit of Marx.

This book is an attempt to trace the development of these ideas. Beginning with Marx and his background, the idea of communism is presented as it has developed into the bewildering variety of meanings that it holds today. Therefore, the book is not only about modern communism in the sense of showing how, why, and when it developed, but also into what it developed. There are, however, so many books on communism and Marxism. Why another?

The answer has to be a personal one, stemming from teaching university courses on communism for over seven years. During this time I have used many different books as texts, and have continued to experience the same difficulty. Books that attempted to tell the whole story were so general and so lacking in significant detail that they were practically useless. Books on specific parts of the course, such as Lichtheim's *Marxism,* contained so many small details that students would read it only if great pressure were applied. McLellan's *Marx Before Marxism* and Meyer's *Leninism,* for example, are very good books, but several texts would be necessary, each with a different style and approach to the subject.

The decision to write my own text stems from a desire to tell the whole, detailed story simply and accurately, without the carping, nit-picking criticisms of the cold warriors, or the smothering ideological jargon of the professional Marxist. In attempting to walk a line between the two I am probably subject to the liberal dilemma—being criticized from both sides. But like Luther here I stand, sympathetic, but critical in regard to Marx, and sympathetic to what Lenin tried to do, yet very critical of what he did do, even though some advances were made. Mao's successful adaptation of Marxism to tradition in China arouses less criticism, but that does not mean that I would urge Maoism on my American contemporaries.

Moreover, new adaptations of Marxism are necessary to test its applicability to countries such as the United States or to the new awareness of a global system of international cooperation. In the last fifteen years one such adaptation has been seen in the development of the New Left in the United States and Western Europe. A more exciting and promising adaptation of Marxism for the future lies in the blending of the enduring aspects of Marxism with a general theory of systems to provide an international framework of humanistic survival in the twenty-first century.

The book, therefore, begins with the background of Marx and ends by evaluating the New Left and describing how Marxism and a general theory of systems fit together for the future. The title of the book is an expression of my own belief that Marxism does contain a promise, the promise of a humanized future for all people both present and future, but that the promise of Marxism is at the same time heavily tarnished. Can the "discolorations" be removed?

The purpose of the book is most definitely not to gain converts to *any* position, but simply to teach. Some people use Marxian dogma or jargon without understanding either it or the society to which they uncritically wish to apply it. Some black groups, some colleagues, some feminist groups, even a few student ecology groups profess a Marxism that I do not often understand. Other people react with *hostility* to a communism they do not at all comprehend. This book is for all those people.

Telling the whole story, of course, would be beyond the scope of any book if one meant to include every detail and nuance of meaning. I do not think that this is necessary to accomplish what I have in mind. Details that would not help the reader's understanding have been omitted. Although such judgments are based on extensive teaching experience they are personal ones. In several places in the text I wanted to add a footnote which read: "Details to be supplied by the professor." This book should communicate the whole story on its own, but it was written for use in a classroom where only a semester's time-constraints limit the amount of additional material that a teacher might supply.

Although footnotes have been kept to a minimum, I have included occasional statements in the words of the person whose ideas are being described so that all of the original flavor has not been lost. Suggested readings at the end of each chapter highlight books found to be useful in addition to those cited in the footnotes. In addition, a conscious attempt was made to avoid language sexism throughout the book.

Writing about ideological subjects always seems to require the use of a vocabulary unfamiliar to the student. Instead of becoming involved with definitions in the text or with many lengthy footnotes, a glossary of possible problem words and concepts is included at the end of the book. Glossary entries are in bold-faced type when they first appear in the text. Readers are urged to consult the glossary and the index for assistance.

If errors of grammar, style, or fact occur in what follows it has not been for want of effective and constructive criticism. My wife, Suzanne, would often come home from work during my sabbatical to discover not a waiting dinner but a waiting chapter. Her patience and contributions were monumental. My colleagues and friends—Tom Greene, George Klein, Mel Cherno, and Robbin Hough—read either all or parts of the manuscript. Their assistance was invaluable. My typist, Marian Wilson, performed with great speed and skill, and my editor, Linda Lowell, provided technical criticisms that were very beneficial. To all these busy people I send my warmest thanks. If any errors remain, the responsibility is my own.

Contents

PART I   MARXISM

Chapter 1	The Background of Marxism	**1**
Chapter 2	The Development of Marxism	**19**
Chapter 3	Historical Materialism	**35**
Chapter 4	The Marxian Future	**51**
Chapter 5	The Interregnum: Marxism in Europe 1870-1917	**65**

PART II   THE BOLSHEVIZATION OF MARXISM

Chapter 6	Russia and Lenin	**83**
Chapter 7	Bolshevism in Practice	**103**
Chapter 8	The Expansion of Bolshevism	**123**

PART III   ALTERNATIVES TO BOLSHEVISM

Chapter 9   China: Theory and Practice   **149**

Chapter 10   Minor Chords   **171**

PART IV   NEW DIRECTIONS FOR MARXISM

Chapter 11   The United States: The Communist Party and
                the New Left—A Study in Contrasts   **195**

Chapter 12   Toward the Twenty-First Century: Marxism in
                the Future   **213**

GLOSSARY   **231**

INDEX   **249**

PART I

Marxism

1

The Background of Marxism

Marxism can be perceived as a combination of three elements: British economics, French political ideology, and German philosophy. The economics is the direct result of the industrial revolution; the political ideology represents the aftermath of the French Revolution; and the philosophy is that of Georg W. F. Hegel and his followers. When Karl Marx was growing up in the Rhineland this trinity dominated intellectual life; therefore, examining these three elements will provide insights that will make Marxism much more understandable.

The Industrial Revolution

The industrial revolution was not something that began and ended on specific dates. Indeed, it is not yet over. The dates given as to when it did begin are somewhat arbitrary. However, a very significant shift in British capitalism occurred in the period from 1780 to 1790—a shift from mercantile to industrial capitalism. Earlier British economics was characterized by *cottage industry*—a "putting-out" system which was loosely organized by merchants. The individual craftsmen worked under contract to the merchant. These workers were in scattered areas, and production was essentially a hand-tool operation.

After 1780 production increasingly became a factory operation with machinery doing much more of the manufacturing than ever before. These factories required enormous quantities of laborers who now became concentrated in one area, rather than scattered. A factory was usually located near a source of transportation—the sea or a navigable river. Thus, several factories could be located within a limited area. Central industrial centers quickly grew, and around them clustered the newly developed industrial working class. This spatial concentration was called *urbanization*.

Why did such changes occur in Britain at that particular time? The explanation is simple—a number of factors happened to mature simultaneously around 1780, and taken together they help to explain why the industrial revolution occurred.

A very important factor was inventiveness—the development of the technology necessary for a factory economy. This was encouraged in Britain by offering prizes for industrial inventions, developing good patent laws, and producing enormous long-range profits for the inventors. These inventions created the machinery that made the factories possible. At first, the inventions were concentrated in the cotton industry, a key industry at that time. However, the technological explosion in cotton manufacturing created inventiveness in other areas, such as using steam for land transportation. This led to the railroad, which, in turn, stimulated the metal industry and resulted in better iron and steel. And so it went: an invention in one area triggered inventiveness in many others.

Another very important influence was the nature of British agriculture in the eighteenth century. The European world was predominantly agricultural. Even though there were many towns, they were centered around farming. East of the Elbe River were vast estates containing millions of acres of land and perpetuating serfdom, absentee landlordism, and very traditional farming methods. West of the Elbe were more independent farmers who sold crop surpluses to the urban or town market. A few areas, however, had been pushed even further in the direction of a capitalist agriculture, notably northern Italy, the Netherlands, and England. In England, landownership was very concentrated, but the average cultivator was a medium-sized tenant farmer who operated with hired labor. This reduced individual farming and, when coupled with a rising population, created a surplus of laborers who began the urban migration. These tendencies in the rural areas were encouraged by the conversion of English agriculture to wool production; enclosure acts which made more land available for commercial farming; and Corn Laws which maintained an artificially high domestic price for grains until the mid-nineteenth century.

A number of other factors were also significant at that time. England possessed a worldwide market; a very stable government; sufficient raw materials; no real transportation problems because of the surrounding sea; and sufficient risk capital to make industrialization operable. By combining inventiveness, surplus labor, and the snowballing impact of innovation, a comprehension of the industrial revolution begins to emerge.

The results included a dramatic alteration in the life-style of most English families. A great many more goods, which would raise the standard of living for all the English population, were being produced by the new industries. However, by the early nineteenth century it certainly did not seem as though the working class was benefiting at all. The workers' cottages were in the lowest, dampest, and worst sections of the city. Usually, each cottage had several families living in one or two rooms. Disease was rampant. Not that they were worse off than they had been in the country. On the contrary, they were probably better off in the city. However, that made their new condition even more deplorable; the rural poverty was a scattered, out-of-sight poverty, whereas the terrible conditions of life and work in the cities were open for people to see and smell. Scattered primitive sanitation facilities were one thing, but *concentrated* primitive sanitation was quite another.

In the country one might hedge against slack times by working in a garden; in the city this was not possible and the low-paid worker was extremely vulnerable to the periodic economic crises. Hunger was common. One at least saw daylight in the country, but in the city gas-lighted factories made it possible to begin and end the day in darkness. Work days were very long. In the country work rhythms were seasonal, but in the city one was subjected to the discipline of the machine, which was often treated far better than the person who operated it. Women were employed at lower wages than men and children began working at eight years or earlier. Entire families eked out their existence in the poorly lit, crowded, and seldom policed working class sections of the city.

The obvious plight of the working class had three decisive consequences, none of which is entirely exclusive of the others. The first was the humanitarian concern about labor's condition, which resulted in parliamentary legislation in 1802, 1819, 1825, 1831, and 1833. The most important of these was the Factory Act of 1833. Some details of that act might create an understanding of what life was like. The act provided that children under nine were no longer to be employed. Also, children between the ages of nine and thirteen could work no more than a 48-hour week and must receive two hours of schooling each day. Those fortunate children between the ages of thirteen and eighteen were now prohibited from working more than 68 hours per week. The act only applied to the large textile industries, and it was poorly enforced. Even so, this was an advance, and further legislation would improve conditions still more. But during the first half of the nineteenth century such legislation had a very minimal impact on the conditions of workers and their families.

A second result of the workers' condition was the beginning of organized activity in labor unions. Initially prohibited as a result of fears stimulated by the French Revolution, labor unions became legal in 1825; however, they met strong opposition. In 1830 an attempt was made to bring all the small unions together into one large Grand National Consolidated Trades Union. A few months later a subunit of this union was formed in Dorchester by six workers. They were arrested and received prison terms of seven years. The Grand National quickly dissolved. In 1838 the labor movement became more political and expressed its opposition by means of a charter which demanded universal manhood suffrage and other reforms that would have given the workers a better chance to be represented in the government, but this too failed. By 1848 the *Chartist movement,* as it had come to be called, collapsed.

A third result of the workers' plight was the development of socialism. One of the individuals behind the Grand National Consolidated Trades Union movement was Robert Owen. Owen was an industrialist in the cotton industry who, in 1789, borrowed £100 and twenty years later bought out his partners for £84,000 in cash. Owen became a socialist because of his concern for his own workers, which resulted in improving the conditions of his labor force, and because of the great difficulty he and others encountered in getting parliament to pass strong reform legislation. Friedrich Engels called Robert Owen the father of English socialism, but Engels realized it was a reformist (nonrevolutionary) sort of socialism. This *reformism* would characterize English socialism throughout the nineteenth century, but it *was* socialism—workers through their cooperatives would become the joint owners of the production process.

The 1820s and 1830s also saw a more theoretical socialism emerge from the *Ricardian* socialists. These economists proceeded on the assumption, sanctified by John Locke, that value was created by human labor. If this were true, they insisted, the laboring class deserved the entire product of industry (with perhaps a pittance for the capitalist owner), for they had created the value in the commodity, instead of vice-versa. This sort of thinking enjoyed a brief heyday and much of Owenite thinking blended with that of the Ricardian socialists, but it all faded into memory around the middle of the century.

What did all this have to do with Marx? The continental industrial revolution began in Belgium around 1810, then reached France and slowly began to penetrate the German area.* It was clearly moving from Britain in an eastward direction. On the western side of Germany lay the Rhineland where Karl Marx was born in 1818. He grew to young adulthood in the area where German industrialization began. In 1833, when Marx was fifteen years old, the *Zollverein,* or Customs Union, was established and was successful in reducing local tariff barriers to the new economy. In 1852, when Marx was thirty-four years old, this Customs Union had spread over most of Germany. The change had occurred during his lifetime. However, Britain became Marx's example for the economic future because France never overcame the small-scale levels of industrialization with which it began, and Germany remained far behind France until after 1871, when industrialization was deliberately encouraged as state policy after German unification.

The French Revolution

The political future of Germany had no stronger influence than that of France because of the impact its revolution had on Europe, which lasted for decades into the nineteenth century. England's political revolution had occurred in the seventeenth century, followed by an industrial revolution; France's revolution occurred in the eighteenth century and was also followed by industrialization. It seemed logical that both types of revolution were next destined for Germany. However, presenting the material in this way makes it seem far more theoretical than it was at that time. Marx, living in the Rhineland, which had been a part of France from 1794 to 1815, could not avoid the consequences of the French Revolution. In order to describe those consequences it is necessary to understand the Revolution itself.

Prerevolutionary France was ruled by absolute monarchs. The society could be divided into two groups—the privileged and the unprivileged. The first group included the First and Second Estates—the clergy and nobility; the second referred to the Third Estate, which comprised about 98 percent of the population. What basically distinguished the first two estates from the third was privilege in regard to taxation—exemption being proof of social status. Naturally this involved the monarch in periodic disputes with the first two orders in the society, for a continuing need for more funds for government was as much a need in the eighteenth century as it is in the twentieth. However, the clergy (high-ranking clergy, not the poor parish priests) and the nobility resisted new taxes on themselves, and that left the large Third Estate to carry the tax burden.

The Third Estate was a very sizable producing group containing many levels of people. From the very poor at the bottom of the group to the very wealthy businessmen at the top, all were contained in this estate. They were the overwhelming majority of the population supporting the thin layer of the privileged, from whom they often received contempt. This situation did not go unnoticed. In fact, a growing body of people was beginning to deplore these circumstances. The ideas of John Locke and Isaac Newton had stimulated the Age of Enlightenment in France, an Age of Reason—a time when the entire universe seemed comprehendible when no problem could long escape the enlightened reason of humans. Although most intellectuals saw a more enlightened monarchy as the solution to France's problems, that enlightenment would soon spread beyond the monarchy, including many other groups as well. This was the theme of the very influential *Encyclopédie,* a seventeen-volume effort on the part of several French intellectuals known as *philosophes.* Their liberalism and humanitarianism helped to undermine confidence in the old ways of doing things.

The French philosopher Charles Montesquieu was an even sharper critic in his hatred of arbitrary government. He wrote *Spirit of the Laws* in 1748, clearly underscoring his belief in the universality of reason as the link between God and humanity. That universal reason was the spirit of the laws, and, for example, differences from one area to another were explainable on the basis of differences in climate. Montesquieu felt that the key to liberty lay in the triadic separation of powers, which he thought he had witnessed in England.

Although not immediately influential, an even more pointed critic was Jean Jacques Rousseau. He not only attacked the present system but civilization as well, with opinions opposing the majority's veneration of the omnipotence of reason. Rousseau insisted that civilization represented false progress, for it began accidentally when reason overcame emotions, and isolation from others smothered simple compassion and patriotism. This condition of alienation resulted in property, which created the need to protect it, and the forces of the poor were marshalled to make secure the property of the rich. As the despot was maintained by force, he could be overthrown in the same way.

At this point Rousseau became involved with how one reinstituted authority subsequent to a revolution (the *Social Contract*), thus his real influence came after the French Revolution had occurred. He insisted that the sovereignty of the people could not be represented; they would all have to vote on issues, but what would emerge from this direct democracy would be a collective sovereignty called the *General Will* that would in fact be the sovereign. Previous individual liberty would be replaced by *associational liberty* wherein people would obey those laws which they themselves had helped to make. The fact that the citizens might have to be manipulated somewhat did not bother Rousseau. Life would be simple again.

However, these ideas of rationality, feeling, liberty, and humanitarianism were not the immediate causes of the French Revolution. The immediate precipitator was the desire of the first two orders, the privileged ones, to protect their tax exemptions against the new demands of Louis XVI. He was in financial trouble because he had assisted the American colonies against the British to avenge his grandfather's losses to the British in the Seven Years War (1756-63). His depleted treasury pushed him to seek financial advice, but the only solution seemed to be the removal of privileges from groups that had become accustomed to them. The first two orders refused his request, claiming that they had no authority to do anything so drastic without a meeting of the medieval *States General,* which had not met since 1614. This was an assembly made up of representatives of all three estates. Since the three estates would meet with equal numbers of representatives for each, the first two could dominate the third, keep their privileges, and once again the Third Estate would be picking up the burden.

An aristocratic revolt was what finally started the trouble, but it quickly turned into a revolt of the Third Estate, which unwisely saw in the forthcoming States General meeting a means of redressing past wrongs. This was especially true when its demands for double representation were met, and, as an equal, it faced the other two estates considered together.

It should surprise no one that when the States General finally met in May of 1789 the issue of whether to vote as estate blocks, which gave an advantage to the first two orders, or whether to vote by head count deadlocked the meetings. This frustration led the Third Estate representatives to start meeting by themselves, and what made their action revolutionary was their declaration that *they* constituted the National Assembly of France. The king locked their meeting place, but they moved to an indoor tennis court where they took an oath not to disband until they had written a constitution for France. Reluctantly, a week later, the king recognized the *fait accompli.* The aristocratic revolt had quickly become a revolution from below.

In July rumors circulated that the king was intending to use force to unseat the Assembly, and this caused mobs to storm the prison known as the Bastille in order to protect the Assembly and the revolution. Things were decidedly moving. In August 1789 the Assembly passed laws abolishing the feudal system. Most manorial obligations were removed, special tax privileges were abolished, and differentially taxed geographical districts were made equal with the rest. These were items of great benefit to business and professional people, the leading group of the Third Estate, and had the effect of opening all offices in the government to all citizens, regardless of birth. Later the same month, the famous Declaration of the

Rights of Man and Citizen guaranteed freedom of speech, press, assembly, religion, equality before the law, universal tax obligations, rights of private property, and the right to due process.

These were efforts by the Assembly to implement liberty, equality of opportunity, and fraternity that continued in 1791 with a new constitution limiting the monarchy, and with the Civil Constitution of the Clergy making clergymen employees of the state. This last step was necessary since church lands had been confiscated for revenue. Clergymen would still receive stipends, but only if they declared allegiance to the new state. This proved to be very difficult for many. The Pope objected strenuously. The king tried to leave France, but he was brought back and placed under a semblance of house arrest. The question was now more frequently heard: what do we do with the king? Newly-developing republicans argued that he could not be trusted; he had just proven that by his attempted flight. Most assemblymen, however, distrusted republicanism as a dangerously radical doctrine, and the limited monarchy continued.

Events quickly took charge, however, for the impending war with Prussia and Austria (as well as England after 1793) demanded the Assembly's attention. The republicans wanted war because they hoped Louis' unreliability would become manifest. The royalists backed war because they thought that no matter what happened the king would win. If France were victorious he would gain prestige. If France lost, the victorious Prussians would reestablish him on his throne. But even the best of plans occasionally falls apart. The war went badly at first and the outcome would have been worse if Prussia had not been preoccupied with dismembering Poland. Rumors of Louis' treason became so prevalent that the Assembly met in 1792 to write yet another constitution that ended the monarchy and established a republic. Although the new government faced an expanded war and tremendous dissension at home, French revolutionary morale was high, especially after the king was executed on January 21, 1793, for "multiple crimes."

In June of 1793, political struggling in the Assembly resulted in the triumph of the Jacobin faction led by men such as Robespierre, an idealist and humanist who implemented the notion that the ends justify the means. Increasingly the revolutionary path was narrowed; opposition to the new General Will was labelled counterrevolutionary and punished by the guillotine. The *Reign of Terror,* that period of hysteria in France, was often matched by terrorism in other countries against those whose governments felt were in support of the Jacobins. As the circle of terror widened in France, however, opposition began to grow. When the war started to go well and more attention could be directed to domestic affairs, the Jacobins were overthrown and became victims themselves. By 1795 another constitution was written which was more conservative, and the franchise was more restricted.

This seeming return to the past, which many thought had been left forever, sparked a radical uprising in 1796 by people who sincerely believed the revolution must be resumed. They wanted to confiscate wealth and generalize equality. The legacy of liberty, equality, and brotherhood had not yet been accomplished, thus the attempted coup; but it failed. The result of that failure was the development of a radical legacy of the 1790s that became an ideology structuring the aspirations of revolutionaries throughout the next seventy-five years. This would be particularly true after 1815.

Liberty, equality, and brotherhood—how could they be achieved? Of the many possible answers, two stood out. Napoleon would bring them about by force of French arms, bringing the fruits of the Revolution to people all over Europe. From 1799 until his defeats in 1814 and 1815, that is exactly what he tried to do, and with considerable success, for Europe would never again be the same.

Another answer came from a man executed for his views in 1797. His name was **François N. Babeuf.** In 1796 he had led a group called the Conspiracy of the Equals. This man emphasized that the urban and rural poor should seize the power of the state, expropriate the rich, and make property communal rather than private. Consumption would be socialized by placing the fruit of every person's work in a common store from which all could draw according to their needs. **Private property** had created masters and slaves. Communal property would teach everyone that no person could become richer or more powerful than his fellow equals, and would assure to everyone as much as they needed. Although he was executed in 1797, Babeuf's ideas were preserved by one of his followers, Philippe Buonarrotti, who transmitted *Babouvism* to the revolutionaries and liberals of the early nineteenth century.

These ideas of a frustrated revolution haunted Paris and contributed to uprisings in 1827, 1830, 1834, 1848, and 1871. The ideology of liberty, equality, and fraternity, along with the revolutionary atmosphere of Paris, caused it to become the home for European radicals who had been exiled from their own countries because of their views.

These revolutionary ideas would, however, be extremely unpopular in the period from 1815 to 1848. That time has been labelled the *Restoration* period by historians because, after the defeat of Napoleon, the returning monarchs attempted to reestablish life as it had been before the Revolution. Prince Metternich of Austria exemplified this conservatism. Change was still seen as possible, but evolutionary rather than revolutionary change. The pace of change that was acceptable under those conditions was too often microscopic. Police became much more efficient in developing dossiers, spying on conversations, and reading mail. Bureaucracies were often staffed with men who brought a near-military discipline to civilian life.

This period also saw a remarkable revival in the outward forms of religious life as churches were restored, and church leaders responded with a warm support of the restored governments. The revolutionaries were anti-church, and the new conservative monarchs saw the church as a bulwark against rapid change and a criticism of religion as a critique of themselves. Even so, pressures for change were present and could not be denied. In the western Germanic area population was on the increase, which forced more persons to move to the urban centers. The Customs Union assisted the new industry, and outputs in mine ores, steel, and textiles began to increase. In the Rhineland area particularly the new **bourgeoisie** was beginning to demand parliamentary representation as in England, more freedom of expression and stronger legal guarantees. In a climate of industrial revolution and rapid change lay the city of Trier where Marx was born.

Philosophy

Nineteenth century Europe was heir to another revolution extending from approximately 1789 to 1848. This was called the *Romantic Revolution* because it was a reaction to the rationalism of the previous century. During the eighteenth century, European thought was skeptical and irreligious, teaching that a human was reason in a body living in a rational universe. Progress was uncritically accepted by most thinkers, a rational development that was rapidly dispelling unknowns. It was no wonder that education seemed to these people to be a panacea for world problems and that sin was considered ignorance.

However, this was too abstract to last. The Romantic Revolution represented a revival of the importance of feeling, a move from generalizations to particulars, from thought to experience. Histories of particular peoples began to be written, and heroic stories were written in the vernacular of the people. Voltaire lost popularity as Shakespeare gained. All over Europe this revolution caused an explosion of genius that seemed to have no end—whether in poetry, painting, or music.

Politically, many of the Romantics stood for liberty, diversity, self-reliance, and the opportunity for self-development, but they certainly differed on how people could attain those goals. Progress they also believed in, but one central theme of the Romantics made this progress clearly distinct from that in the Age of Reason: the notion that society was a living organism. They replaced the mechanistic world with an organic interrelationship that was an extension of the notion of a biological organism including the whole world. Thus the progress that they discussed was evolutionary progress as in biology—an inevitable movement in history from the simple to the more complex. Change came about gradually, and in small doses, but relentlessly.

Saint Simon saw three stages in historical development: infancy (Ancient Egypt); youth (Greco-Roman times); and maturity (now) where modern technology would create a plenty that would be justly distributed. Auguste Comte, his pupil, saw three stages as well. His included infancy, where religion played a large role; youth, wherein humans metaphysically created abstractions and gave power to them; and maturity, the present, when abstractions could be dropped and positive levels of thought could be reached by seeing objects and their interrelationships empirically in nature. German Idealism (*Hegelianism*) also saw history evolving in three stages from past to present, a story which explained the present in terms of the past, and thought of the universe as an evolving organic unity.

However, Hegelianism deserves much more consideration here. It was this philosophy that sparked Karl Marx to become known as one of the foremost revolutionaries in Europe. At first glance this is difficult to understand because Hegelianism does not seem revolutionary at all. What is first necessary is to determine what it was that Hegel concluded, and then, equally important, what people did with his system after his death. Only then does this philosophical background assume its true significance.

Georg W. F. Hegel (1770-1831) was a German Idealist, perhaps the best representative of that school of philosophy, and certainly the most influential. When the word "idealist" is used in its philosophic sense, it does not necessarily refer to the high ideals of a person, but to someone believing that ideas are real while material things are not. An idealist believes that what we think of as material objects are in truth collections of universals, such as hardness, smoothness, and so on. Material things are a reflection of ideal reality. On the other hand, a materialist in philosophic terminology is not necessarily one who lusts after a suburban home with three bathrooms and two cars. A materialist is a believer in the reality of material things, and that ideas are a reflection of that material world. The basic difference lies in where one puts the reality: in idea, or in matter.

To describe Hegel as a German Idealist is first to describe him as an idealist, and second, to place him in that school of philosophy that followed Immanuel Kant in Germany in the late eighteenth and early nineteenth centuries. Kant had become very influential by writing his *Critique of Pure Reason* in 1781. In this rather heavy volume he had responded to the challenge from the empirical writings of John Locke as well as the skeptical empiricism of David Hume. These two men seemed to deny any importance to reason in the knowing process by insisting that all of our knowledge was derived from sense impressions on the mind which, after a time, created an order permitting rational thought to take place. Additionally, Hume insisted that rules, such as cause and effect, that the mind developed were not necessarily applicable to the outside world at all, but were basically internal rules of the thinking mind.

Kant responded by insisting that although in the knowing process the mind was dependent on sense impressions for knowledge, it did not mean that the mind came empty to the sense data. Logically, prior to the arrival of the sense data, the mind possessed principles which could channel the data, structure it, and make sense out of it. In terms of perception, Kant felt that the a priori principles were space and time. In terms of conception, the twelve categories were the a priori principles. The mind was an active participant in the knowing process, even though it was still true that knowledge was dependent on sense impressions.

Thus far, Kant had only seemed to respond to empiricism by creating a more active role for reason in the knowing process, but he went beyond this. He examined "knowing" very carefully and concluded that sense impressions are appearances—these are what the mind is equipped to handle. This is logical, for when one looks at a tree, the tree is not in his mind but, rather, an image or picture. Kant believed that what was behind that appearance could not be known. It was unknowable because our minds could only deal with appearance, not with the thing-in-itself. This also meant that the mind was incapable of moving beyond the terrestrial world of appearance in terms of knowing. Whether anything such as God was out there could not be known even though it might be believed.

Philosophers who followed Kant expanded this system by destroying the limits he had placed on human reason. The key was the "thing-in-itself," that unknowable something existing behind appearance in the world. Subsequent philosophers played with that concept. If the thing-in-itself is unknowable, they said, it cannot exist. Existence, they insisted, is a predicate of something, and nothing can be predicated about that which cannot ever be known. It was not merely that the thing-in-itself was unknown, but that it was by Kant's definition unknowable. Existence was one of the categories that applied to appearance, and so was cause. Neither existence nor cause could apply to that which was unknowable, and in this way subsequent idealist philosophy did away with the thing-in-itself. In so doing, any possibility of a material anchor for appearance was removed. The world was now idea, thought, or reason.

Hegel continued this kind of thinking and expanded on it by creating a philosophic system that sought to explain the entire universe. In so doing, he showed a decided affection for triads, explaining things in three's. The basis of the universe, Hegel believed, was reason. Reason was its self-explanatory principle, not a reason, but Reason itself. From this starting point he sought to deduce, or explain, the whole universe.

An overview of the entire system is a triad that can be diagrammed as follows:

Idea in itself   Idea outside itself
or   or
The Logical Idea   Nature

Idea in and for itself
or
Spirit

The *Logical Idea* contained the Kantian categories—but in pure thought, in terms of universals unconnected with sense data. *Nature* was used to describe the world of plants, minerals, and animals; this world was a necessary and logical consequence of pure thought. Not that thought created a stone, but that the thought of stone was deduced from pure thought. Remember that this is **idealism**—a stone is a collection of universals such as greyness and smoothness. Shortly after the emergence of animals, humans particularly, consciousness begins. Once this has happened, the way is open for the third part of the triad—*Spirit*—to emerge as the synthesis of the universal triad, a unity of Logical Idea and Nature emerging in human consciousness and developing to a full unity between humanity and absolute.

This development proceeded dialectically. Hegel needed this notion of the **dialectic,** the simultaneous coexistence of opposites, because he wanted to be able to deduce the universe from its most basic category, *Being.* Pure Being, he felt, was devoid of any determinations about it, and was therefore *Nothing* (non-Being) as well as Being. The one seemed to move into the other and back again, and the process of that movement was *Becoming.* Hegel could then continue the progressive deductions. The idea of the dialectic had already had a long history up to this point as a confrontation of opposites. Hegel refined this to make his dialectical theory argue for the simultaneous presence of opposites in the same "thing." These opposites coexisted in tension which sought resolution, which was the motor of progress from one level to another. An example of this might be life and death. A person is both alive and dying at the same time. Although a morbid thought, it does make sense. Conversely, although it is dead, the fossil "lives" in other forms.

A simplified way of stating this is to give names to the three points on the triad. *Thesis* (affirmative) confronted by *antithesis* (negative) and resolved by *synthesis* (both thesis and antithesis in a higher form). In this sense, for the overview of his system, the Logical Idea was the thesis, Nature was the antithesis, and Spirit was the resolution or synthesis. As the whole of the philosophy could be understood as a dialectical triad, so also each of the parts of this triangle was subdivided into triads which allowed

Hegel to show his chain of deduction from the first principle, Reason, through Logic to Nature, through Nature to the Spirit, and through the Spirit to the final resolution.

The whole of his system was dialectical. The universe logically began with Reason, or Absolute Idea, then Nature appeared as the Idea going outside of itself. This large dialectical conflict resulted in the Spirit, moving again by dialectical tension to a complete resolution in which the Absolute Idea was again reunified with itself. Idea returned to itself, not as abstract idea, however, but as the living spirit of humanity, mind existing in the world. His philosophy was cosmic in scope and reminds one of similar sagas in religion where God (or the same thing by another name) initially existed by itself, then created the so-called material world which became alienated from God; this tension was resolved by the coming of some mediator, through whom God and the human were reunited. This was not what Hegel was saying, but it sounds very similar.

The history of humanity is contained in the third phase of the large triad, the synthesis of Spirit. The Spirit moved dialectically, progressively unfolding in three manifestations. The first was where it was inward, personal, and subjective: as consciousness of self but nothing else. The second phase (negative-antithetical) was objective Spirit. This was the externalization of subjective Spirit in the institutions, mores, customs, and so on, into which a person was born. This would be a consciousness of the whole but as somethng external to the self. The normal movement of an individual was through the family (thesis), civil society (antithesis), and the state (synthesis), but this triad was one of the subdivisions of the objective Spirit, or Spirit externalized. Spirit could not stop here. Both subjective and objective manifestations of the Spirit must be transcended by the synthesis—absolute Spirit which would be both subject and object at the same time—a reunification of Spirit and human, moving through its own triad of art, religion, and philosophy to complete the fulfillment and the overcoming of alienation. In the final form, philosophy (and Hegel rather immodestly meant his own philosophy), there is knowledge of the absolute by the absolute (I know that I am *All*), an awareness of absolute reason by absolute reason in the mind of the human who has attained this philosophic awareness. This was spoken of as "finding freedom," a freedom that transcended and blended subject and object into one.

This was Hegelianism, a complicated, idealistic explanation of the whole universe by means of a dialectical development of Reason or Idea from itself to itself. A story of Idea that became alienated from itself only to rediscover itself in higher form.

Similar to the Romantics, Hegel's theory of human history, a part of the total system, appeared to evolve in stages that reflected development of human consciousness. The first stage of world history was the *Oriental,* a despotic period because only one person knew that he was *All.* The second period was the *Greco-Roman* in which some could know their freedom. The third and final stage was the *Germanic,* when all could know their freedom through Hegel's philosophy. Hegel's historical saga was one of dialectical development. Conflicts generated tension, thus pushing further development. Warfare was not necessarily evil, for it allowed the Spirit to take up residence in the victorious nation, thus moving its own development forward. This history was a tale of the overcoming of alienation within the absolute, and in the phase of the Spirit this overcoming was accomplished *in the consciousness of humans,* making it the transcendence of human alienation as well.

In addition, this historical philosophy appeared to conclude with a glorification of the state. Actually he was referring to the idea of the state as the means by which rational laws and rational people would come together—a unity of subject and object. But Hegel expressed his views in such a way that later one-sided adaptations of his thought were inevitable. His descriptions of the state, drawn from the empirical world and idealized, tended to justify or legitimate the status quo. The dynamic tension of the dialectic was much easier to see in the past than in the present. Thus when Hegel described the state and spoke of the monarch as the embodiment of the Spirit through whom the Spirit to the common people was mediated, he sounded both antidemocratic and pro-Prussian. However, Hegel was not a Prussian chauvinist. The actual state was still too external, too objective, something that confronted people as "other." The Spirit, nonetheless, was close to final realization as it moved through its triad in art and religion—particularly Christianity—toward its resolution in philosophy. Humans would see that the ideal or philosophized state was the collective expression of themselves, identical with themselves. Hegel's language was not always clear, and it seemed to many as though he were praising the Prussian state as that objectivity wherein humans could best find their freedom.

This complicated philosophy did not hold together very well after Hegel's death in 1831. His philosophy had become enormously influential, but people tended to emphasize that part of it which appealed to them most. Conservatives, in this Restoration period, quite naturally emphasized Hegel's apparent approval of the Prussian state and used his arguments to strengthen that state. This seemed to be common sense at that time because Prussia was a dominant Germanic entity of the thirty-six or so German areas, and pressure for German unity was very strong. Therefore, the conservatives played down Hegel's emphasis on conflict, as the motor of change, and played up his emphasis on the state.

Those on the left tended to do just the opposite. They emphasized conflict as the means of progress, and they attempted to move history in the direction of philosophy—absolute freedom. These *Young Hegelians* began with a critique of religion, not simply because they disliked religion, but because religion, particularly Christianity, was not the final phase but the step just prior to philosophy. They felt that they had to help move the state beyond religion. However, they attempted this at a time when religion was very warmly endorsed by the state as the bulwark against revolutionary change, and a time when the ruler of Prussia, Frederick William III, had been recently converted to a pietistic Christianity. The Young Hegelians quickly ran into considerable trouble, and it was at that point that Karl Marx went to the University of Berlin. Where were many of the Young Hegelians located? At the University of Berlin.

It is difficult to imagine how Marx could have avoided Hegelianism, for after Hegel's death in 1831 the University went through a "Hegel period" somewhat like the period following the assassination of President Kennedy. Almost every course Marx could have taken on the campus at that time would have brought him back to Hegel. The most active group on campus seeking the implementation of Hegelianism was the group of bright graduate students who constituted a Berlin contingent of the Young Hegelians. Marx became involved with them, and his life was changed from that point on.

The world in which Karl Marx grew up was dominated by three separate developments: the industrial revolution, particularly in England; radical political ideology, emanating from the frustrations of the French Revolution; and pressure for change, emerging out of the Young Hegelian interpretation of German Idealism. These were the forces that shaped him. His genius lay in putting them together.

*The German area will be called Germany for simplicity, even though the term was not technically accurate until after 1871.

Suggested Readings

Cole, G.D.H. *Introduction to Economic History, 1750-1950.* London: Macmillan, 1954.

Cox, Oliver. *The Foundations of Capitalism.* New York: Philosophical Library, 1959.

Engels, Frederick. *The Condition of the Working Class in England.* Translated by W.O. Henderson and W.H. Chaloner. Stanford: Stanford University Press, 1958.

Hobsbawn, E. J. *The Age of Revolution.* London: Weidenfeld & Nicolson, 1962.

Kaufmann, Walter. *Hegel's Political Philosophy.* New York: Atherton, 1970.

McManners, John. *Lectures on European History 1789-1914.* New York: Barnes & Noble, 1967.

Plant, Raymond. *Hegel.* Bloomington: Indiana University Press, 1973.

Soboul, Albert. *The Sans-Culottes.* Translated by Remy Inglis Hall. Garden City, N.Y.: Doubleday, 1962.

Stace, W.T. *The Philosophy of Hegel.* London: Dover, 1955.

Sydenham, M.J. *The French Revolution.* New York: Capricorn, 1966.

2

The Development of Marxism

Karl Marx was born on May 5, 1818, in an old city of approximately 12,000 people in the Moselle River valley, about twenty miles from the border of France. He was born into a well-to-do Jewish family living in a good neighborhood in Trier. His father was a lawyer to the high court of appeals, who had been forced to become a Lutheran in 1817 in order to keep his job. Karl's mother was uneducated like most women of that day, and she was quite domestic. There were several other children in the family, growing up in a quiet but changing Rhineland that was now being administered by Prussia. In his lifetime Marx made very little money, was quite dependent on his few friends, never stopped trying to achieve, and seldom finished what he had set out to accomplish; nonetheless, he bequeathed a considerable legacy to future generations. Marx lived to be sixty-four years old.

In the fall of 1835 when Karl was seventeen, this oldest son of the Marx family left home for the University of Bonn, not too far to the north. He was not a serious student during that year, and, like many another freshmen, he seemed to have difficulty adjusting to his new freedom. He was arrested for riotous and drunken behavior, and there were rumors of his involvement in a duel. Also, his studies appeared to be low on his list of priorities. His father decided that Karl should transfer to the fairly new but already prestigious University of Berlin, and Karl did this in the fall of 1836.

He was eighteen years old, and wanted to be a poet. However, what motivated his poetic impulses was frustrated love for Jenny, the girl back home, rather than talent. Only two poems were published in his lifetime and even a sympathetic biographer like Franz Mehring saw little poetic talent.[1] It did not take Karl long to decide that law offered a more promising career, and he threw himself into the study of jurisprudence. Almost immediately, he began to rewrite the history of law. Marx translated difficult articles into German for his own use, and before long he encountered the dominant philosophy at the University: Hegelianism. He did not care for it at first, but he was depressed after discouragement with his history of law and an abortive resurgence of his poetic drives. Marx wrote his father in 1837:

> A curtain had fallen, my holy of holies had been shattered, and new gods had to be found.
> Setting out from idealism—which, let me say in passing, I had compared to and nourished with that of Kant and Fichte—I hit upon seeking the Idea in the real itself. If formerly the gods had dwelt above the world, they had now become its center.
> I had read fragments of Hegel's philosophy and had found its grotesque craggy melody unpleasing. I wished to dive into the ocean once again but with the definite intention of discovering our mental nature to be just as determined, concrete, and firmly established as our physical—no longer to practice the art of fencing but to bring pure pearls into the sunlight.[2]

He then tried to write a new philosophy of religion, nature, and history. He failed in this as well and became ill.

> While out of sorts, I had got to know Hegel from beginning to end. . . .
> . . . [I]n Stralow I became a member of a Doctors' Club to which some instructors and my most intimate friend in Berlin, Dr. [Adolph] Rutenberg, belong. In discussions many a conflicting opinion was voiced, and I was more and more chained to the current world philosophy from which I had thought to escape.[3]

Marx said that he had gotten to know Hegelianism, and in the next sentence had mentioned the Doctors' Club, a segment of the leftist Young Hegelians. The milieu in which Karl would come to understand Hegel would be this particular group. Meeting at coffeehouses, they would hold long discussions, argue about interpretations, and in general have an enjoyable time. The Young Hegelians sought to implement

Hegelianism, but as idealists. The reforms they sought were in the mind rather than in the empirical world, but the physical world kept intruding. Eduard Gans, a very popular professor and a disciple of Hegel, had written in 1836 that the sort of progress recently seen in the world (the industrial revolution) was not universally progressive. Had slavery been abolished? Not at all. Look at the factories where

> . . . hundreds of emaciated and miserable men and women . . . sacrifice their health for the service and profit of a single man. . . .
> Is it not possible to awaken in these miserable proletarians a moral conscience and lead them to take an active part in the work that at present they execute automatically? The view that the state should provide for the needs of the most numerous and poorest class is one of the most profound of our time. . . .[4]

This reflected Gans' preference for *Saint Simonianism,* a French brand of socialism which was beginning to gain influence in the Rhineland as well as in Berlin. However, the industrial problems that gave rise to it were barely visible in Prussia. The Young Hegelians would not become socialists until after Marx had left Berlin. In the later 1830s they were struggling with their philosophy. Idealism was frustrating when it prevented political criticism, and they wanted to criticize. The quiet acceptance of the status quo was what characterized the conservative interpreters of Hegel, not the Doctors' Club. The leftist Hegelians valued conflict as the motor of progressive change in history. Their philosophic system emphasized the past as the explanation of the present, however, and presented history as a completed cosmic story. They strained at the limits of idealism. Political activity had to be rationalized into the system, but this meant that the future was as important as the past and present—that the cosmic story was not as yet finished. Yet, as idealism, Hegelianism should resolve empirical problems in idea or in the mind.

Even so there was an emphasis in Hegelianism on mastering and identifying with the rational aspects of the external world. The quest for rationality led the Young Hegelians to evaluate theology critically, and this became a critique of religion. In 1835 David Strauss, one of the group, wrote *Life of Jesus,* which described the Gospels as myths. This conclusion aroused considerable opposition from outside the group which, in turn, increased their theological criticism. This was an attempt to *apply* philosophy, to descend from the heights of theory to *praxis,* which Cieszkowski, a Polish count, had described as practical philosophy whose concrete impact on life and social conditions amounted to the use of critical philosophy within concrete activity.[5] Praxis became the tool for applying philosophy—informed criticism that clarified issues and resolved contradictions in the concrete or empirical society that stood in the way of the realization of philosophy.

While Marx was a part of the Doctors' Club, its praxis lay particularly in the religious area. One of Karl's close friends at that time, Bruno Bauer, an instructor in theology at Berlin and then at Bonn, gradually became so involved with this praxis that in 1841 he published a critique denying the historical existence of Jesus. He had become an atheist. Another Young Hegelian, Ludwig Feuerbach, published in that same year his *Essence of Christianity*. This was a very influential book in Marx's development, but at the time he was very busy, and Feuerbach's impact was somewhat delayed.

Marx received his Ph.D. from the University of Jena in 1841. It was simpler to get the degree from Jena because all he had to do was mail in his dissertation, and his friends had been pressuring him to finish. Bruno Bauer, in particular, had been urging Karl to finish so that Marx could come to the University of Bonn. Together, he thought, they could start a new journal, the *Archives of Atheism,* and really startle the old professors. Unfortunately for these plans, Bruno was in deep trouble in Bonn. His atheism crept into his lectures, and conflicts with colleagues became common. After all, an atheist in a theology department did not please everyone. Bruno was fired, and Marx's chances of joining him there evaporated.

At this point Marx badly needed an income. He wanted to marry Jenny, but his allowance from home was disappearing. His father had died in 1838, and by this time his mother felt he should support himself. An older member of the club, Arnold Ruge, asked Karl to write an article for his journal, the *Deutsche Jahrbucher,* criticizing the censorship laws recently promulgated by the new monarch, Frederick William IV. Although the new laws loosened censorship in general, they did not apply to religious criticism—a major activity of the Young Hegelians. Marx agreed to write a critical article, and without realizing it a life pattern was established. What else could he do? He was a philosopher, a philosopher of praxis. Therefore, he became a social critic.

Marx wrote that the protection of the Christian religion by the state was actually a blending of politics and religion; it was basing the state on faith and Christianity rather than on reason. This was a confusion of political and Christian principles resulting in an official denomination.[6] Criticism of religion, Marx was discovering, led directly to a criticism of the state.

His critical attitudes toward religion and the Prussian government were shared by large numbers of liberals in the Rhineland. The Rhenish left was a composite of belief in democracy, dislike for the anachronism that was the Prussian monarchy, and a touch of French socialism. This mix explained the editorial policies of a new newspaper in Cologne, the *Rheinische Zeitung*. The initial editors were two former law students from Berlin who had been sympathetic toward the Young Hegelians and began to solicit articles from them to publish in the paper. The Young Hegelians were delighted to have a vehicle for the expression of their views. Their philosophical language obscured their antireligious and increasingly socialist tendencies for a time, but they began to have serious difficulties with the censor. This was unfortunate for the paper's existence. It had only conditional permission to publish during a probationary period.

In 1842 Karl was asked to become the new editor and save the paper. He took the position even though it meant he had to fire the old editor, a former friend named Rutenberg. This man was very angry and went back to Berlin to complain about Karl to the Young Hegelians, but Marx did not care. The group had evolved since he had left. Under the influence of Bauer they had become militant socialists—staging demonstrations and fistfights, and begging for the poor. Marx thought they had gone mad. He cut off their flow of articles and tried to save the newspaper.

This experience pushed Marx further away from purely speculative philosophy toward a stronger philosophy of praxis. He continued his struggle against religion and the state in his articles, sounding in the process very democratic. The state, he wrote, was not an association of believers, but a free association of moral human beings aiming at an actualization of their freedom. The individual found satisfaction in the life of the whole, and the whole in the attitude of the individual.[7] In other words, there was a reciprocity within that association, and anything which interfered with that identity of the whole with the one, such as private property which separated people, had to be transcended. Marx became aware that property and wealth had caused an externalization of self in the things that were owned, and had created a class rather than an associational representation in the Prussian legislature. This meant a furthering of the distance between himself and Hegel. Now both the religious aspects of idealism and Hegel's evident approval of the Prussian monarchy must be thoroughly critiqued. After the newspaper was suppressed in early 1843, that was what Marx began to do.

He still did not accept socialism, but he was surrounded by it. A person who was very active behind the scenes at the newspaper was Moses Hess. He had also studied philosophy, but Moses had become a Communist.

He had already converted Frederick Engels and the Russian, Mikhail Bakunin. Moses began a small discussion group in the editorial offices of the paper, and Marx joined them when he came in October 1842. Hess was not successful in convincing Marx, probably because Karl had not yet had time to really study what these people were discussing. He could not accept socialism or communism as the next step in history simply because such a step would be desirable. History moved by dialectical resolution of opposites, said this student of Hegel, not because the next step was good. Nonetheless, more and more people were becoming aware of socialism. Lorenz von Stein had unwittingly spread socialist ideas in writing *Socialism and Communism in Contemporary France.* He had intended to warn the Prussian government of the dangers of these ideas, especially communist ideas. He distinguished between socialism and communism, maintaining that socialism was more of a philanthropic movement such as **Fourier's** that sought a peaceful reorganization of society, but he felt communism was dangerous. It had emerged as the new ideology of the also new **proletariat** in France. The new working class had absorbed the revolutionary ideas of the *san-culottes* during the Reign of Terror and particularly of Conspiracy of the Equals. As a result, the proletariat had become the special concern of French Communists. These ideas surrounded Marx, but they would not appear as his ideas until late 1843 and 1844.

A major influence in that transition was Ludwig Feuerbach's impact on Marx. In February 1843 the *Anekdota* contained not only Marx's first article but a piece written by Feuerbach as well. This article, entitled "Preliminary Theses for a Reform of Philosophy," was a continuation of his earlier work on religion. In 1843 the two works together had a very strong effect on Marx, made stronger by the fact that he was moving in this direction on his own. Feuerbach gave him much sharper reasons to continue.

In 1841 Feuerbach had defined the religious phenomenon as the projection or objectification of finite human experience into an infinite object of worship. People had created God, not the other way around. In order to understand religion, he wrote, one had to reverse the order of subject and predicate; instead of God creating humans, people created God. The deity was predicate of humanity, and the rise of religion was a particular historical fact. The God concept was a projection or externalization of something within the human essence, something people abstracted from themselves; then as time passed they forgot the source and foolishly worshiped their own creation.

Imagine, for example, that a carpenter is pounding a nail when suddenly the hammer strikes his thumb. The workman curses the hammer loudly and violently throws it down. What is he doing? Cursing the spirit of the hammer? Attempting to exorcise the evil by throwing it down? Whether these words are used or not, the workman just described is attributing power to that hammer, a power that struck his thumb. He has made a fetish by giving an inanimate object human characteristics. The man is giving the hammer part of his own essence by externalizing it in the hammer. Feuerbach felt that this was what happened when people created God. They took from themselves and gave to an abstract concept their own best qualities; then they compounded their mistake by abasing themselves before it. The concept had come back to haunt them as an "other" to them, external to their essence. This artificial separation of the human essence was religion, and it was also alienation. Humans had to take back that essence into themselves before their alienation could be overcome and their truly human existence could be realized. The important thing, he insisted, was not the question of theism or atheism, but the denial or affirmation of humanity (species-man). Arguments about these abstract concepts prevented humans from dealing with the real problems of real people. Years were spent debating whether bread became body and wine became blood, while real people were hungry and thirsty.

In the 1843 article he applied the same critique to speculative philosophy, or Hegelianism. Philosophy represented the same abstraction of a limited, local feature of human experience into an absolute principle that was made universally valid. The subject-predicate reversal had to take place in philosophy as well as in religion. Instead of considering Idea as subject—from which nature, religion, and philosophy were predicated —this must be reversed in order to place it in its true form. Hegel had to be read "transformationally" in order to get at the truth. Hegel had erred in that he had emptied empirical reality of intrinsic value and meaning, had mystified it—preserving intact the features of the empirical order while allegorically ascribing to them an ideal quality. This led to an uncritical acceptance of empirical evils.[8]

During the summer of 1843 Karl had time to study and think. His experiences on the newspaper, his attitudes concerning religion and the state, and now Feuerbach pushed him toward a criticism of Hegel's major political work. This resulted in Marx's *Critique of Hegel's Philosophy of Right*. His desire to criticize religion had led him to criticize the state and now Hegel. In so doing Marx described his own conclusions about political theory and much of what later became known as Marxism.

Using Feuerbach's expression, Marx described humans as a species that had not only individual needs but species or group needs as well. Men and women were social animals, that is, part of their essence was social. They could not really be human outside of society. This was an old idea even then, for Aristotle had described a person outside the *polis* as either a beast or a god. In other words, Marx was stating that by definition humans lived in society, and that the social forms in which they lived were functional to them, they were species-forms. There was a built-in reciprocity that was not simply desirable but vital to the human essence. People required communal being *(Gemeinwesen)* as much as they needed air to breathe. The actual forms of the communal being such as family, society, and state, derived from those needs and in turn fulfilled them. The reciprocity was a *sine qua non* of human existence, and to describe one side was to describe the other.

Moreover, the human was conscious of this bond with others, this human nature that was possessed in common with other people. Consciousness of species helped elevate humans above the animal world. This awareness of species existence demanded that there be no separation between the individual and society as there was between the believer and God. Yet that separation existed: there was a gap between the state and society. The state seemed external to the human, as an "other" to them. Hegel had resolved this in the ideal sphere, in human consciousness that had transcended the problem. Marx, by this time, sought resolution in the *empirical world*. His experiences had taught him that there was an actual bifurcation in political life between the propertied interests represented in the legislature and those who were unpropertied and therefore unrepresented. Thus, "[at] its highest levels the state appears as private property, whereas private property should appear as property of the state. Instead of making private property a civil quality, Hegel makes political citizenship, existence, and sentiment a quality of private property."[9]

The vehicle for overcoming this **alienation** in human political life was in erasing that separation between society and the political state through universal suffrage.[10] This meant that the state as such would be abolished, for it would be the expression of the political sentiment of the entire civil society and indistinguishable from its human components.

Once his eyes were opened to discover alienation as separation in the human essence, Marx found it in other areas as well. Money and money worship were also symbols of human alienation—tendencies to externalize the human essence in abstract concepts. In 1843 Marx entered a discussion of the problem of Jews in European society by equating "jewishness" with money worship as a means of driving his point home. Money, he wrote, was the jealous god of Israel, degrading all other gods, and it attained its highest development in the Christian community.[11] The Christians had become the best "Jews" in this respect. The species relationship among humans, such as the relations between a man and a woman, had become objects of commerce in which the woman was bought and sold.[12] Alienation, best symbolized by religion, was to be found everywhere.

As long as man is captivated in religion, knows his nature only as object-ified, and thereby converts his nature into an *alien* illusory being, so un-der the dominion of egoistic need he can only act practically, only prac-tically produce objects, by subordinating both his products and his activity to the domination of an alien being, bestowing upon them the significance of an alien entity of money.[13]

Again Marx needed a job, especially since he had married Jenny in the summer of 1843. Arnold Ruge came to the rescue again, promising an editorial position on a new journal if Karl would move his family to Paris to get away from the Prussian censors. At the end of 1843 Karl and Jenny went to Paris, a move from the philosophical and backward Germanic area to the more advanced and revolutionary France.

Almost immediately another transition occurred in Marx's writing. The means of achieving the universal reciprocity necessary for a really hu-man existence had been universal suffrage. Now it became the dialectical triumph of a universal class: the proletariat. The notion of praxis now took on new dimensions. Informed criticism now became *revolution,* ma-terial force overthrowing material force. This praxis he identified with the proletariat. For if the overthrowing were to be done by any of the old groups there would only be the substitution of one slavery for another. The criticism of religion, he wrote, had ended with the doctrine that man was the supreme being for man. Therefore, all conditions that debased, enslaved, neglected, and made man contemptible had to be destroyed. Who would be able to do it completely, without reinstituting a particular interest? The proletariat.[14] Why the proletariat? What made the working class the companion of philosophy and the class that could bring about a universal revolution?

First, Marx was seeing the whole in the part. Society was an organic relationship, a unity of reciprocity, and he could not consider a part of that whole without seeing at the same time its relation to the whole within a changing context. This meant that Marx would use a word as a window through which the central concept of alienation would be clearly visible. Other words windowed on that concept as well and expressed similar rela-tionships: if A = B and B = C, then A = C. If one accepts the notion that human nature in essence is a nature outside (but including) the indi-vidual (i.e., species-nature) and that the species-person is a unity, then anything that separates parts of the whole from each other is evil and must be destroyed. Marx identified this separation of the human from species-nature as alienation, which was symbolized by religion. In Paris in 1844, he came to view the proletariat as he did religion.

. . .the critique of religion is the prerequisite of every critique.
The wretchedness of religion is at once an expression of and a protest against real wretchedness. Religion is the sigh of the oppressed creature,

the heart of a heartless world and the soul of soulless conditions. It is the opium of the people.

The abolition of religion as the illusory happiness of the people is a demand for their true happiness.

It is the task of history, therefore, once the other-world of truth has vanished, to establish the truth of this world. It is above all the task of philosophy, which is in the service of history, to unmask human self-alienation in its secular forms, once its sacred form has been unmasked.[15]

In one sense what Marx said here was that his atheism was in fact humanism, and that the religious opiate created a dream world of future justice which allowed people to ignore the here and now—thereby reinforcing the exploitative status quo. He was also saying that there were *secular forms of religion,* factors in the empirical world that symbolized real alienation just as there were in the heavenly world of the blue mist. That secular factor which represented alienation completely was the working class or proletariat.

Hegel was being read transformationally, and that meant that the Absolute was not Reason externalizing itself and returning to itself—what Hegel had really meant was that humans, as species-humans, externalized themselves through their mastery over nature. For Marx, Hegel's Spirit became the human that produces and creates. This creative and productive species-human was humanity as it ought to be, as it was going to become. The objects that people had produced made up their environment—the world of nature that surrounded them. Therefore, that natural world was also part of the human whole, an expansion of human nature, and a bond between people realized in society.[16] Who were the producers in society? The workers. The humans, *par excellence.*

The world just described was the "ought to be" world not the "is" world. Empirical reality revealed that nature was seen by people as outside their natures, as an "other" to them. The tree outside the window or the road that leads to town were not viewed as ingredients of *human* nature. There was a reason for that artificial separation. That reason was alienation in the heart of the human essence—in labor. The productive activity that distinguished human from animal activity, that creativeness that tied the whole together into a human whole, was deeply divided; all of the products of human labor confronted people as alien, not just nature. The result was an illusion of individuality.

What constitutes the externalization of labor? First is the fact that labor is *external* to the laborer—that is, it is not part of his nature—and that the worker does not affirm himself in his work but denies himself, feels miserable and unhappy, develops no free physical and mental energy but mortifies his flesh and ruins his mind. The worker, therefore, feels at ease only outside work, and during work he is outside himself. It is not the satisfaction of a need but only a *means* to satisfy other needs.

Finally, the external nature of work for the worker appears in the fact that it is not his own but another person's, that in work he does not belong to himself but to someone else.

. . . the activity of the worker is not his own spontaneous activity. It belongs to another. It is the loss of his own self.

The result, therefore, is that man (the worker) feels that he is acting freely only in his animal functions—eating, drinking, and procreating, or at most in his shelter and finery—while in his human functions he feels only like an animal. The animalistic becomes the human and the human the animalistic.[17]

In other words, the whole world of productive activity which ought to have been the glorious end of the human had become the means for the exercise of his or her animal life. A person worked in order to live, rather than lived in order to work. The proletariat represented in the real world what religion had symbolized in the heavenly world—alienation in the essence of the human condition. Private property was another symbol of externalized human essence, and that meant that the bourgeoisie was just as alienated as the proletariat. In the course of history that alienation had deepened to the point where Marx saw people as alienated from their labor, tools, products, fellow humans, nature, and basically from themselves.

How could this be overcome? Just as religion had been abolished by criticism, so must these other secular symbols of alienation be destroyed. The proletariat, the universal class, must become conscious of its condition and its role; overthrow that which prevents it from its destiny, and the triumphant result would be communism. Just as the other side of atheism was **humanism,** so also the other side of the destruction of private property by the proletariat was a destruction of themselves as proletarians, and an end to alienation, ". . . the return of man himself as a *social,* i.e. really human, being, a complete and conscious return which assimilates all the wealth of previous development."[18]

This was a philosophical understanding of the proletariat. Empirical observations of the conditions of the working class further developed the concept and gave it empirical weight but in its essence the concept of the proletariat did not derive from an analysis of working-class problems, but from an analysis of religion. In the process, the working class had become the redeemer which would emancipate all of humanity by freeing itself. Marx's philosophical notions were now wedded to Frederick Engels' observations of the English workers. The result was a proletariat that represented the human essence both in alienation and beyond—in communism. An example of Marx's thinking is provided in the following quotation. Note how he *derives* the concept of private property.

> *Private property* is thus product, result, and necessary consequence of *externalized labor*, of the external relation of the worker to nature and to himself.

> *Private property* thus is derived, through analysis, from the concept of *externalized labor*, that is, *externalized man*, alienated labor, alienated life, and *alienated* man.

> [Private property] . . . is rather a consequence of externalized labor, just as gods are *originally* not the cause but the effect of an aberration of the human mind. Later this relationship reverses.[19]

The proletariat was also a **class**. Since coming to Paris Marx had intensively studied French history to give him a better understanding of the French Revolution. His conclusions were the generally accepted ones of that time, namely that French history, and by generalization all history, could only be understood as class conflict. History was a record of conflict between classes, and groups received class designations by virtue of economic factors pertaining to their period. In order for history to exist at all, Marx wrote, the production of goods necessary to sustain life must take place. Production was the basis of human history, but it was an alienated or separated production from the beginning. Marx described this separation as between thoughtless activity and inactive thought, enjoyment and labor, and production and consumption—in short, between owners and nonowners of the means of production.[20] A class was such by virtue of its relation to the means of production. It was a part of the division of labor in society. Conflict was implicit in that division of labor, and the dialectical resolution of that conflict moved history forward (see chapter 3).

Moving to Paris not only placed Marx squarely in the center of French revolutionary socialism, but also his use of the proletariat as the agent class pushed him in the direction of economics, particularly the more advanced economics of England. He felt a solid economic analysis would demonstrate in very clear fashion the accuracy of his blend of philosophical and empirical perspectives. The study of economics had now become a prime necessity in his life.

However, his planned critique of political economy was never finished. He was diverted from his economic studies by the philosophical struggles in Germany; activities of other revolutionaries that required his refutation; and by joining the Communist League in 1847. This group, an expanded version of a German émigré organization, asked Marx and Engels to write a definitive description of the aims and beliefs of the League. They did, and the result was the *Communist Manifesto* which carefully distinguished Marxian communism from more utopian variants and urged the workers of the world to unite under the leadership of the League so as to bring about the revolution.

In 1848 revolutions actually did break out in Paris, Vienna, Berlin, and elsewhere. The League and the *Manifesto* had not caused these uprisings, but both the League and Marx attempted to involve themselves on the side of the workers. Since Prussia was very unstable at that moment, Marx was able to go back to Cologne and reestablish the newspaper.[21] His articles placed him on the left of the Cologne Workers' Association, the democratic movement in the Rhineland. However, when the uprisings failed and stability returned, Marx again had to leave. After a brief stopover in Paris, he and his family moved to London which would be his home for the rest of his life. The hope raised in him by the recent revolutions persisted, even though the Communist League proved to be shortlived. His confidence in the impending revolution made him even more eager to pursue his economic studies.

During 1850 and 1851 Marx spent long hours in the reading room of the British Museum, preparing himself to write his long-postponed critique of capitalist economy. However, he never did finish it. Only portions of it were ever published, including the *Contribution to a Critique of Political Economy,* in 1859. Another portion was the first volume of *Capital,* which Marx published in 1867.[22] Fortunately, his research notebooks remained available.[23] *The Grundrisse* (main principles) was written in 1857 and 1858 and it constitutes a very important synthesis of his economic studies with his more philosophical past. The *Grundrisse* points back to the Hegelian-Feuerbachian period as well as forward to the critique of capitalism and the coming of communism. The notebooks make very clear that Marx the economic critic was still basically the philosopher turned social critic, for human alienation was manifested in economic history as well as in the capitalist mode of production in his day. Even though he was studying empirical economics and describing actual economic practices, he described economic factors as the predominant influence in an organic, social unity wherein the externalization of the human essence had reached its peak.

Living in London had not caused him to forget Germany either. That country and its problems remained a vital concern to him. In the preface to the German edition of *Capital,* Marx urged the German reader to take no comfort from the fact that the described English conditions were not German ones, for they soon would be. "The country that is more developed industrially only shows, to the less developed, the image of its own future."[24] This was why he was so critical of the development of socialism in Germany, so compelled to help shape it in his *Critique of the Gotha Program* in 1875.

Through all of this activity Marx did not neglect involvement in political affairs while in England. He was very active in the International Workingmen's Association that began in 1864. From 1868 to 1871 he was a leading figure behind that movement to unify the workers of the world. He even helped the association to collapse when it appeared to be coming under the wrong (i.e., anarchist) leadership.

In all of these matters, Marx was assisted both financially and mentally by his close friend, Frederick Engels. When they had first met in Cologne in 1842, Karl had been cool. After all, Frederick was one of the new breed of Young Hegelians. By 1844 their views had begun to coincide, and a lifelong friendship emerged. Engels continued to work as a manufacturer to support himself and Karl's family, and Karl consulted him repeatedly to sharpen his thoughts and share his problems.

In March of 1883 Karl Marx died in his sleep. Engels lived until 1895, and during the intervening twelve years he continued their work to the best of his ability; but the revolution they both had sought had failed to come. Nonetheless, Marx left a legacy for future generations which included a full description of how and why history was inevitably leading to that revolution which would usher in the truly human age. It was to be deeply influential.

Suggested Readings

Hook, Sidney. *From Hegel to Marx.* Ann Arbor: University of Michigan Press, 1962.

Hyppolite, Jean. *Studies on Marx and Hegel.* Translated by John O'Neill. New York: Harper Torchbooks, 1969.

Lichtheim, George. *The Origins of Socialism.* New York: Praeger, 1969.

Marcuse, Herbert. *Reason and Revolution.* Boston: Beacon, 1960.

McLellan, David. *Karl Marx, His Life and His Thought.* New York/London: Harper and Row, 1973.

Ollman, Bertell. *Alienation: Marx's Conception of Man in Capitalist Society.* New York: Cambridge University Press, 1971.

Tucker, Robert. *Philosophy and Myth in Karl Marx.* New York: Cambridge University Press, 1961.

NOTES

[1] Franz Mehring, *Karl Marx* (1918; reprinted Ann Arbor: University of Michigan Press, 1962), p. 11.

[2] Excerpt from *Writings of the Young Marx on Philosophy and Society,* edited and translated by Loyd D. Easton and Kurt H. Guddat, pp. 46-47. Copyright © 1967 by Loyd D. Easton and Kurt H. Guddat. Reprinted by permission of Doubleday & Company, Inc.

[3] Ibid., p. 48.

[4] Eduard Gans, *Ruckblicke auf Personen und Zustände* (Berlin, 1836), p. 99ff.; quoted in David McLellan, *Marx Before Marxism* (New York: Harper Torchbooks, 1970), p. 51.

[5] A. von Cieszkowski, *Prolegomena zur Historiosophie* (Berlin, 1838), p. 142; quoted in McLellan, *Marx Before Marxism,* p. 65.

[6] Marx, "Comments on the Latest Prussian Censorship Instruction," in Easton and Guddat, *Writings of the Young Marx,* p. 77. The *Deutsche Jahrbücher* was itself suppressed, and this article appeared in the first and only issue of Ruge's *Anekdota* (February 1843).

[7] Marx, "Leading Article in No. 179 of the *Kölnische Zeitung:* "Religion, Free Press, and Philosophy," in Easton and Guddat, *Writings of the Young Marx,* pp. 118, 120.

[8] "Editor's Introduction," in *Karl Marx—Critique of Hegel's Philosophy of Right,* ed. and trans. Joseph O'Malley (Cambridge: University Press, 1970), p. xxxvii.

[9] Ibid., p. 111.

[10] Ibid., p. 121.

[11]Karl Marx, "On the Jewish Question," in Easton and Guddat, *Writings of the Young Marx*, p. 245.

[12]Ibid., p. 246.

[13]Ibid., p. 248. Excerpt reprinted by permission of Doubleday & Company, Inc.

[14]Karl Marx, "A Contribution to the Critique of Hegel's Philosophy of Right, Introduction," in O'Malley, *Critique of Hegel's Philosophy*, p. 142. Marx intended this short article to be the beginning of his larger unpublished *Critique of Hegel's Philosophy of Right*. The Introduction was published in the new journal, *Deutsch-Französische Jahrbücher* (Paris, 1844), in its first issue. The journal meant to blend French political thought with German philosophy, hence the title, but it sold badly in France and was confiscated in Germany. The same article is under a different title, "Toward the Critique of Hegel's Philosophy of Law: Introduction," in Easton and Guddat, *Writings of the Young Marx*, pp. 249-64.

[15]From O'Malley, trans. and ed., *Karl Marx—Critique of Hegel's Philosophy of Right* (Cambridge: University Press, 1970), pp. 131-32. Reprinted by permission of the publisher.

[16]Karl Marx, "Economic and Philosophical Manuscripts," (1844), in *Karl Marx—Early Writings*, trans. and ed. T. B. Bottomore (New York: McGraw-Hill, 1963), p. 157. See also Easton and Guddat, *Writings of the Young Marx*, pp. 305-6.

[17]Excerpt from Easton and Guddat, *Writings of the Young Marx on Philosophy and Society*, p. 292. Reprinted by permission of Doubleday & Company, Inc.

[18]From *Karl Marx—Early Writings*, trans. and ed. T. B. Bottomore. (New York: McGraw-Hill), p. 155. Copyright 1963 by McGraw-Hill. Used by permission of McGraw-Hill Book Company.

[19]Excerpt from Easton and Guddat, *Writings of the Young Marx on Philosophy and Society*, pp. 297-98 (emphasis Marx's). Reprinted by permission of Doubleday & Company, Inc.

[20]Marx and Engels, "The German Ideology," in Easton and Guddat, *Writings of the Young Marx*, p. 423 ff.

[21]The Prussian government had pressured France to expel him, and while living in Brussels he had been forced to give up his Prussian citizenship. After he wrote the *Manifesto* the Belgian government did not want his presence either.

[22]Vols. II and III were published after his death by Engels in 1885 and 1894.

[23]A partial translation is available in English. See David McLellan, trans. and ed., *The Grundrisse* (New York: Harper Torchbooks, 1971).

[24]Karl Marx, "Preface to the First German Edition of *Capital*," in *Marx-Engels Selected Works* (Moscow: Progress Publishers, 1969), 2: 87.

3

Historical
Materialism

History has often been used by philosophers to show how their own particular interpretations of contemporary life have necessarily developed out of events of the past. If the historical saga is believed, the philosopher will be believed. Thomas Hobbes proved the necessity of a strong sovereign in England by historical argument. John Locke did the same thing to prove the supremacy of property and parliament a few years later. Rousseau demonstrated the desirability of the commune; Machiavelli the necessity of a strong prince; and Hegel the ideal state by means of historical tales.

Marx also used history to reveal the inevitable necessity of the proletarian revolution with an interpretation that saw its primary elements as social, producing humanity. The reduction of life to its minimum elements revealed that production was crucial if *any* history at all was to take place. Humans, who by definition lived in society, produced subsistence and surplus which made continuous life possible. Therefore history ought not to be understood as a saga of kings and empires, for these were results or consequences of the more basic ingredient—social production.

From his Hegelian background, Marx had the notion that history was a single story. Replacing Hegel's Spirit with the human meant that the past was an organic unity which described *human* progress in the manner in which people made their living—in production. The romantic notion of evolutionary progress was strengthened by the dialectic which functioned as the motor of historical progress. History—the history of social production—moved forward as a result of the dialectical tensions seeking resolution, not in the world of the mind or idea, but in the empirical world of material things. Hegel was de-idealized, but the dialectical framework would still be used as an explanation of empirical reality—past, present, and future, a **materialism** that actualized in praxis the idealistic philosophy which gave it birth.

Historical materialism was thus the manner in which Marx justified his allegedly scientific comprehension of the present and his confident predictions about the future. He summed it up in 1859.[1] In the social production of their life people enter into definite relations of production, not because they desire to, but because they cannot help themselves. These relations of production correspond to the stage of development of the material productive forces. In other words, in history there have been different manifestations of these relations of production, reflecting differences in the stage of development. History was divided or grouped by these stages of material production.

The relations of production at any given time constituted the economic structure of society. Exactly what those relations would be was determined by the stage of production that was being described. The economic structure was the real basis of the whole society of that period, the foundation on which were constructed particular legal and political arrangements that reflected the economic base. Even the social and intellectual consciousness of the period was conditioned by that economic foundation—it could not be escaped.

When Marx wrote this way he was often interpreted as maintaining an economic **determinism**—the notion that everything else was the effect of the economic cause, which seemed to be a very rigid understanding of society. If this were true, Marx's ideas would be like a devil theory, a simple explanation for everything; and easy explanations of complex history are and ought to be quickly refuted. Although this was how Marx sounded, Engels wrote, this ought not to be the way that he is understood.

> . . . According to the materialist conception of history, the *ultimately* determining element in history is the production and reproduction of real life. More than this neither Marx nor I have ever asserted. Hence if somebody twists this into saying that the economic element is the *only* determining one, he transforms that proposition into a meaningless, abstract, senseless phrase. The economic situation is the basis, but the various elements of the superstructure . . . also exercise their influence upon the course of the historical struggles and in many cases preponderate in determining their *form*. There is an interaction of all these elements in which . . . the economic movement finally asserts itself as necessary.[2]

Marx and I are ourselves partly to blame for the fact that the younger people sometimes lay more stress on the economic side than is due to it. We had to emphasize the main principle *vis-à-vis* our adversaries, who denied it, and we had not always the time, the place or the opportunity to give their due to the other elements involved in the interaction.[3]

Even if this is the correct understanding of the relationship of social factors in any given period, it is still clear that the economic factor was basic to Marx's analysis of history. There was an interaction, but within limits. People were determined by the relations of production in their society in the sense that they were not free to choose this or that form of society. They were born into an already existing society that was an edifice reflecting the economic base, but during their lives people developed their productive facilities further by inventions and the like, so that it could be said that they were partially determining their own relations of production. Marx understood society as a product of human reciprocal action affected by the dominant relations of production or manner of producing at that time period.[4]

This development by succeeding generations of people ultimately had an impact on the relations of production. The mode of production did not simply continue developing, for there was an internal dynamic at work that was not necessarily perceived by the people involved at that time. This was the dialectic. The development of the productive forces, Marx wrote, reached a stage where new development came into conflict with the existing relations of production or relations of property. Further development was then hampered and restricted by those old relations. "Then begins an epoch of social revolution."[5]

Since the economic factor was basic, the alteration in the relations of production caused changes in the entire **superstructure.** But such transformations did not occur often in this line of development. They would only take place when the progress in production could no longer be handled by the existing economic arrangement, when the room for new developments was exhausted. What emerged from this social revolution was a new relation of production that had been quietly gathering strength while still in the old economic mode. The new grew in the womb of the old until it was ready to become dominant, then it also had its prime followed by its eventual decline while still another new relation of production was gathering muscle for the next major transformation of society.

Human history thus seemed to be made up of a series of stages of economic development. Marx was really describing European development here—a history that evolved from primitive communism to the ancient or slave society, then to the feudal period, and finally to the capitalism of

Marx's own day. This would in turn be followed by the communism of the future (see chapter 4). However, there was another possible sequence that Marx was aware of—namely Asiatic society or oriental despotism. This kind of society emerged out of primitive communism in areas where the state quickly grew dominant because of its monopoly over the irrigation systems on which the agriculture of those societies was dependent. Oriental despotisms such as in Egypt, China, India, and elsewhere differed from the line of European development by not going through the same stages and by their astonishing durability over time.

Aside from this exception, historical materialism was a story of progressing stages of economic development moved by the dialectical confrontation of opposites seeking resolution. These opposites were opposing relations of production or relations of property that resolved into higher and newer stages of production relations. This opposition or conflict was manifested in class warfare. Class, the collective expression of each individual's relation to the means of production, was a reflection of both the dominant production relations and the new relation growing within the framework of the old. Human history could therefore also be expressed as a record of class conflict—the manner in which the economic conflict was fought.

The "gens" stage was a primitive period at the beginning of civilization.[6] Production was communal, that is, a primitive communism prevailed. This included the family, for group marriage was common. The goods that were produced communally were not usually for exchange, as in trade, but for use within the community. It was a matriarchal society that included a small amount of manufacture, but in the beginning it was a hunting and gathering type of society.

When agriculture emerged as a significant form of food production, things began to change. Private property began to manifest itself in the economic base. The line of descent and inheritance altered from the mother's line to the father's, group marriage gave way to monogamy, and *individual* possessions began to supplant *social* possessions. At this point slavery was introduced as a means of increasing the production of agricultural goods. This was the new relation of production that would grow within the old communal relations and was a direct result of private property's emergence within this communal society. As surplus products could now be produced, trade increased, and production for exchange became common. This made slavery an even more necessary institution. When this reached the point where the old communal relations were a barrier to further progress, a social revolution occurred and a new relation of property emerged: the ancient or slave society. Private property was then enshrined in the relations of production in the form of the two major classes—the owners and the slaves.

Alienation was furthered by the association of labor with slaves. Work became a despised occupation. The expansion of slavery to increase the production of surpluses pushed trade higher and higher. In this context arose the merchant who arranged trade between various parties. The use of money as the symbol for goods developed rapidly. There was economic expansion on a worldwide scale, but it was a production based on slave labor. Such expansion was expensive, and taxes had to be constantly increased. Money lent at exorbitant rates by merchants impoverished many. The expansion of empire, as in the case of Rome, led to an expansion of citizenship or the development of a large mass of freemen to whom labor was repugnant. All of this had a cumulative effect. A new class of impoverished free and freed people broke up the large landed estates that had been worked by slave labor but had become unprofitable, and subsistence agriculture reappeared. However, the new class was relatively powerless, and, as the old empires disintegrated, feudalism was born.

This was not a very clear description of history. There was no indication of exactly how the dialectical relationship of classes developed as an inevitable outgrowth of productive development. The necessity seemed *post hoc*, as someone's hindsight making the Second World War a necessary and inevitable consequence of the Versailles Treaty. The closer one came, however, to Marx's own day the clearer his explanation became. This suggests that the division of labor in Marx's time was generalized, through the concept of class conflict in history, into a pattern read onto history. His analysis of contemporary society, he felt, was true—indeed scientific; and if that were so, then history *must* reveal those same patterns in other forms. History was progress; progress was inevitable, and it was dialectical. Marx had all of this before he looked at history, and what he found confirmed his theoretical conclusions.

Feudalism, the next stage, was characterized by small-scale peasant agriculture and handicrafts on a local level. The division of labor was between the serf and the lord, between whom the reciprocity of protection and labor existed. In general the worker owned the means of production, his own tools, but he was a serf, performing forced labor for the lord, paying rent to the lord, and normally not able to leave the lord's service. Towns dotted the landscape but they were rural in nature. The small amount of manufacturing that took place in the towns was performed by hand, protected from competition by strong guild restrictions.

As stability returned so did the merchants, but initially trade was very local. However, developments in Europe, such as the compass, permitted more distant travel. The Crusades opened people's eyes to other areas, and geographical discoveries dramatically expanded the availability of gold and silver. All this contributed to a tremendous increase in trade and a desire for the production of commodities for exchange. Increasingly the

old relations of production became dependent on the merchant as the nobility and the serf became dysfunctional. The rise of those who controlled
the money that greased the wheel of state could not be suppressed for
long. The restrictions of the old relations of production had to be transcended. Again a revolution would occur, and there would be a new con-
figuration in those production relationships—this time capitalism—and
the division of labor between the proletariat and the bourgeoisie.

This was the last period in the "prehistory" of humanity, the period
contemporaneous with Marx. Historical materialism changed from a description of the past to an analysis of the present. There was a solid reason
for this. The ". . . evolution of the economic formation of society is viewed
as a process of natural history . . . ,"[7] but it was an evolution according
to what Marx called the rational (his own) rather than the mystified
(Hegel's) dialectic. That evolution revealed properly (dialectically) had a
stunning impact on those who read about it,

> . . . because it includes in its comprehension and affirmative recognition
> of the existing state of things, at the same time also, the recognition of
> the negation of that state, of its inevitable breaking up; because it re-
> gards every historically developed social form as in fluid movement,
> and therefore takes into account its transient nature not less than its
> momentary existence; because it lets nothing impose upon it, and is in
> its essence critical and revolutionary.[8]

Capitalism had a beginning, therefore, but it would also have an end.
Marx was combatting the general tendency to see in one's own time the
complete culmination of history, to see in the institutions of one's society
a sacred hand that made them givens which ought not to be tampered
with. His analysis of capitalism was a part of historical materialism. Its
analysis was designed to reveal the temporary nature of the bourgeois relations of production.

In that description of capitalism Marx also revealed the depths of human alienation especially experienced by the proletariat. The progress in
technological ability throughout history was matched by "progress" in
alienation. It was vitally important that the working class become aware
of this fact, as well as cognizant of the transitory character of capitalism
due to the inevitable flow of the dialectic in history. This knowledge
would create **class consciousness,** hope, and revolution.

Marx began his analysis by asking questions: what was value? What
was the value of a commodity that had been produced and was now on the
marketplace? If one assumed that value was price, what was the basis of

that price or value? Here Marx used a concept that had been a part of John Locke's justification of private property and a part of Ricardo's analysis of capitalism: the labor theory of value. The value of any commodity was determined by the amount of labor time expended in its manufacture. This was corrected to account for lazy individuals or new innovations by rephrasing the statement to read, "The value of any commodity is the result of the *socially necessary* labor time expended on its manufacture." A commodity that had used up eight hours of this labor time was twice as valuable as one requiring only four.

However, the produced commodity was not simply the result of human labor time because there were machines and raw materials involved as well. This was no problem because the machinery and raw materials were themselves commodities whose value derived from human labor time. A machine, for example, represented "stored" human labor. Raw materials had an extraction cost that could be similarly considered. The commodity concept not only referred to the finished product but to the intermediary products as well. One might be the consumer of a finished automobile, but the capitalist was a consumer of such things as steel or machinery.

Labor was also a commodity. Living labor in the bourgeois relations of production was free—not bound to the land or owned by a slave master. The worker could contract with an employer. Wages reflected the laborer's value or the cost of sustaining the worker in that capacity. Wages below this level caused starvation, and wages above this level assumed a philanthropy among capitalists that Marx did not believe was there. Wages, on the average, tended to be subsistence wages.

In the production process living labor was blended with frozen labor to create commodities. Costs to the capitalist were expenditures for the three commodity categories of raw materials, machinery, and labor time. However, the price of the finished product did not reflect this cost base alone. An article that cost $5 to produce sold for $7. Where did this extra value come from? It came from **surplus value,** a value created by labor which was not part of the costs of production because the worker was not paid for it.

Imagine being hired for $10 per day. During the day living labor is blended with objectified labor (machinery and raw materials) to create products of value. Further suppose that goods valued at $10 are created during the morning's work. If the worker goes home at this point, the capitalist receives an equivalent return. However, the worker is kept on the job, and during the afternoon's work products are created for which the laborer receives no remuneration. This was the basis of profit. This was surplus value, occurring in a system of production which denied the workers a large portion of the fruit of their own productivity. At the heart of the bourgeois relations of production lay exploitation and theft.

This was not simply a distribution problem distinct from capitalism itself. It was an essential aspect of that process.[9] If the capitalists had to pay the full equivalent to the workers, they would cease to be capitalists. Profit was exploitation, and without it the system would not operate.

Was Marx intending to deny the bourgeoisie a return on their investments? By no means. He was not writing a moralistic tract, but a scientific analysis. The other side of this exploitative character of capitalism was that labor only became productive when taken into capital and utilized under capitalist discipline. Of course alienation deepened and the workers confronted "stored" labor as an alien "other." However, in order for capitalism to exist, labor must be turned into wealth. This was done by a production process stimulated by the greed of the capitalist that, however deplorable, dramatically increased productivity and the amount of goods available for consumption.[10] The chains of minimal subsistence would be broken forever because of the wealth produced by capitalism.

Capitalism was, in other words, an ongoing and valuable historical stage of production that was thoroughly based on labor. Where, for example, did the capitalist get the money to invest? From personal labor or the labor of ancestors. Invested money came back with a return in the following year. Where did the extra money come from? From capitalized surplus value owing its existence to unpaid labor. The proletariat, by its own surplus labor, created the capital destined to employ additional labor in the following year. Bourgeois property insured the legal right to appropriate the product of unpaid labor. This kept the system moving and expanding.

However, there was another force at work here that Marx described. There was a dialectical tension between labor and capital that would eventually need resolution. *Within* bourgeois society was being created the force that would destroy the system, the new relation of production growing in the womb of the old. This was the proletariat, gradually assuming its universal character in a variety of ways.

Although capitalism was based on private property, the proletariat was being taught to live and work socialistically. Large numbers of workers had been brought together under one factory roof where they had been taught through the discipline of capitalism to work *together* in **commodity production.** The goods that were produced were not the result of a single worker's activities, but resulted from the labor of them all. It was a joint product, a social product. To whom did it belong? To the capitalist, the owner of the means of production. If the bourgeoisie were ignored for a moment, it was clear that the ownership of the product was the social or human collectivity and not a single individual. Moreover, these urban workers were concentrated in living quarters around the factories. They were not only working together, they were living together and were bound together by their propertyless condition. Within the framework of capitalism, socialism was beginning to emerge.

The dialectic was also involved in the surplus production that made capitalism the creator of great wealth. This productivity was achieved by an extensive overspecialization of labor that had converted the worker into a crippled monstrosity by forcing dexterity in a very limited area while ignoring the rest of his or her productive capabilities. [11] The individual was turned into a machine-like creature, performing over and over again the same operation which gave the laborer skills which could not be sold anywhere else. The wealth that capitalism was producing, however valuable as a prerequisite for the later sharing of socialism and communism, was crippling the worker at the same time.

The fact that labor created the capital destined to employ additional workers the following year meant also that the proletariat was, in general, not paid enough to be able to consume the very products that it made. As capital expanded, production expanded, and this ought to have meant increases in wages due to shortages of labor. However, ruthless competition among capitalists had the opposite effect—the smaller bourgeoisie was forced into the working class, while the shrinking remainder concentrated in monopolies. The more concentrated industry permitted greater utilization of machinery and greater efficiency, resulting in a cheapening of the product and a falling rate of profit that were consequences of the smaller size of the *active* work force. With the increase of the total capital, therefore, there was a corresponding decrease in the demand for labor. The laboring population thus produced, along with the capital necessary for capitalist expansion, the means by which it was made superfluous.

This was the cause of the growing industrial reserve army, the ranks of the unemployed. The larger the number of unemployed the greater the pressure on the active work force to take less remuneration and more overwork in order to keep their jobs. Classical economists had maintained that as capitalist expansion took place, wages would increase as well until additional laborers entering the job market brought the wages down again. (The "invisible hand" of Adam Smith at work.) Marx insisted, however, that long before the workers would benefit, the increasing concentration of industry into monopolies would introduce so many new machines that the proletariat would be worse off rather than temporarily better off. This was called the absolute general law of capitalist accumulation—the greater the social wealth, the greater the absolute mass of the proletariat, and the greater the size of the industrial reserve army. The greater the ranks of the unemployed, of course, the more extensive the scope of pauperism. On the one hand was social wealth, the production of which was capitalism's historic vocation; on the other hand was a misery of constantly expanding proportions.

This society of a growing proletariat and a shrinking bourgeoisie was exacerbated by periodic crises of increasing dimensions. Cycles of boom and depression followed from the lack of connection between the producer and the consumer and from the depression of the overall wages of the increasingly large proletariat. The pressures on the capitalist encouraged rapid production resulting in overproduction in the context of a shrinking market. Consumers, including workers, had less money to buy the commodities produced by an expanding capitalist economy. Crises had already occurred, and they would again, more and more frequently, and with greater severity.

This was an inevitable flow of events. Capitalism was creating within itself the seeds of its own destruction. As the **negation** of capitalism developed, the ability of the bourgeoisie to retard this process lessened. The results were a deepening of the misery of the proletariat; a greater concentration of capitalists; a larger industrial reserve army; and finally the pauperized proletariat would find itself the overwhelming majority of the population opposing a handful of capitalists. At this point the giant contradiction, implicit in the relations of production from their inception, became very, very clear. The thoroughly socialized proletariat was confronted by the old relations of property which permitted very few to benefit from the poverty of the masses. The capitalist relations of production which had created so much wealth had now exhausted their historic function—they had become fetters on continued progress. Marx believed that the proletariat would see this, and see themselves for what they really were. Their consciousness of unnecessary servitude, coupled with a sense of their power, would bring about the revolution.

Just as previous modes of production had been altered by revolution so would the present system. A social revolution would take place, radically changing the mode of production, thereby also abolishing the old superstructure based on those relations of production. This conflict of classes would culminate in the smashing of the existing state, but that was the consequence of the social revolution, not its primary purpose. The revolution would occur in the resolution of the dialectical conflict within the economic base of the society.[12]

Although probably beginning in one country, the revolution would quickly become worldwide. Workers had no country in this type of struggle. Nationalism was itself part of the bourgeois mystique and would be a restraint on proletarian development. Workers all over the world would quickly ascertain that they had nothing to lose but their chains and everything to gain—a world based on the fruits of their own collective labor organized into a society that marked the beginnings of truly *human* history.

Marx's Revolutionary Theory

Historical materialism described the past leading up to the present, and the present leading to the future—a future made possible by the praxis of revolution. That was the theory. The application of the theory was, however, extraordinarily difficult. History's contrariness in following predicted lines caused Marx and Engels to frequently reinterpret events and to readjust their theory. As a result, the revolutionary praxis, which was a key element in their legacy, became confused and ambiguous. They became confused about the character of that revolution, its timing, whether the proletariat or a party should lead it, and whether the struggle would be violent or peaceful.

One of the first mistakes, later admitted by Engels, lay in considering the French Revolution a prototype of the revolution to come. At the time that their ideas about revolution were maturing, they were affected by the French Revolution and by the revolutionary **ideology** in Paris. Engels wrote that he and Marx were under the spell of the French Revolution(s) when they were writing and acting in 1848-49. "It was, therefore, natural and unavoidable that our conceptions of the nature and course of the 'social' revolution proclaimed in Paris in February 1848, of the revolution of the proletariat, should be strongly coloured by the memories of the prototypes of 1789 and 1830." [13] The proletarian revolution was considered a struggle of good against evil, of progressive forces against exhausted minions of the *ancien régime*. The deprived would triumph over the depraved.

However, the revolutions in 1848 failed. Engels, from the vantage point of 1895, attributed their error to failing to see that a new economic prosperity had doomed the revolution. [14] In 1848, however, they had felt that the new prosperity was very shaky, that conditions remained ripe for revolution. *"A new revolution is possible only in consequence of a new crisis. It is, however, just as certain as this crisis."* [15] The tie between crisis and revolution caused Marx to predict revolutions that never developed. Frustration caused him to equate significant events, such as the discovery of gold in California, or the invention of the steam locomotive, with the imminence of crisis and revolution.

In 1895 Engels seemed embarrassed by their earlier predictions. We were wrong, he said, because the state of economic development on the continent was not yet ripe for the elimination of capitalism. [16] This was a sensible response but a weak one. The massive inroads into proletarian revolutionary fervor made by the extension of the suffrage and the early successes of unions were late-nineteenth-century phenomena. In mid-century Marx had seen the extension of suffrage as a means of unchaining the class struggle. [17] The ripeness of economic conditions appeared to be a function of revolution, not the reverse. Marx wrote to Engels in 1856 that the proletarian revolution in Germany depended on the possibility of backing from a second edition of the Peasant War of the sixteenth century. [18] If the proletariat needed help from peasants when the time came, historical materialism was not as clear a picture as Marx had thought. Could it also be that the proletariat might attain power "ahead of time"? This was a real possibility to Engels. This would be a seizure of power *before* economic conditions were ripe! The proletariat would then be undertaking *untimely communist experiments.*[19]

What had happened to the theory that the proletariat would be the vast majority of the pauperized population? Did the existence of an "advanced party" cancel that out as a necessity? The Communist League had been a group which alone knew the line of march, the correct path to follow. [20] In 1867 Marx described the **International** as a powerful engine in "our" hands. [21] Near the effective demise of the International, in 1872, Marx and Engels wrote a resolution for the Hague Congress of the International that said:

> In its struggle against the collective power of the possessing classes the proletariat can act as a class only by constituting itself a distinct political party . . . . This . . . is indispensable to ensure the triumph of the social revolution. . . .[22]

In 1875 Engels identified the Eisenacher wing of the German Social Democrats as "our party." [23] The masses were important, no question, but the correct party was important as well.

Did this mean that the party would work for revolution against the system, or for reform from within? Theoretically the answer was simple—violence. Material force against material force was necessary to overthrow the bourgeoisie. Perhaps because of the existence of the German Social Democratic Workers' party that had formed at Eisenach in 1869, perhaps because he changed his mind, or perhaps because, as with economic determinism, he had never intended to sound so proviolence, Marx wrote in 1872:

We know of the allowances we must make for the institutions, customs and traditions of the various countries; and we do not deny that there are countries such as America, England, and I would add Holland if I knew your institutions better, where the working people may achieve their goal by peaceful means. If that is true, we must also recognize that in most of the continental countries it is force that will have to be the lever of our revolutions; it is force that we shall some day have to resort to in order to establish a reign of labour. [24]

Although qualified, this statement allowed for the possibility of a peaceful transition to socialism in democratic countries. Engels went so far in 1895 as to suggest that perhaps the ballot box might have replaced the barricades in Germany as well. [25] He qualified this by referring to the possible necessity of violence, but it was certainly true that both Marx and Engels confused the issue. Violence might still be necessary, but peaceful methods might bring about proletarian success as well. This was true even in Germany, where, after 1890, the socialist party could participate in national elections.

The legacy left by historical materialism was not as clear as might have been desired. Many different interpretations resulted. Marx felt that his ideas were often used in a very superficial manner by others, as an excuse not to study history themselves. The results were interpretations of "Marxism" that he disavowed. Speaking of French "Marxists" of the 1870s, Engels wrote, Marx said, "All I know is that I am not a Marxist."[26]

Even though history quietly refused to step into the pattern that Marx had constructed, he continued to believe that the revolution was imminent until his death.

For Marx was before all else a revolutionist. His real mission in life was to contribute, in one way or another, to the overthrow of capitalist society and of the state institutions which it had brought into being, to contribute to the liberation of the modern proletariat, which *he* was the first to make conscious of its own position and its needs, conscious of the conditions of its emancipation. [27]

Regardless of whether or not others agreed with him, Marx felt that he had found the solution to the riddle of history and the means of ending the enslavement and alienation of humans everywhere. That solution was communism.

Suggested Readings

Avineri, Shlomo. *The Social and Political Thought of Karl Marx.* New York: Cambridge University Press, 1968.

Bober, M.M. *Karl Marx's Interpretation of History.* New York: W.W. Norton, 1965.

Caute, David, ed. *Essential Writings of Karl Marx.* New York: Macmillan, 1967.

Cole, G.D.H. *The Meaning of Marxism.* Ann Arbor: University of Michigan Press, 1948.

Hook, Sidney. *Marx and the Marxists.* New York: Van Nostrand, 1955.

Padover, Saul K., ed. and trans. *Karl Marx On Revolution.* New York: McGraw-Hill, 1971.

Wittfogel, Karl A. *Oriental Despotism, A Comparative Study of Total Power.* New Haven: Yale University Press, 1957.

NOTES

[1] Karl Marx, "Preface to *A Contribution to the Critique of Political Economy*," *Marx-Engels Selected Works* (Moscow: Progress Publishers, 1970), 1: 503-4.

[2] Engels, "Letter to J. Bloch in Königsberg" (September 1890), ibid., 3: 487.

[3] Ibid., p. 488.

[4] The foregoing paragraph is paraphrased from Marx's "Letter to P.V. Annenkov in Paris," ibid., 1, especially pp. 518, 522.

[5] Marx, "Preface to *A Contribution to the Critique of Political Economy*," ibid., p. 504.

[6] For extensive detail, see Engels, "The Origin of the Family, Private Property and the State," ibid., 3: 191-334. This work was partially based on Lewis Morgan's *Ancient Society* (1877) and Marx's notes on that book, to which Engels added his own research.

[7] Karl Marx, "Preface to the First German Edition of the First Volume of *Capital*," ibid., 2: 89.

[8] Karl Marx, "Afterword to the Second German Edition of the First Volume of *Capital*," ibid., p. 98.

[9] Karl Marx, "Productive Power in Capitalist and Communist Society," in McLellan, *The Grundrisse,* p. 151.

[10] For a fuller discussion of this point by Marx, see "The Contributions of Labour and Capital to the Production Process," ibid., pp. 87ff.

48

[11]The term "overspecialization of labor" is used here to avoid confusing it with the more common "division of labor," which had a more general, alienative meaning in most of Marx's writings.

[12]See an excellent discussion of these points in Robert Tucker, "The Marxian Revolutionary Idea," in *Why Revolution?* ed. Clifford Paynton and Robert Blackey (Cambridge: Schenkman, 1971), pp. 214-29.

[13]Engels, "Preface to Marx's Class Struggles in France, 1848-1850," *Marx-Engels Selected Works* 1: 189.

[14]Ibid., p. 187.

[15]Karl Marx, "The Class Struggles in France 1848-1850," ibid., p. 289.

[16]Engels, "Preface to Marx's Class Struggles in France, 1848-1850," ibid., pp. 191-92.

[17]Marx, "The Class Struggles in France 1848-1850," ibid., p. 223.

[18]Marx, "Letter to Engels in Manchester, April 16, 1856," ibid., p. 529.

[19]Engels, "Letter to J. Wedemeyer, April 12, 1853," *Marx-Engels Selected Correspondence* (Moscow: Foreign Languages Publishing House, n.d.), p. 94.

[20]Marx and Engels, "The Manifesto of the Communist Party," *Marx-Engels Selected Works* 1: 120.

[21]Marx, "Letter to Engels, September 11, 1867," *Marx-Engels Selected Works in Two Volumes* (London: Martin Lawrence, Ltd.), 2: 614.

[22]Marx and Engels, "From the Resolutions of the General Congress Held in the Hague," *Marx-Engels Selected Works* 2: 291.

[23]Engels, "Letter to August Bebel, March 18-28, 1875," ibid., 3: 31.

[24]Marx, "The Hague Congress," ibid., 2: 293.

[25]Engels, "Preface to Marx's Class Struggles in France 1848-1850," ibid., 1: 201.

[26]Engels, "Letter to C. Schmidt in Berlin, August 5, 1890," ibid., 3: 484.

[27]Engels, "Speech at the Graveside of Karl Marx," ibid., p. 163.

The Marxian Future

The future would be communism. When individual awareness of alienation—its cause and its cure—had spread among workers to the point where life itself was seen as a living contradiction, proletarian activity would be revolutionary. The praxis of changed humans would seek to transform the conditions of their existence. The resulting revolution could not be a partial one. Caused by an absolute nadir of humanity, it could only result in a total, universal emancipation. By the time of the revolution the proletariat no longer represented a class similar to those in the past—it represented everyone. In freeing itself, the working class liberated all humans as well.

Communism was both means and goal. Marx's struggle against religion had become a battle against the society that required religion, against the social pervasion of the religious principle. Overcoming that alienation would be the great task of the revolution, but in the process it would make atheism unnecessary. The denial of God had been an affirmation of the human, but that would no longer be necessary. The human would be affirmed in every aspect of life. Thus the goal of the future was not atheism but the return of the human to full essential being. Similarly, if communism were thought of as the abolition of private property, what Marx meant was the appropriation of the human essence in and for humans.[1] This was communism as means to an end.

The position of communism is the negation of the negation and hence, for the next stage of historical development, the necessary *actual* phase of man's emancipation and rehabilitation. *Communism* is the necessary form and dynamic principle of the immediate future but not as such the goal of human development—the form of human society.[2]

The abolition of private property would not be, after all, something that one did continuously; it would be done *in order that* practical communism (humanism) might come into being.

The first step taken by the proletarian revolutionaries, therefore, would be the destruction of private property. This was not construed as burning down someone's house, or as a refined welfare distribution of the wealth of the society, but as a basic alteration in the **mode of production.** The **means of production** would be socialized and the division of labor in the relations of production would be forever ended. No longer would there be owners and nonowners of the means of production, for all would own collectively. In order to accomplish this vital task, however, the proletariat would need power.

. . . the proletarian class will first have to possess itself of the organized political force of the State and with this aid stamp out the resistance of the Capitalist class and re-organize society . . . [carrying out] that economic revolution of society without which the whole victory must end in a defeat and in a massacre of the working class like that after the Paris Commune.[3]

Between capitalist and communist society lies the period of the revolutionary transformation of the one into the other. Corresponding to this is also a political transition period in which the state can be nothing but *the revolutionary dictatorship of the proletariat.*[4]

Anarchists, such as Bakunin, wanted to *destroy* the state. That was what the revolution was all about to them. Marx and Engels, on the other hand, wanted to *use* the power of the state to socialize the means of production and to crush opposition from former capitalists. Engels wrote that the proletariat would not use the state in the interests of freedom, but in order to hold down its adversaries by force.[5] Actually, the notions of freedom and state were unlikely as simultaneous conceptions, in that they agreed with **anarchism.**

. . . and as soon as it becomes possible to speak of freedom the state as such ceases to exist. We would therefore propose to replace *state* everywhere by *Gemeinwesen*, a good old German word which can very well convey the meaning of the French word *'commune.'*[6]

In the meantime the state would be useful to the proletariat. Workers would not forget what the state actually was—a reflection of the dominant relations of production in that it was a machine for the oppression of one class by another. No—the state was an evil thing *at best*, and the proletariat immediately would amputate as much as possible of its worst parts.[7]

Such use of the power of the state would only be temporary. When the means of production were socialized the division of labor would be abolished. This meant that classes reflecting a division of labor could not arise. The need for the oppressive arm of the ruling class in a context of classlessness made no sense. Therefore the state's functions would only be for the transition period. How long would that be? Engels answered, rather ambiguously, ". . . until such time as a generation reared in new, free social conditions is able to throw the entire lumber of the state on the scrap heap."[8] At that point it would cease to exist.

> When at last [the state] becomes the real representative of the whole of society, it renders itself unnecessary. As soon as there is no longer any social class to be held in subjection; as soon as class rule, and the individual struggle for existence based upon our present anarchy in production, with the collisions and excesses arising from these, are removed, nothing more remains to be repressed, and a special repressive force, a state, is no longer necessary. The first act by virtue of which the state really constitutes itself the representative of the whole of society—the taking possession of the means of production in the name of society—this is, at the same time, its last independent act as a state. State interference in social relations becomes, in one domain after another, superfluous, and then dies out of itself . . . .[9]

These ideas were based on the belief that the socialized relations of production would deeply influence the new environment and the people in it. This was a key element in scientific socialism, and failure to comprehend this will make Marx's comprehension of the future read like a fairy tale, out of touch with what is called "reality." Marx felt that what one might call "human nature" was, to a large extent, a reflection of the dominant relations of production—not entirely caused by it but deeply conditioned nonetheless. The people living in the capitalist relations of production were products of their environment. Humans would also change when that environment dramatically altered in communism because of the way in which the superstructure would begin to reflect the social relations of production. People were products of heredity, of course, but to a much greater extent they were a reflection of their environment—the institutional superstructure that surrounded them from birth. In a deeper sense the human had always been social—it was part of the essence. Previous relations of production, however, reflecting the perniciousness of private property, had obscured that natural social character by forcing all kinds of "separations" into it. What passed for human character in the bourgeois period was in fact a travesty of real human nature. The socialization of the means of production meant an overcoming of alienation in real life, and that meant the return of a true human nature to people. The bourgeois individual with a passion for private acquisition at the expense of society would fade away. The new person with returned human essence would, after a short time lag, be a social person.

This new essence was even superior to that with which the human began in primitive communism. In that earlier period people had been alienated from nature, from a world considered outside themselves because it could not be understood. All of subsequent history, however, had demonstrated increasing human ability to conquer that "outside nature," to impose human will upon it, so that by the time of communism the nature which surrounded the human was in fact a part of *human* nature and a bond with other people. The new human nature would therefore be the most complete human essence—and *human* history could only then begin. As with the prodigal son, people had in their long history eaten of the bitter husks of alienation, had rejected them, and would return to themselves wiser and richer.

The revolutionary dictatorship of the proletariat would be communism as means. It would socialize the means of production, destroy capitalist opposition, and abolish institutions that reflected the alienated past. But in so doing the proletariat would be proceeding dialectically, that is, it would build a qualitatively new phenomenon on the basis of what was of enduring value in the old. The abolition of private property would destroy property that separated people from each other, transcending *bourgeois* property. This would not mean that everyone would claim the shirt that a person wore, or that people would have to take turns wearing a dress. Property that was the basis of production and that separated people into classes of haves and have-nots was to be abolished. The articles of consumption would belong to all people as a human right, but they would be consumed individually. In communism, you could say that this dress or that shirt was *yours,* but it would actually be a meaningless concept. Private property as privilege for the few would be abolished, replaced by the possession of social property for the purposes of consumption.

Other institutions would follow a similar path. Democracy, for all of its freedoms and pretensions of freedom, was nonetheless a bourgeois state. Vulgar democracy, Marx wrote, saw the millennium in the democratic republic. The proponents of democracy did not suspect that it was the last form of the state in bourgeois society—the one in which the class struggle had to be fought to a conclusion.[10] Engels, much later, described the democratic republic as the last form of bourgeois rule and the one in which that rule went to pieces.[11] That kind of democracy had to be transcended; but the solution was again built on the enduring qualities of the old. The revolution was a social one that had political ramifications. The new form that the social organization would take would be built on the past form in the process of transcending it. Social organization would be a democracy without the bourgeois adjective, a democracy that would have exchanged past illusion for reality. With the withering of the state the administration of people would change to the administration of things.

Communism as means would produce a communism of practice. The new social form was to be called "association" or "community":

> The working class in the course of its development will substitute for the old civil society an association which will exclude classes and their antagonism, and there will be no more political power properly so-called, since political power is precisely the official expression of antagonism in civil society.[12]

The abolition of the division of labor could not last without a communal organization of society. Only in association with others was it possible for personal freedom to exist. Instead of the pretense of democracy made impossible by the division of labor, the genuine community was an organization in which individuals gained their freedom in and through their association. If people were really to assert themselves as individuals, really rule themselves, the association was necessary.[13]

Therefore, the new association would not be political in the sense of factional power politics, but it would be democratic in a real sense of the word. The people would really rule. Human social organization would then become the result of their own free action. People would become their own masters in their own society. Exactly how this organization would work in practice was not described. This was one of the many details left to work out for itself in the future. Marx and Engels were not prescribing the minutiae of the future—in their view that would have linked them with the **utopian socialism** they had condemned; they were deducing general descriptions on the basis of their conviction that the abolition of alienation in the relations of production would have profound social consequences. A clue to the possible mechanics of the association was provided by Engels when he generalized about the worth of two methods utilized by the brief **Paris Commune** of 1871 (i.e., filling all posts by universal suffrage with easy recall, and the paying of those elected officials no more than that received by other workers).[14]

The association was, therefore, not anarchic. There would be authority in the new system. Not political authority, of course, but an authority that would be more like self-discipline arising from *social* consciousness and *voluntary* cooperation. An orchestra, for example, is a disciplined group of people coordinated or blended by the conductor. If everyone played the notes that pleased them individually, music would only rarely emerge. Remember that this was to be a different sort of democracy. People would be masters of their own society, but humans were not simply individuals—they were simultaneously social. Marx and Engels were writing about all people, not just a few. That human collective would have to be disciplined and coordinated, and the people would have to do this themselves. The bread had to get to the grocery store, the wheat to the mills, and the milk to the children. This would require that people perform their tasks in concert with each other, just as musicians created music by playing together according to a plan.

This was expressed by Engels when he attacked anarchist critics by asking: How do those people propose to run a factory or work a railroad, or steer a ship without a deciding will and a unified direction?[15] Marx put it in much the same way in *Capital*. There would have to be regulation of working hours, division of social work, accounting—functions previously performed by capitalism. As a matter of fact, Marx continued:

> ... all labours, in which many individuals cooperate, necessarily require for the connection and unity of the process one commanding will, and this performs a function which does not refer to fragmentary operations, but to the combined labour of the workshop, in the same way as does that of a director of an orchestra. This is a kind of productive labour which must be performed in every mode of production requiring a combination of labours.[16]

Authority must be present, but it would be restricted in scope to that which was absolutely necessary under the new conditions of production.[17]

Communism in practice, therefore, meant democratic freedoms in a real sense—not understood as private individual autonomy in an absolute sense, but as free participants in a social entity that required operation according to a single rational plan. The whole point of that plan was to be consumption; this was not production for exchange but production for *use*. Those products deemed, by the people themselves, as necessary or desirable for human life would be produced. That production required discipline and coordination, a plan of operation that developed from below but represented social authority nonetheless. Humans together would thereby determine the conditions under which they lived. The social authority, the plan, would function as the head controlling the body—making progressive movement possible. The result would be an unbroken, progressive development of industry and a practically limitless growth in production, an abundance made possible by unfettering the very productive capitalist system. Removing the private extraction of profit and proceeding according to a rational plan, wealth would be created that would change life as much as a river flowing over former desert sands brought new green life. Engels wrote that there would be

> ... an unbroken, constantly accelerated development of the productive forces, and therewith ... a practically unlimited increase of production itself. Nor is this all. The socialised appropriation of the means of production does away, not only with the present artificial restrictions upon production, but also with the positive waste and devastation of productive forces and products that are at the present time the inevitable concomitants of production, and that reach their height in the crises. Further, it sets free for the community at large a mass of means of production and of products, by doing away with the senseless extravagance of the ruling classes of today and their political representatives. The possibility of securing for every member of society, by means of socialised production, an existence not only fully sufficient materially, and becoming day by day more full, but an existence guaranteeing to all the free development and exercise of their physical and mental faculties—this possibility is now for the first time here, but *it is here.*[18]

Communism in practice would mean association, planned production, and abundance. This would mean, of course, that people would have to work. A difference would exist, however. Formerly work was a means to animal life, but now work would be an expression of human life. Productive labor was here understood as opportunity for the individual to develop and utilize all of his or her faculties whether physical or mental. Productive labor would become more like a hobby, something you want to do because you can do it and it is fun to do. It would be perspiration that would not be minded, made especially pleasant by the inability of any group to place its labor on some other group's shoulders. Adding to this pleasure would be the notion of working at different sorts of tasks rather than being bored with only one. Individuals had interests that led in many directions, and associational labor would bring this multidimensionality into the daily life of the worker. One might, for example, be a teacher in the morning, a bricklayer in the afternoon, and a movie critic in the evening. The talents of persons, heretofore only latent, would be allowed to flower. This would still be labor, but with a profound difference.

Private housework would be transformed into a public industry. This implied child care centers, public dining facilities, and perhaps a corps of "maids" performing vital cleaning functions as part of their social labor. The dominance of women by men, a necessity as long as the division of labor made the male the breadwinner, was already being decimated in capitalism. Under communism the woman would be an equal partner with the man, married for love and only as long as love endured. The entire relationship between men and women, and women and society, would alter considerably.[19]

Agriculture would also be transformed by associational, rationally planned labor. Land would be withdrawn from private ownership, transformed into social property, and worked by cooperative associations of agricultural workers as part of their social labor. This communal activity would allow for greater production on the combined farms, a production which would be coordinated in the single rational plan for the entire worldwide association. The differences between town and country would diminish. The large cities would be broken up and the rural areas would lose their sense of stuporous isolation. Scattered industry would gain purer water and agriculture would benefit from nearby industry. City sewage could then be used as agricultural fertilizer. The results of the combination of the best in city and country would be cleaner air, more spacious and abundant housing, and an even distribution of the population.[20]

Communism in practice would mean association or community living; the authority of rational planning; a substantial difference in people; alterations in the character and kind of work that one did; and the abolition of artificial distinctions between various kinds of work, sexes, and locale. It would also mean a new distribution of the wealth of the society, an inevitable result of the socialization of the means of production. This too was a part of the rational plan.

Before one could speak of distribution to individual people, however, one would have to supply the needs of the basis of their lives—the productive engine. First, society should replace the used-up portions of the means of production such as raw materials and worn out or out-of-date machinery. Second, society should budget for production expansion. Third, a reserve fund for contingencies would be wise. Fourth, there would have to be an allocation for nonproducing but associated costs of production, such as administration, schools, public health, and unemployment compensation. This would come off the top. The remainder would be divided among the individual producers in the society as social dividends.[21]

The manner of that distribution would depend on the character of the society. In the initial period following the revolution a communism would exist that was still economically, morally, and intellectually stamped with birthmarks from the old, capitalist society. This time lag reflected Marx's belief that things could not be completely changed overnight. It would be a new society, but still deeply affected by the old. In this first phase workers would not exchange their products as social wealth, even though there would be a direct relation between labor and product. The *value* of the product would still be expressed in external "monetary" terminology, resulting in the laborers being individually rewarded. A person's labor time would entitle the worker to receive a certificate stating that, after deductions, he or she should receive from the common store goods equivalent to that labor time. The workers would receive back from society the exact amount, less deductions, that had been put in by their labor. This would be a different distribution from the past in that money would not exist as the medium of exchange. In another sense, this initial period would resemble the capitalism of the past in that there would be an exchange of equal values. A given amount of labor in one form would be traded for an equal amount of labor in another form.

What could be wrong with that? Would that not be equality? True, but it would be, Marx insisted, an equality that papered over inequality. Some workers were stronger, both physically and mentally—they could produce more and work longer hours than others as a part of their natural endowment. The labor of everyone was valued, but it would not be the fact that everyone was laboring but the *measure* of that individual labor in intensity or duration that would be the basis of reward. In addition, some workers would require more of a reward than would others—just to stay even. Some would be married with large families to support, others would be single. In other words, this initial equality would raise to a social right the unequal natural endowments and unequal needs of the people. The result would not be new classes, but some would be richer than others.

To overcome this problem social right, instead of being equal, would have to be unequal. This could not occur until society itself had moved so far from capitalism that it was only a historical memory.

> In a higher phase of communist society, after the enslaving subordination of the individual to the division of labour, and therewith also the antithesis between mental and physical labour, has vanished; after labour has become not only a means of life but life's prime want; after the productive forces have also increased with the all-round development of the individual, and all the springs of cooperative wealth flow more abundantly—only then can the narrow horizon of bourgeois right be crossed in its entirety and society inscribe on its banners: From each according to his ability, to each according to his needs![22]

The distribution of social wealth, after deductions, would then be unequal and satisfy the needs of humans from the common store. Needs which people formerly spent their entire life trying to satisfy would then be easily fulfilled, and with everyone working they would be consuming as much as was necessary. The satisfaction of all reasonable needs would be assured to everyone in an ever-increasing measure.[23]

The anarchy of capitalist production and distribution would be replaced by the association's rational plan, coordinating production so that the talents of individuals would be fully used, and coordinating distribution so that needs would be satisfied. This would mean that some people would be entrusted with the administration of the plan, but those administrators would be as conditioned by the socialized mode of production as the rest of the society. Administration would not be a vehicle for making more money—there would be no money to make more of—nor a device to exercise power over people. Administrators would be in those positions because of administrative talents. They would perform other functions according to their other talents as well and would receive, as would everyone else, a satisfaction of needs from the common store. They could very well be elected and easily recalled. These were details, however, that Marx and Engels left for the future members of the association to decide for themselves. As Robinson Crusoe on an *individual* basis created his own world in fiction, so would the association members, on a *social* basis, create their world in reality.

Communism in practice would also mean an economics of time. The plan would implement measures that would reduce the amount of time necessary for the production of wheat or cattle, for example. This time saving would give society more opportunity for other forms of production, both material and intellectual. The massive introduction of machinery into the productive process in capitalism had made active labor in production less imperative. Whereas surplus labor had previously fed the wealth of the few, in communism this lowered work requirement would result in leisure time for all—time in which all members of society could develop their education in the arts, sciences, and so on, thanks to the free time and means available to all.[24] Semi-automated industry was, even under capitalism, placing production on the level of an automatic process requiring supervision and regulation and little else. Under communism, further savings in labor time would increase this leisure, resulting in a further improvement of the production process and qualitative differences in the people themselves. Humans living and working in the association would be renewing both themselves and the world of wealth that they had created.[25] Because of this, what was really worth preserving in historically inherited culture, science, art, and human relations would not only be preserved but converted into the common property of the whole of society and further developed.[26]

Communism in practice would have a final social benefit—peace. The proletariat would have already demonstrated in its revolution that the narrow confines of nationalism had been left far behind. The association would be worldwide, and the conflict between classes would have disappeared. Since needs would be satisfied and talents directed into social channels, hostility between groups of people or between individuals would wither away. Engels wrote glowingly about the American Iroquois tribe in primitive communism: "Everything runs smoothly without soldiers, gendarmes or police; without nobles, kings, governors, prefects or judges; without prisons; without trials. All quarrels and disputes are settled by the whole body of those concerned."[27]

However wonderful, that society was doomed to perish—but all of the subsequent history of human progress in mastering nature and improving production did not diminish the beauty of that primitive communist beginning. The communism of the future would be far richer because it would be totally unalienated, fully human, and worldwide. The socialized means of production proceeding according to rational plan for the benefit of everyone would put an end to crime and an end to war. A new society would spring up, Marx wrote, whose international rule would be peace, because its national ruler would be everywhere the same: labor.[28]

The internal dynamic of history would culminate, therefore, in the start of *human* history that was, in a way, a return to the beginnings of prehistory. In Hegel that internal logic was implemented through the activity of individuals who had risen above mundane affairs—people such as Alexander the Great, Caesar, and Napoleon. Their personal interests became synonymous with the universal interest of the Spirit which moved them. To Marx the internal dynamic moved through classes in history, dramatically altering relations of production until the proletariat, representing universal interests, by socializing those production relations, would create a human plateau. Communism as means would result in communism in practice, a union of philosophy and praxis in the world of material reality.

Marx had written to his father in 1837 that he was seeking the Idea in the real itself so that he could discover human mental nature to be just as determined, concrete, and firmly established in its broad outlines, as was physical nature.[29] By blending a transformed Hegel with French revolutionary politics and British economics he felt he had unlocked the secrets of history and pointed the way to human emancipation for all of time.

Was he correct? An answer to that question ought to be an informed one—informed about what happened to his ideas after his death in the world he had fought to change.

Suggested Readings

Denno, Theodore. *The Communist Millennium—The Soviet View.* The Hague: Martinus Nijhoff, 1964.

Fischer, Ernst, ed., and Bostock, Anna, trans. *The Essential Marx.* New York: Herder & Herder, 1971.

Freedman, Robert, ed. *Marxist Social Thought.* New York: Harcourt, Brace & World, 1968.

Hyppolite, Jean. *Studies on Marx and Hegel,* ed. and trans. John O'Neill. New York: Harper Torchbooks, 1969.

Meyer, Alfred G. *Communism.* New York: Random House, 1967.

Tucker, Robert C., ed. *The Marx-Engels Reader.* New York: W.W. Norton, 1972.

NOTES

[1] Excerpt from Karl Marx, "Economic and Philosophical Manuscripts (1844)," in Easton and Guddat, *Writings of the Young Marx on Philosophy and Society,* p. 304. Reprinted by permission of Doubleday & Company, Inc.

[2] Ibid., p. 314.

[3] Engels, "Letter to Phillip Van Patten, April 18, 1883," *Marx-Engels Selected Correspondence,* p. 437.

[4] Marx, "Critique of the Gotha Program," *Marx-Engels Selected Works* 3: 26.

[5] Engels, "Letter to A. Bebel, March 18-28, 1875," ibid., p. 35.

[6] Ibid.

[7] Engels, "Introduction to 'The Civil War in France,' " ibid., 2: 189.

[8] Ibid.

[9] Engels, "Socialism: Utopian and Scientific," ibid., 3: 147.

[10] Marx, "Critique of the Gotha Program," ibid., 3: 27.

[11] Engels, "Letter to Eduard Bernstein, March 24, 1884," *Marx-Engels Selected Correspondence,* p. 445.

[12] Marx, *The Poverty of Philosophy* (Moscow: Foreign Languages Publishing House), p. 167.

[13] Marx and Engels, "Feuerbach. Opposition of the Materialistic and Idealistic Outlook" (Chap. 1 of *The German Ideology*), *Marx-Engels Selected Works* 1: 65-66.

[14] Engels, "Introduction to 'The Civil War in France,' " ibid., 2: 188.

[15] Engels, "Letter to T. Cuno in Milan, January 24, 1872," ibid., pp. 425-26.

[16]Marx, as quoted in Irving Fetscher, "Marx, Engels, and the Future Society," in *The Future of the Communist Society*, ed. Laqueur and Labedz. New York: Praeger, 1962, p. 101. Reprinted with permission of the publisher.

[17]Engels, "On Authority," *Marx-Engels Selected Works* 2 : 378.

[18]Engels, "Socialism: Utopian and Scientific," ibid., 3: 148-49.

[19]Engels, "Origin of the Family, Private Property and the State," ibid., pp. 248-55.

[20]See Engels, *Herr Eugene Duhring's Revolution in Science* (Anti-Duhring) (New York: International Publishers, 1939), pp. 323-24; and his *The Housing Question* (New York: International Publishers, n. d.), pp. 36, 95-96.

[21]Marx, "Critique of the Gotha Program," *Marx-Engels Selected Works* 3: 16-17.

[22]Ibid., p. 19. This section on distribution is paraphrased from this article. Marx was here attacking the program which joined two wings of the German Social Democrats at Gotha in 1875. A major point made in this critique was that overconcern about distribution was vulgar socialism. *Distribution must not be considered independently of the mode of production.* Much later, "welfare socialism" resulted from a failure to recognize this (see chap. 5).

[23]Engels, "Karl Marx," ibid., p. 86.

[24]Marx, "The Position of Labour in Capitalist and Communist Society," in McLellan, *The Grundrisse—Karl Marx,* p. 142. See also "General and Specific Labour," ibid., pp. 74-76.

[25]Marx, "Leisure and Free Time in Communist Society," ibid., pp. 148-49.

[26]Engels, *The Housing Question*, pp. 29-30.

[27]Engels, "Origin of the Family, Private Property and the State," *Marx-Engels Selected Works* 3: 266.

[28]Marx, "First Address of the General Council of the International Working Men's Association on the Franco-Prussian War," ibid., 2: 193-94.

[29]Marx, "Letter to His Father: On a Turning Point in Life (1837)," in Easton and Guddat, p. 46.

5

The Interregnum:
Marxism in Europe
1870-1917

Marxism was a faith that history moved according to predictable patterns, and that activity by individuals and groups could hasten or hamper the inevitable socialist triumph. During the period 1870-1917, Marx's ideas were very influential in the developing labor movement, but they competed with other varieties of socialism and less ideological concerns about working-class conditions. In places, times, and circumstances of which Marx could not always be aware, his ideas were developed by other people in response to specific situations in their own countries. The repository for his somewhat ambiguous legacy was concentrated in the working-class parties of Europe which formed the heart of the Second International (1889-1914)[1]. The internationalism of this movement, however, was a facade behind which national political development took place. This would become very clear in 1914.

Britain, France, Germany, Poland, and Russia were certainly not the only areas where Marxist ideas were important in beginning programs and organizations—Marx's influence was worldwide.[2] The European parties, however, were the leaders and models for other organizations. They all faced similar problems, and the European solutions were duplicated in the rest of the world.

Those problems were divisive. The most significant issue was reform versus revolution. All other problems were subsets of this basic question as, for example, the issue of the relationship between the working-class party and the trade unions or peasantry, or the question of the national versus the international implementation of communist ideas. Part of the problem lay in Marxism itself, for the reticence of Marx and Engels to speculate about the socialist future, a reticence shared by later Marxists, made the goal rather ambiguous. The lack of a clear finish line made the race exhausting and bewildering, giving more time for the problems related to the methods of accomplishing goals. The result was that each organization became riddled with internal differences that were uneasily held together by a perceived need for unified action.

The development of *German Social Democracy* during this period provides a focus for a discussion of these problems as they developed. The Germans were the most organized, perhaps the closest to Marx, and the dominant group in the Second International. Other European parties patterned themselves after the German organization.

German Social Democracy had its roots in the General German Workers' Association begun by Ferdinand Lassalle (1825-1864) in 1863. Lassalle, who himself "Frenchified" his given name of Lasal, was a flamboyant, vain, ambitious Hegelian who had never understood Marx's inversion of Hegelianism.[3] Lassalle saw socialism as an idea whose time had come in the developing spirit of the German people. He believed that universal suffrage would transform the state so as to make it an instrument of the general good of the entire population. As a result he began competing with the liberal progressives for working-class reforms to be granted by the state.

Engels did not like Lassalle. Marx cooperated with him until 1861, but then began to complain that he was stealing some of his ideas. In 1862, just as Prince Otto von Bismarck (1815-1898) was coming into real power in Germany, Marx sent Wilhelm Liebknecht (1826-1900) to Germany to begin an organization along Marxist lines, but Liebknecht was quickly expelled from Prussia. The General German Workers' Association thus began more in isolation from Marx than in cooperation with him. Opposition to Lassalle in 1863 from within Germany resulted in the formation of a *League of German Workers' Educational Society*. Liebknecht and August Bebel (1840-1913) used the League as a vehicle to set up the German Social Democratic party (SPD) at Eisenach in 1869. Many members of the association deserted to join the new movement. The new group maintained that it was necessary to side with the more progressive elements of the middle class against the aristocrats and autocrats, because only by defeating German autocracy could the German workers have a chance of victory. This position was reminiscent of Marx's own activities in Cologne in 1848-49. Stay independent of the middle class but support the more progressive elements so as to defeat the common enemy—the autocratic state.

This was difficult to practice right from the beginning. The socialists were already gaining victories at the polls. Bismarck had granted manhood suffrage to the North German Confederation in 1867, and both von Schweitzer, the Lassalean leader, and Liebknecht had won seats in the Reichstag. The problem was: how far should support of the progressive elements go? And how could real cooperation take place if working-class independence had to be jealously guarded? Later opportunities for participating in ruling coalitions were crucified by that rule of independence and separation; yet, years of partial cooperation in legislatures created such a dependency on parliamentary activity that revolution began to sound very much like rocking a canoe in deep water. The problems of later years grew from such early seeds.

The Social Democrats and the Lassalean association continued as rivals for only a short time. In the aftermath of the Franco-Prussian War and Bismarck's hostility after crushing the Paris Commune in 1871, the two groups were drawn together. In 1875 they united under the leadership of the more Marxist Eisenacher group into the German Social Democratic party at Gotha. Interestingly enough, this was done without prior consultation with Marx, and, as has been noted, he was very critical of the Gotha Program. He felt that it contained far too much Lassalle and not enough Marx. Liebknecht, however, suppressed the Marxian critique; it did not become generally known until after 1890 when the new Social Democratic Program (the *Erfurt Program*) was revised to take these criticisms into account—comments that were then sixteen years out of date.

In the meantime Bismarck's antisocialist hostility took other forms. Attempts in 1878 to assassinate the emperor gave Bismarck the excuse to push through antisocialist legislation. This drive was given added strength by an 1878 papal Encyclical, *Quod Apostilici Muneris,* which denounced socialism, communism, and nihilism as a deadly plague. The antisocialist laws that emerged in 1878 remained in force until 1890 and forbade the existence of any organization that sought to subvert the state or social order by advocating any form of socialism, social democracy, or communism. The SPD had to go underground, and socialist candidates for legislative seats had to be very careful. The organization was divorced from day-to-day involvement, and it had to operate from Switzerland. This isolation preserved the Marxist revolutionary notions intact in theory even though practice was increasingly reformist as the socialism was watered down in order to be legal. The hostility between socialism and the church, which the papal Encyclical had furthered, prevented the sort of cooperation between Christian socialists and Social Democrats that resulted in ethical socialism in Britain. This led G.D.H. Cole to remark:

> Indeed, for the German, Social Democracy was not so much a political creed as an entire culture, sharply separated both from the culture of the German *bourgeoisie* and from the rival culture which found its inspiration in the Catholic Church. Both Catholics and Social Democrats sought the allegiance of the whole man, in hostility to the no less exacting claims of the Prussian-dominated State.[4]

Emerging from the forced isolation in 1891, the Erfurt Program described a revolutionary Marxism that reflected past frustrations but not present conditions. Phrases such as "the increasing misery of the proletariat" were articulated in the face of vast improvements in working-class life. The capitalism that theory described as dying because of its internal contradictions was still very much alive. Theory and practice were wide apart as the Social Democrats came into the Second International, and they came as leaders. Germany, in the last quarter of the century, had replaced France as the foremost industrial nation of Europe, and the duration of the German organization as well as the scope of it made the Germans the leaders of the international movement.

In France the forcible suppression of the Paris Commune had made socialist organizations impossible for a time. In 1879 Jules Guesde (1845-1922) led a Federation of Socialist Workers of France out of a Marseilles Labor Congress just as amnesty for former Communards was declared by the French government. Guesde had been exiled after the Commune in 1871 and had been impressed with German Social Democracy while in Switzerland.[5] Wilhelm Liebknecht helped him set up a French Marxist party on the German model. In 1880 Guesde visited Marx in London and received additional help from Karl's son-in-law, Paul La Fargue, in organizing a French group based on the Gotha Program of 1875. However, this was only part of the French Left. There were Mutualists who wanted to cooperate with the bourgeoisie; Anarchists opposing any political action; Blanquists; trade unionists who wanted any political party to be subordinate to the union organizations; and vague Integrationists who were willing to use any means to gain the socialist objective. The Guesdists wanted to use the French parliament as the Germans did theirs, for propaganda purposes and secondarily for reforms, but others under Paul Brousse (1854-1912) felt that the goals of worker-delegates should be to gain whatever beneficial reforms were possible.

Another dimension of differences was in the problem created by the continued vitality of the peasant class. Individual proprietors of small landholdings were, theoretically, relics of feudalism who should disappear. However, they did not in France, nor elsewhere for that matter. The Guesdists sought peasant support by stressing the great wrongs done to both the peasantry and the small capitalist by finance capital and unfair taxation. To other socialists this position seemed to be combining class warfare with class cooperation, and they were very antagonistic. Attempts to solve this issue in other countries met similar problems. The peasantry could be partially redefined as a rural proletariat, but this did not satisfy very many. The problem grew more serious the further east one went.

These differences resulted in the formation of two rival French groups in 1882. The *Possibilists* under Paul Brousse gained control of the Federation of Socialist Workers of France, renaming it the *Socialist Revolutionary Workers'* party (dropping the "revolutionary" within a few years); and the *Guesdists* formed the *French Workers'* party on a centralized Marxist model. While this split was hardening, trade unions gained the right to exist, and by 1885 a struggle had emerged over which of the two competing political groups should control the Federation of National Unions. The Guesdists were victorious, but only temporarily. Their view of unions (*syndicats*) was similar to that of the Germans. There was supposed to be an increasing misery of the proletariat; therefore, unions could not improve the workers' condition—only the conquest of political power could.[6] This relegated the unions to a subordinate position, but this failed to recognize that the independent spirit of the French unions was not similar to that of the German ones. The right to combine in unions in Germany came after the working-class representatives were already in legislatures—this fostered dependence. In France the timing of both organizations was sufficiently simultaneous, fostering mutual independence. In Britain where the unions existed well in advance of the socialist parties, parties such as *Independent Labor* grew out of the union movement and sought to represent it in Parliament. Basic differences between national parties thus developed quite naturally.

Besides demanding greater independence, the French syndicats were much more influenced by anarchism than were other unions. They were more excited by American labor's agitation for an eight-hour working day, and much more caught up with the notion of the general strike as the workers' major weapon. Sorel later described this as the "myth" of the general strike that had captured the imagination of the syndicats. This, he thought, gave workers a very efficacious method of action; they could threaten the general strike and inspire *fear*.[7] It was just the opposite in Germany, and Guesde's advocacy of German concepts in France was a continually losing battle. When the Second International decided to use May Day as the American groups were doing—as a day to celebrate labor—the Germans saw this as an opportunity to demonstrate for the eight-hour day, but the French saw it as a rehearsal for the general strike to introduce a socialism containing worker control of industry organized by the syndicats.

By 1893 Fernand Pelloutier (1867-1901) began leading Syndicalism, calling for industrial action to establish a new society without any interfering political parties. Pelloutier's successor, Victor Griffeulhes (1875-1922), was even more outspoken in his distrust of intellectuals. Griffeulhes was also interesting in that he disliked the mutton-headed suggestibility of the workers as well, and felt, like **Blanqui**, that a conscious minority would have lead them.[8] For roughly the same reasons Lenin later developed a similar attitude toward the working class. This belief in insurrection or the threat of it, and the general strike's efficacy in bringing about the new order, was in sharp contrast to the overt reformism of socialists such as Millerand, Viviani, and Briand—people who became members of the very governments that felt compelled to put down the strikes called by the unions. Somehow the French Left held all this together most of the time, but not without considerable effort.

Marxist socialism began in England with the temporary cooperation of Marx. H.M. Hyndman (1842-1921) began a group called the *Democratic Federation* in 1881. At first, he seemed to be attempting to resurrect Chartism, and Marx discouraged that. When Hyndman published his *England for All,* however, he used Marx's ideas without giving him credit. This annoyed Engels very much, and he talked Marx into breaking with Hyndman. As a result, Marxist socialism developed in England in isolation from Marx and against the active hostility of Engels. The Federation quickly got into further trouble by supporting Irish independence from Great Britain at a time when anti-Irish feeling in Britain was very strong. For a time this kept British workers out of the movement, and the revolutionary socialism that the Federation (renamed the *Social Democratic Federation* in 1884) was preaching emanated more from foreign workers who had moved to Britain and had joined the SDF than from indigenous workers.[9]

The 1884 extension of suffrage to include more workers tended to discourage revolutionary attitudes even though there was a serious economic depression in 1886. In any event, Hyndman's group was too factionalized to take advantage of the depression, for in 1884 William Morris had broken away to form the *Socialist League.* The League quickly became anarchistic, and during that same year the SDF had lost members to the newly formed *Fabian Society*—a reformist group stressing an ethical socialism that was very influential in the 1890s.

A further difficulty for Marxist socialism in Britain was that the new unions which developed in the late 1880s were socialistic bargaining agencies for the improvement of working conditions and wages. Sparked by strikes in 1888, the new unions resembled Robert Owen's ideas far more than Karl Marx's; they wanted representation in Parliament—not revolution. Out of their frustration with the Liberals arose the *Independent Labor* party in 1893. The interests which the Labor party sought to represent were specifically unionist in nature. Early successes in municipal elections led to improvements in education, wages, slum clearance, and work for unemployed. These achievements confirmed the reformist, pragmatic trend of British socialism. As Caute points out, the language of this socialism still sounded Marxist, but this was an adoption of Marxist categories and teleology while his methods of combat tended to be rejected.[10]

Moving westward from Germany, one witnessed more reformism than revolutionary attitudes—more union independence and even union dominance of the working-class political parties. Moving eastward, the opposite effect could be seen.

During this period, Poland was divided between Prussian, Austrian, and Russian domination. The socialism that developed there was influenced both by the most dominant country ruling Poland as well as by differences in economic development from west to east. Moreover, effective unions, especially in Russian east Poland, simply did not exist. The socialism that developed in the Prussian and Austrian sections came under the influence of the German Social Democrats. However, that developing in the Russian portion not only identified with the Russian revolutionary movement against the Tsar, but developed as a radical protest movement without trade unions involved in a day-to-day struggle. This meant that the revolutionary aspects of Marx's theory received far less challenge. This was furthered by the illegality of the Russian and east Polish organizations when they developed—they were never able to operate openly. They had to be clandestine, utilizing secret cells in factories and organizing conspiratorial meetings.[11]

The socialist movement in the Marxist sense began in 1881 in Poland and in 1883 in Russia. The Polish group, *The Proletariat,* was formed by Ludwig Warinski (1856-1889) and Stanislaw Mendelssohn (1857-1913); the Russian group was begun by a converted populist named Georgii Plekhanov (1857-1918), who named his movement *The Emancipation of Labor Group.* This was by no means the first socialist organization in Russia, merely the first Marxist group and the one that Lenin joined in the 1890s (see chapter 6). Russian Marxism was also a mixture of reform and revolution, but the specific conditions in Russia eventually caused the balance to shift in the direction of revolution.

The original Polish group did not last long. In 1885 Russian authorities arrested most of its leaders, but in 1887 it was revived and began to form unions and organize strikes. During the next year the Proletariat separated into two wings—one economic and the other political. The economic half became the *Polish Workers' League,* and the political half kept the name Proletariat and concentrated on underground political action. The most important of the Polish socialists in that political movement was Rosa Luxemburg (1870-1919), who fled to Switzerland to avoid arrest, met the exiled Plekhanov and others, and became a Marxist. At this point her attention was still in a Russian direction. When May Day strikes in 1892 resulted in Polish workers being shot by cossacks, the Workers' League and the Proletariat recombined to form the *Polish Socialist* party which Rosa represented at the International Congress that was held in Zurich in 1893. The split between the workers and the political ideologies had not lasted long, but a new source of division was on the horizon.

Another Polish socialist group, largely made up of émigrés living in London, was far more concerned with Polish national independence than with international socialism. Rosa could not agree with this new emphasis. Polish independence was important but not that important, so the movement split again. The nationalists kept the party name (PSP), while the splinter group which included Rosa took the name of the *Social Democratic Party of the Kingdom of Poland* (Russian Poland). In 1899 Lithuania was added to the name, as a small Lithuanian contingent led by Felix E. Dzerzhinsky (1877-1926) joined the movement. This Luxemburg group advocated an internationalism more real than that put forward by other groups. Her internationalism was furthered by the dismemberment of her own country. Plekhanov's and Lenin's similar attitudes were further aided by their émigré status. Another contributing factor for all three was the weakness of their movement in Poland and Russia. The strength of Marxist socialism lay elsewhere. They had to be internationalists because, otherwise, their notion of a socialist revolution for their countries did not make sense.

As internationalists and revolutionists they represented a left wing of the Second International, but they too had their differences. Rosa Luxemburg believed in a conspiratorial party which would gain a mass worker following by taking up the proletarian struggle for economic gains and democratic liberties. The party would lead the workers into strikes and from this mass activity would come a revolutionary consciousness as well as the numbers the party now lacked. Her group, however, was organized democratically. She would have it no other way, for she could not conceive of a revolution that did not have a massive following, nor of a party that was too distinct from the masses. Felix Dzerzhinsky sought a much tighter control by the party leadership, which he felt would result in a more unified and successful revolution. This impatience with democratic niceties, which also characterized Lenin a short time later, reflected in a sense German ideas of centralization and discipline but was dedicated to conspiratorial political revolution rather than reform. Therefore, in the Russian area of Europe there was a strong tendency to allow the goal to take over the method, whereas in Europe the method of struggle generally determined the goal. G.D.H. Cole described this as follows:

> On the other hand, in the more advanced countries and especially where there was some experience and tradition of bourgeois democracy and constitutional government, 'the Revolution' did not necessarily mean blood. It was possible to envisage it as coming in a bloodless or almost bloodless fashion, something like the following: (a) the building up of a body of mass-support behind a parliamentary party; (b) the winning of a parliamentary majority by that party; (c) the voting in the Popular Chamber of a measure proclaiming a new Constitution, or summoning a Constituent Assembly to make one; (d) the rejection of this measure by the Upper Chamber and by the Crown or the executive authority; (e) the presentation by the Popular Chamber of an ultimatum to these resistant powers, backed perhaps by the threat of a general strike, or even of insurrection; (f) the surrender of the ruling classes in face of this ultimatum because they realized that the popular movement was too strong for them to resist; and (g) the meeting of a Constituent Assembly to pass a new set of basic laws which would destroy the old order and lay the foundations of a Socialist society.[12]

Socialist leaders such as Guesde, Liebknecht, Bebel, and the new leader of the German party, Karl Kautsky (1854-1938), worked in this frame of reference. They were in fact democrats, as well as socialists, who felt that they had no right to make the revolution without at least the assent of the majority of the people. This proclivity dominated Western Europe. However, in Eastern Europe and particularly in Russia, where there were very few democratic traditions to encourage this feeling, the balance shifted toward a revolution led by a minority in the name of the majority.

The fragile unity of the Marxist movements was severely strained in the 1890s with the emergence of *revisionism* in the German party. This brought the struggle between reform and revolution out into the open. Although, as has been noted, this conflict was there from the beginning, it was an unacknowledged difficulty. Karl Kautsky, until 1917 the editor of the party journal, *Neue Zeit,* stood for a Marxist orthodoxy that included an acceptance of surplus value; capitalist contradictions; the increasing misery of the proletariat; the dropping of the small capitalists into the ranks of the proletariat as the class division widened by monopolization and growth of big business; and the progressive socialization of the working force. Even though he believed all this, his notion of revolution was based on an evolutionary model. Working for the revolution meant working for the proletariat, but never to the extent of increasing the power of the bourgeois state. This limited the scope of permissible social legislation. Kautsky was for parliamentary activity on behalf of the workers but refused to conceive of that activity in any coalition with bourgeois parties, and this limited the effectiveness of the parliamentary group. He had a profound faith in the socialist future that would develop after a majority of the people were socialists, and for this reason disagreed sharply with Lenin in 1917 about the dictatorship of the proletariat in Russia—before such a majority had been reached. Kautsky's workers' state was one that would come about by peaceful methods; he disliked violence intensely. Although he believed that a disciplined and unified proletariat was necessary to achieve this victory, it would do so through democratic means. The revolution became synonymous with socialism, rather than the means.

This reformist strain was dominant, but it was couched in revolutionary terminology. This uneasy compromise was embarrassingly shattered by Eduard Bernstein (1850-1932) in the mid-1890s. Although a German, Eduard had lived in England for several years. He had become very close to Frederick Engels before the latter's death in 1895, but he had also been deeply influenced by the Fabians, then at the height of their significance in England. Beginning in 1896 with articles published in *Neue Zeit*, he radically criticized Marxism and stirred up controversy and condemnation within party ranks and from the International. In 1899 he summarized his ideas in a book called *Evolutionary Socialism (Die Voraussetzungen des Sozialismus und die Aufgaben der Sozialdemokratie)*.

Bernstein had no intention of destroying Marxism; he just wanted to purge it of things that Marx had been mistaken about, things that history had revealed to have been untrue. First, he attacked the general reticence about discussing future socialism as an attitude that led to the idea that after capitalism there would be a sudden leap into a socialism that would solve all problems. This eschatological view of revolution was utopian—speculation about it was not. Failure to probe the future created the utopian attitude. Second, he challenged the idea that capitalism was in its death throes. These two points are related. Many worker reforms in Germany had been put off until after the success of socialism to avoid giving more power to a bourgeois state. If capitalism still had considerable vitality, those reforms were still a very long way off. Whereas in Lenin's thinking this possibility encouraged an imminent revolution of a different sort, to Bernstein it meant that

... Socialism would come, not as a system constructed by Socialists on the morrow of their conquest of power, but by an accumulation of piecemeal changes which would be brought about by social action within the limits set by the sheer necessities of economic development. There would be, in his view, no sudden transition from capitalist to Socialist society, but rather a gradual transformation of the one into the other; and it would not be possible to say that the great change had occurred at any one point in this evolutionary process.[13]

This was not so much a denial of the class struggle as it was of determinism. Bernstein suggested a freeing of socialist thinking from all determinism, however generalized. Marx's predictions about the pauperization of the working class were just not coming true. His idea that capitalists would become fewer and fewer was vitiated by newly developed joint stock companies with a diffusion of shareholding. Additionally, Bernstein said that there were many small businesses still functioning, and land ownership appeared to be moving into more hands rather than fewer. The middle class was not dying out but gaining strength. Since economic determinism was not working as it should according to predictions, and since attempts at political reform were achieving success, Bernstein saw no difficulty in removing the one and substituting the other.

Third, Bernstein argued that workers would not be able to take over the many industries in the country immediately; the industries would therefore have to remain in hands that knew how to operate them. This meant a transition period, during which Bernstein called for consumer **cooperatives,** but not producer co-ops, leaving industry in private hands for a considerable period. In addition, the notion of the dictatorship of the proletariat was not sufficiently democratic for this transition period and would also have to be removed from socialist theory. Even the idea of internationalism was attacked, for he felt that workers did in fact have countries. They should have been about the business of safeguarding their national interests even if that meant supporting colonial expansion. After all, the higher civilization had a right to dominate the lower culture.

Naturally this line of argument had to be condemned by the German party, but Bernstein was never expelled. The party passed condemning resolutions at conferences. This mild response gave mute testimony to the strength of Bernstein's ideas within the party, even though they were too radical for *official* acceptance.[14] By the time these notions were fully debated Wilhelm Liebknecht had died, Bebel was getting quite old, even Kautsky's influence was beginning to wane. New leaders were taking over. The old orthodoxy was still important, but they did not see the life-death significance of Bernstein's critique that the left wing did.

Rosa Luxemburg actually began disengaging herself from the SPD because she felt so strongly that Bernstein ought to have been expelled. Her concern about strike activity in Poland to create the revolutionary consciousness was very different from Bernstein's almost British preoccupation with reform. Rosa's attitudes were hardened by the 1905 revolution in Russia that had repercussions in Russian Poland. She went back to Poland to help organize insurrections and strikes that could assist the Russian revolutionaries. She tried to start peasant uprisings and encouraged even very small strikes as moving in the right direction. This caused considerable trouble between her and the Polish Socialist party, now led by Jozef Pilsudski (1867-1935). The PSP, more dominated by nationalism, had a great hatred of Russia, so Rosa's pro-Russian activities were condemned. This and revisionism in Germany pushed her in the direction of the Russian movement even more, especially since the German party only toyed with the idea of support for the Russian rebels in 1905 by talking about the possibility of a German general strike. By 1906, however, the leadership of the German unions made the SPD promise to avoid such ideas without prior consultation with the unions. The division between East and West became clearer.

The unions had a point: conditions in Germany seemed to be getting better all the time, and there was no sense in upsetting this progress. This denial of international worker solidarity received sharp emphasis in 1914. Bebel had died the year before, and Hugo Haase (1863-1919) had taken over the SPD. When war broke out, the majority of the party voted for the war, and the minority opposition went along for the sake of party unity until 1917, when it formed the *Independent Socialist* party. However, their secession at that point allowed the "Majority Socialists" to move further to the right, and this right-wing heart of the old party soon formed the nucleus of the governing coalition for the *Weimar Republic* that emerged in 1918. The SPD had been a very strong party. Although it had had a solid youth program, an effective female wing, many publications, and great influence in the International, the inner conflict present from its beginning had finally resolved the SPD into a group whose socialism was more a remembered orthodoxy than a program for implementation.

In France the divorce between revolutionary syndicats and party continued into the twentieth century. The *United Socialist* party under Jean Jaurès (1859-1914) practiced reform tactics similar to those of the Germans, but the French had an even more divided party. This became obvious in 1906 when the issue of trade union autonomy from the party was approved by a *party* vote of 148 to 130. The party was deeply divided. The minority was the Guesdist group, which had failed in its attempt to make the French party more revolutionary; the majority, led by Jaurès, was headed by a person who sought through politics the completion of the work of the French Revolution. Jaurès was a humanist liberal whose notion of revolution was quite consistent with reform. He, like Kautsky, was against destructive violence. Thus, led by a moderate and cut off from the more revolutionary unions, French socialism also thought in Marxist terms but acted in terms of an ethical socialism similar to that of the British Fabians. In 1914 even Guesde deserted his former convictions and became a minister in the war government.

The revolutionary syndicalism of the late nineteenth century also weakened progressively in the twentieth. Although theoretically supporting unified action through the idea of the general strike, the syndicats were essentially local in character, ideologically divided among themselves, inadequate in strike funds, and weak in leadership after 1909. Although occasionally resurgent, syndicalism faded.

In Britain the weakening of revolutionary socialism continued. The Independent Labor party which represented the new unions was predominantly a reformist group only occasionally bothered by a more militant left wing. Labor party activity was designed to improve the lot of the working class. Class war was being replaced by demands for class reconciliation. The Social Democratic Federation grew weaker as a counterforce to this reformism, and other efforts were equally insufficient to tip the balance the other way. In 1903 a Scottish faction of the SDF formed a small *Socialist Labor* party modelled after Daniel DeLeon's militant and revolutionary organization in the United States.[15] In 1905 another secession from the SDF resulted in the *Socialist* party of Great Britain under the leadership of C.L. Fitzgerald. This group stood for the full adoption of socialism as soon as possible, but it was very small and existed mainly in London. Its secession weakened the SDF still further.

The period from 1910 to 1914 was one of great labor unrest in Britain. Strikes were common, and the unions grew steadily. This impetus created the movement for one big union to represent every worker, and a desire for worker control of industry—desires that resembled French Syndicalist arguments as well as the ideological statements coming out of the *International Workers of the World* in the United States. Such activity in Britain resulted in the *National Guilds* movement which called for chartered guilds and union management of industry. This was an effort to institute worker control from below. This idea emerged in other areas later, Russia included, and was contemptuously condemned by Lenin as a left-wing disorder.

During the war years until 1916 most of the socialists and workers supported the British war effort. After the German peace offer of December 1916 was rejected and the Russians had their March 1917 revolution, with workers demonstrating in the streets for peace, a new note of militancy invaded the placidity of British socialism. This militancy was heightened by military conscription which began in 1916 and seemed particularly to draw men from the engineering and building trades. Unrest in these industries gave rise to the "shop stewards" movement, an expression of militant revolutionism from the rank and file of the workers without the support of the reformist union leadership, However, the war's end in 1918 terminated this brief rebellion.[16]

By 1917, therefore, revolutionary socialism was waning west of the Elbe River and successfully fighting for its life to the east. The war had ended the international pretensions of the Second International, and this freed Luxemburg and Lenin to articulate the more revolutionary view with less socialist oppostion. Attempts to mend the war wounds of the International, such as at Zimmerwald in September 1915, were failures. In 1916 the left opposition, led by Luxemburg, formed the *Spartacus League,* but it was very small and drew mainly from among unskilled workers. Other new left groups began to affiliate with Lenin's *Bolsheviks.*

In March of 1917 when the small Independent Socialist party of Germany was formed, the Spartacus League became its affiliate. However, the cooperation did not last long. The new German government that emerged in 1918 saw the Spartacus group as a definite threat to the rather shaky postwar state. The Spartacus people sounded Bolshevistic but they were really a weak group still trying to run things democratically; they were not the threat that the government imagined. In the confusion, its leaders—Karl Liebknecht (Wilhelm's son) and Rosa Luxemburg—were murdered in 1919.

The socialism that was evolving in Germany was dominated by the right-wing Majority Socialists. After the January 1919 elections the Independent Socialists could have formed a governing coalition with the Majority Socialists, but the Independents refused to cooperate in a coalition as they had so often in the past. The Majority Socialists did not have these scruples, and formed a coalition with bourgeois parties. The Weimar Republic, ostensibly socialist, became the new form of the German state.

Poland, in the postwar period, was a newly independent country led by the socialist-nationalist Pilsudski. He quickly developed new and compelling reasons for a dislike of Russia during a brief war between the two countries in 1921.

Russia came out of the war years very much in chaos. Within Russia, socialism was weak and deeply divided, but the radicalizing events of 1917 eventually tipped the balance between reform and revolution in the direction of revolution. Russia, as a result, would never again be an unimportant country.

Suggested Readings

Adamic, Louis. *Dynamite: The Story of Class Violence in America*. New York: Viking Press, 1931.

Anderson, Evelyn. *Hammer or Anvil: The Story of the German Working-Class Movement*. London: Victor Gollancz, 1945.

Cole, G.D.H. *A History of Socialist Thought*, 5 vols. London: Macmillan & Co., 1953-60.

————. *A Short History of the British Working-Class Movement 1789-1947*. London: George Allen & Unwin, 1947.

Coser, Lewis A. "Marxist Thought in the First Quarter of the 20th Century," *American Journal of Sociology* 78,1 (July 1972): 173 ff.

Harrington, Michael. *Socialism*. New York: Saturday Review Press, 1970.

Nettl, Peter. *Rosa Luxemburg*. London: Oxford University Press, 1969.

Turin, S.P. *From Peter the Great to Lenin*. New York: Augustus M. Kelly Reprint, 1968.

NOTES

[1]There is some ambiguity as to the actual termination date of the Second International. Since postwar efforts to continue the organization were failures, the effective termination date appears to have been 1914, when militant nationalism triumphed over international worker solidarity. The termination date of the First International was also unclear. As a result of infighting between Marxists and Bakunists, the headquarters were moved to America where the International quietly died some four years later. The effective date would appear to have been 1872.

[2]In this chapter Russia will be discussed only as a part of the European movement. In chapter 6 the concentration will be entirely on Russia.

[3]G.D.H. Cole, *A History of Socialist Thought*, vol. 2, *Socialist Thought, Marxism and Anarchism 1850-1890* (London: St. Martin's Press, Macmillan & Co., 1961), p. 72 ff.

[4]Ibid., p. 265. Reprinted by permission of the publisher.

[5]Switzerland was a melting pot of revolutionary ideas in the 1870-1900 period. Here one found the exiled Germans, French, Poles, and Russians. The fact that they acted as exiled *nationals* most of the time belied the international character of their movement. A comprehensive study of their interactions needs to be made.

[6]Note how attempts to hasten the "social revolution" were turning into a struggle for *political* power within the context of the bourgeois relations of production. This was fully developed, for example, in Germany when Lenin was still a high school student.

[7]Georges Sorel, "Class War and the Ethics of Violence," in *The Anarchists,* ed. Irving L. Horowitz, (New York: Dell, 1964), p. 533. The idea of the general strike was also advocated earlier in Britain by Owenite and Chartist groups but without much success.

[8]G.D.H. Cole, *A History of Socialist Thought* 3, part 1, *The Second International 1889-1914* (London: Macmillan & Co., 1960), p. 348.

[9]A similar phenomenon occurred in the early development of American socialism. Revolutionary socialism was not indigenous, but came with foreign workers, especially Germans, from Europe. Even European factions were recreated on American soil. In 1877 this led the *National Republican* (Washington, D.C.) to editorialize on July 21: "The fact is clearly manifest that communist ideas are very widely entertained in America by the workmen employed in mines and factories and by the railroads. This poison was introduced into our social system by European laborers." Cited in Robert V. Bruce, *1877: Year of Violence* (New York: New Bobbs-Merrill Co., 1959), p. 225. The Palmer raids of 1920 were by no means the first anticommunist efforts in the United States.

[10]David Caute, *The Left in Europe Since 1789* (New York: McGraw-Hill, 1966), p. 58.

[11]Governments seem unable to learn that forcing groups underground encourages revolutionary development rather than the opposite. This is true, for example, of some black groups in the United States, as it was of early American union development.

[12]Cole, *The Second International 1889-1914* 3, part 2: 946. Reprinted by permission of the publisher.

[13]Ibid., 3, part 1: 277. Reprinted by permission of the publisher.

[14]As an illustration of how time can drastically alter the position of the "center," the idea of a gradual transition to socialism through democratic means was considered *left-wing* in the 1974 SPD. See *New York Times,* 4 October 1974, p. 10.

[15]DeLeon's group strongly advocated revolutionary socialism, but it declined sharply after the 1901 formation of the reformist *American Socialist* party.

[16]This resembled the decline of student militancy when American overt involvement in Vietnam was ended (see chapter 11).

PART II

The Bolshevization of Marxism

Russia and Lenin

The Russian Empire in 1850 was a backward, slowly industrializing society. It had been kept out of the mainstream of western development by the Mongol occupation of Russia from the twelfth to the fifteenth centuries, and by Russia's religious evolvement out of the Eastern branch of the church, which prevented the country from participating in the homogenizing influences of the Roman papacy. The beginnings of industrialization or modernization can be traced to ' Peter the Great (1696-1725), a despotic tyrant who forced the Russian nobility to westernize their clothing and social habits and deliberately encouraged and supported the beginnings of cottage industry. In 1699 he further breached Russian custom by adopting the Julian calendar, and by the end of his reign he had begun several schools to train personnel for the new industries.[1] It was a beginning, but a small one.

The eighteenth century witnessed a very slow but steady growth of industrialization, largely created to provide the needs of warfare. The growth progressed against very heavy odds. Russia was very large and grew even more immense under subsequent Tsars and Tsarinas, but lacked adequate transportation facilities. Russia was also poor. An overwhelming majority of her population consisted of serfs engaged in subsistence agriculture. In addition, Russia was easily invaded. These factors caused Russian economic development to proceed in a significantly different fashion from that of Britain. The Russian state provided much more of the entrepreneurial capital, controlled trade, and required a much tighter control of the population.

Only a leviathan state could effectively control all classes of the society. And thus it was that out of centuries of war and agrarian poverty, Russia had created by the beginning of her industrialization in the eighteenth century one of the most total despotisms of human history: a militarized state with a huge and cumbersome bureaucracy; a subservient church stripped of its lands; a servile but frequently treacherous nobility; a peasantry in bondage, occasionally erupting in aimless and bloody rebellions; and a line of autocratic rulers, some progressive and some reactionary, many spurred by megalomaniacal ambitions and paranoic cruelty, which often resulted in the increased impoverishment and suffering of their people.[2]

A major obstacle to more rapid industrialization in the eighteenth and early nineteenth centuries was that the labor force was composed of serfs. These workers were a very small part of the peasant population and were for the most part "possessionary peasants"—permanently attached to the factory where they worked. A smaller subset of these workers were free to move about so long as they paid the *obrok* or tax to their noble. There was a considerable lack of labor mobility.

The nobility were also part of the problem. They had been freed from compulsory service to the crown in 1762 which weakened the basic rationale of serfdom. They were given substantial powers over the peasants on their lands and this made them little lords of the manor—perpetuating a feudalism that was being eroded by efforts at modernization. The nobles were normally better off than the peasants, but under Paul I (1797-1801) they found themselves ruled by a rigid disciplinarian who instituted a police regime in order to regulate details of their dress, way of life, and intellectual pursuits. This led to Paul's murder in 1801—an assassination approved in advance by Paul's oldest son, Alexander.

Peasant response to these conditions was frequently violent. After the nobles were freed from service to the crown, rumors circulated that the serfs would also be liberated. When this did not occur, frustration resulted in the Pugachev rebellion from 1773 to 1774 which briefly seemed to threaten the crown. This would not be the last of the peasant risings by any means, but they accomplished little. The risings were relatively unplanned and far too local in character to gain more than a temporary respite in the peasants' condition. However, the frequency and intensity of these risings did provide a revolutionary excitement and focus among intellectuals in the nineteenth century.

Part of the reason for these peasant rebellions was poor working conditions in the small number of factories. Long hours of labor were sporadically remunerated. Debts to the company store were encouraged by these infrequent wage or in-kind payments, and a vicious poverty cycle was perpetuated. When Catherine II came to the throne in 1762 she noted in her first speech that already there were some forty-nine thousand factory peasants in revolt.[3]

The nobility was heavily in debt to the state and this severely reduced risk capital available for investment in industry or transportation. The state filled the gap. The first major railroad in Russia, between Saint Petersburg and Moscow, was constructed in the 1840s at state expense. There was some private capital at work in the early nineteenth century, but it usually came from sources that were not encouraged to develop a general capitalist mentality. Jews and the religious sect known as the Old Believers became early capitalists and bankers. However, both of these groups rather naturally tended to pool their wealth among themselves rather than save it for general investment. Other entrepreneurs came from the west, including the United States, but these were under Russian state auspices. Nobles might begin factories on their land, but these were also largely underwritten by the state. A few serfs became capitalists, but they were clearly an exception.[4]

Along with this slow industrial development came a gradual awakening of upper-class opposition to the autocratic rule of the tsars. In the Napoleonic wars many Russians were exposed to the French ideas of liberty, equality, and fraternity, which contrasted sharply with repression back home. Secret societies began. The *Union of the Public Good*, organized in 1818, was composed largely of military officers who ostensibly engaged in social work but actually were working for a representative government and the freeing of the serfs. This broke up in 1821, but a year later Colonel Paul Pestel (1793-1826) organized a secret Southern society even though it was then forbidden by law. A Northern society quickly developed in the same year. These two societies were behind the abortive officers' revolt in December of 1825. They had over three thousand troops on their side, but their push for equality, democracy, and a constitutional monarchy was a failure. The new tsar, Nicholas I (1825-1855), easily put them down and had more excuse than ever for a repressive regime. But in another sense this *Decembrist* revolt was not a failure. The frustrated attempt and subsequent martyrdom provided a firm base for the growing revolutionary sentiment among many intellectuals in the nineteenth century.

This revolutionary development should not be exaggerated. Every intellectual was by no means a revolutionary and only a few actually were.

In addition, the radical response to the tsarist autocracy was conditioned by Russian reality. On the one hand it wanted to overcome Russian backwardness, on the other hand it was intimately involved with that force in Russia that had demonstrated rebellious characteristics in the past and that morally deserved a radical improvement in conditions—the peasantry. Even by 1913 only about 4 percent of Russia's population could be called an industrial proletariat. Even that number was misleading. Many of those were still peasants working seasonally in factories or were raw recruits from the country who still had a peasant mental outlook and maintained close ties with their home village.

A desire to modernize Russia, which was part of the radical response, was partially mitigated and partially spurred to greater lengths by the industrialization that gathered momentum after the Russian defeat in the Crimean War (1853-56). Some of the modernizers sought their goal in westernization; many were satisfied by Russian industrial development in the latter nineteenth century and by reforms, such as the *Emancipation Edict* of 1861 which freed the serfs. Other modernizers, however, saw grave dangers to Russian peasant institutions in westernizing, and they both resisted the development of capitalism as harmful and attempted to deny its existence when industrialization was before their eyes.

Overlapping this difference was an overwhelming preoccupation with the peasantry. Russian revolutionary aspirations were so tied to the peasant that the movement as a whole could be called *populism,* desirous of creating an agricultural sort of socialism. The Edict of 1861 had not given more land to the peasant but to the village commune, which then administered the land for its members. This preservation of an ancient village structure seemed to many populists to show the way in which a specifically Russian socialism could develop. Capitalism could be avoided and socialism could build directly on the village commune. Actually these communes were little more than devices to more efficiently collect tsarist taxes, but the populists romanticized them. This was made easier by the social and geographical distance between the populist intellectual and the mundane village commune. Nonetheless, the discontent of the peasantry was real, as was the contact of intellectuals with ideas from Europe through foreign tutors and travel—ideas that gradually focused around the growing number of universities that were created to provide the necessary trained personnel for a modernizing Russia.

Industrialization might have been a necessity for Russian survival in European political terms, but at the same time it became a definite threat to political stability in Russia. Much of the reason for this was due to the fact that industrialization was achieved largely at the expense of the peasantry. The rapid pace of change was not possible without substantial foreign imports of machinery, raw materials, and technology. In turn, this was not possible without saleable exports—chiefly grain. The sale of foodstuffs, in large part, paid for industrialization, trading economic progress for the threat of hunger. However, the expansion of agriculture did not match the growth of industry. The Russian peasant after 1861 had less land to till than before; was saddled with high redemption payments to the state for his emancipation; was unsympathetic to scientific agriculture; and grew in numbers disproportionate to the available land. This did not entirely prevent, but it did discourage the rise of agricultural capitalists who could grow a saleable surplus. Therefore, the industrial drain was from a subsistence agricultural base—a shaky foundation, as was discovered in both 1891 and 1914-15.

The population pressures on the land, coupled with the growth of industry in the cities, pushed the development of an urban proletariat as it had in other countries in the past. Conditions of life in the new factories were often deplorable. According to investigations in 1882-83, some factories forced their laborers to work eighteen hours per day. Debts to the factory store were still encouraged by wage payments once or twice a year. When the workers went out on strikes, fines were levied on the participants or they were drafted into the army. Even though strikes were illegal and costly, they continued to occur. To some extent these strikes were the result of underground labor organizations. The *South Russian Labor Union* was founded in 1874, followed by another in the north in 1878. Although they followed a program similar to that of the First International, their strikes were economic in nature rather than political. The big strike of four thousand workers at Orekhove-Zuevo in 1885, for example, was almost entirely economic even though deeply influenced by ideas of socialism and revolution.[5]

This increased working-class activity, however small, began to attract the attention of some of the populist intellectuals. The shift in focus was made easier by populism's great debacle in 1874, when hundreds had gone to the countryside to "discharge their debt to the peasantry" by teaching them. The peasants had responded by calling the police. This would be roughly similar to student radicals descending en masse on General Motors to "enlighten" the workers of contemporary Detroit. The workers' response would probably be equally hostile. The resulting disillusionment in Russia created tremendous frustrations in the movement, and a substantial part became terroristic—believing that selected acts of political violence would make the peasants revolutionary. Such motivation lay behind the assassination of Alexander II in 1881. The result was not peasant revolutionary consciousness, but more repression from Alexander III.

Around the same time a representative of the smaller, more peaceful wing of the old movement began to see the sense in revolutionary activity among peasants who were working in the urban centers. These people were fairly accessible and were basically peasants. However, this gave the fairly vague agricultural socialism of the past a different base, and Marxism—an anti-autocratic revolutionary socialism based on an urban proletariat—began to make more sense. Marxism had not been unknown before, it just had not seemed to fit as well. Tentative gestures had been made to Marx by some of the populists in the past, and Marx had responded by agreeing that socialism based on the village commune might be a possibility if capitalism had not yet become firmly entrenched, a flexible adaptation of historical materialism by the master himself.

> If the revolution takes place at the right time, if it concentrates all its forces to ensure the free development of the village commune, the latter will soon emerge as the regenerative force in Russian society and as something superior to those countries which are still enslaved by the capitalist regime.[6]

Marxism was here adapted by Marx to fit imagined Russian conditions, but in a few years Russian Marxists began to apply to those Russian conditions a far more rigid Marxism. After 1881 terror seemed counterproductive to most of these people, and the number of believers in a specifically peasant path of socialist development declined spectacularly. New ideas and new methods were needed, but the first was easier than the second. In this context one of the leaders of the more peaceful wing of the old group, Georgii Plekhanov—already an émigré in Switzerland—began to think and write in terms of a European Marxist solution to Russian problems. His Marxism was not new, the difference being that he insisted on Marxism to the exclusion of all other economic and political theories.[7] In 1883 Plekhanov and a few fellow émigrés from Russia formed the *Emancipation of Labor Group,* through which they hoped to influence events in Russia. This did not seem to be an entirely forlorn hope, for in the 1880s secret social democratic organizations developed at Russian universities, loosely affiliated with Plekhanov's group, and mixed with the remnants of the older terroristic group to propagate revolutionary socialist ideas, particularly among students and other intellectuals.

Plekhanov remained in exile and represented the Russian movement abroad. Between 1893 and 1900 he came to be known as one of the major European Marxist theorists, although he was less known than Kautsky or Bernstein. Plekhanov's conversion from populism meant an awareness that capitalism had in fact arrived in Russia and that it could not be turned back. This meant to him that capitalism would have to run its full course before socialism could develop. Although he was an orthodox

Marxist, he became more rigid than Marx himself in his perception of the stages of historical materialism. Plekhanov introduced into Marxist theory a "geographical determinism" which was a statement of Russian peculiarities that required a new adaptation of theory.[8]

The revolutionary struggle for socialism in Russia was particularly against the autocracy. This was, in historical materialism, the role supposedly played by the bourgeoisie. The Russian bourgeoisie, however, was too weak to perform its historic role, and the emerging proletariat was already strong enough to help. Therefore, Plekhanov urged working-class activity in support of bourgeois goals of constitutional government in order to create the preconditions of socialism. This sounded somewhat similar to what the German SPD was advocating, except that the Germans expected the socialist revolution. Plekhanov advocated proletarian support for the bourgeois revolution as the first step, introducing into Russian Marxism the idea of minimum program (bourgeois revolution) and maximum program (the proletarian revolution) that both **Trotsky** and Lenin would later develop further.

Within Russia the gradually developing movement created three leaders who, in the twentieth century, would come to stand for the center, right wing, and left wing of this adapted Marxism. Y.O. Martov (1873-1923) would symbolize the center. Martov came from a prosperous Jewish family and, as a student at the University of Saint Petersburg in the early 1890s, was one of the leaders of the Social Democratic Circle, called the Saint Petersburg Group of Liberation. After he was expelled from the university, Martov became a professional revolutionary in Vilna. Before he was banished to Siberia he worked with the developing Jewish workers' movement there and cooperated with Lenin. In the early twentieth century Martov broke with Lenin and led the moderate Menshevik center.

A.N. Potresov (1869-1934) came from a noble family and also became an active revolutionary in the movement. After Lenin and Martov were arrested and banished in the latter 1890s, Potresov headed the Saint Petersburg organization until his own arrest. He was one of the major links between Plekhanov and this organization. After 1900 Potresov also became disenchanted with Lenin, particularly after the 1905 revolution, and eschewed conspiratorial activities to concentrate attention on accomplishing something within the legal frame of reference. He led the right wing of the movement until 1925 when the Bolsheviks allowed him to leave Russia.

The leader of the left wing was, of course, Lenin. This man also came from a noble family.[9] His name was Vladimir Ilyich Ulyanov (1870-1924), and he was born in Simbirsk (now called Ulyanovsk), a small city along the Volga River. His father was a teacher who became first an inspector and then director of schools in the area. His father's work was so well received that he was made a high-ranking noble by the tsar—a rank that he could pass on to his oldest son. Vladimir's mother was a well-educated daughter of a retired physician. She spoke German and Russian and taught herself English and French. Under her guidance the children put together a weekly family newspaper, edited by the oldest son, Alexander.

This placid family existence was rudely shattered in 1886. The father died in January of that year. Shortly thereafter, Vladimir became an atheist at the age of fifteen, and Alexander, the older brother, became a revolutionary. He was by this time at the University of Saint Petersburg, and he became one of the leaders of the Social Democratic circles there that still retained a carry-over from the terroristic organizations of the recent past. A small group, including Alexander, decided that an appropriate way to commemorate the five-year anniversary of the assassination of Alexander II was to kill Alexander III. The plot failed and Alexander Ilyich, along with the others, was arrested. At his trial he tried to take all the blame on himself, refused a defense attorney, and with his mother in the audience he placed the real guilt on the shoulders of the autocratic regime. He was executed on May 8, 1887.

In the fall of that year Vladimir became a freshman at the University of Kazan. The rest of the family (except for an older sister, Anna, who had been banished to the family estate at Kokushkino) joined him there, but he quickly got into trouble. The University of Kazan had a rigid inspector who implemented the 1884 University Statutes with vigor, making life nearly impossible for liberals and revolutionaries alike. In December student reaction broke out in a demonstration, and Vladimir participated. When the police came they discovered that another "Ulyanov" was involved in antigovernment activities, and he was promptly arrested and expelled from school. He too had to go to Kokushkino for at least a year, and the family went along. This brief "exile" became a critical period for his later development; he read voraciously. He studied textbooks, thinking that he would soon be going back to school. He also read the works of former revolutionary heroes such as Chernyshevski and Dobrolyubov, from whom he developed a strong sense of the necessary dedication a revolutionary must have if he or she wished to be successful. That dedication to revolution presupposed that any means justified the desired end, and that there was no substitute for direct, personal involvement in revolutionary activity. He also began to read Marx with great satisfaction.

Vladimir never did get back to school in the usual sense. In 1890 his mother was finally successful in gaining permission for him to live in Saint Petersburg and study on his own if he chose. In one year he successfully covered enough material to pass his bar examinations in 1891 with very high grades. He seemed headed for a legal career, but he was by this time a revolutionary for whom such a career was meaningless. He left Saint Petersburg for Samara, still unsure of how he should proceed.

The circumstances of 1891-92 provided a partial answer. This was a famine year created by both a bad harvest and export policies which had depleted the grain reserves. In the emergency situation the government permitted the formation of philanthropic groups to deal with assistance to the starving peasants. Some of these groups made genuine attempts to alleviate suffering by providing food and helping to give typhoid shots to peasants. Other groups functioned more as "covers" for obvious radicals. The response to the crisis created a public debate on how best to alleviate the problem. Answers could be divided between hard and soft in the sense that the hard response blamed the famine on the government and saw revolutionary solutions as the only real answer. The soft response saw the solution as feeding the peasants and alleviating their immediate suffering. Vladimir, by advocating the hard response, gave evidence for the first time of a ruthless determination that would continue to characterize him. An acquaintance later recalled that Lenin had responded to the problem by saying:

> The famine is the direct consequence of a particular social order. So long as that order exists, famines are inevitable. They can be abolished only by the abolition of that order of society. Being in this sense inevitable, famine today performs a progressive function. It destroys the peasant economy and throws peasants from the village into the city. Thus the proletariat is formed which speeds the industrialization of the nation. . . . It will cause the peasant to reflect on the fundamental facts of capitalist society. It will destroy his faith in the Tsar and in Tsarism and will in time speed the victory of the revolution.
>
> It is easy to understand the desire of so-called "society" to come to the assistance of the starving, to ameliorate their lot. This "society" is itself part of the bourgeois order. . . . The famine threatens to create serious disturbances and possibly the destruction of the entire bourgeois order. Hence the efforts of the well to do to mitigate the effect of the famine are quite natural. . . . *psychologically this talk of feeding the starving is nothing but an expression of the saccharine sweet sentimentality so characteristic of our intelligentsia.*[10]

This was a total dedication to revolution that contained no sympathetic qualities. It was also a morality that few people could handle. Whatever contributed to the revolution was good. Lenin refused to condemn even the use of terroristic tactics, supposedly avoided by Plekhanov's group. He represented a combination of the Russian revolutionary past and Marxism that made the revolution far more of an end than a means to an end. While Bernstein in England was developing his reformist, revisionist ideas, Lenin's notions were solidifying into a total dedication to revolution.

In August of 1893 he began his life as a professional revolutionary by going to Saint Petersburg where he joined the *Elders Circle,* which was chiefly involved in the propagation of Marxism among factory workers. The Saint Petersburg circle was one of many circles that had evolved out of populist attempts to spread education among first the peasantry, then the working class. Although the circles had become increasingly Marxist under the influence both of the secret Social Democrats and the Marxism already in populism, they were still basically educatory devices taught by intellectuals who sought to spread general knowledge, in order that specific revolutionary consciousness might develop. Often, more time was spent in general education than on Marxism. It was a nonactivist approach.

In the 1890s this had begun to change. Newer Marxists shared less of the populist background, and the spontaneous activity of the Jewish and Polish workers stimulated change. What really discouraged the Marxist intellectuals was that so many of the workers they educated did not become revolutionaries. Some immigrated to America; others went on to higher education at universities; some went into business! Many Marxists had begun to describe the circles as useless.

The demand for immediate change came from worker activity. Polish workers in 1890 were cooperating with the Proletariat group and were using May Day as a day of demonstrations. In 1891 the worker response was much larger than in the previous year, and by 1892 their activity had caused the Russian authorities to occupy the city of Lotz with troops. This was far more exciting than teaching general subjects to semi-illiterate workers. By 1893 the new workers' agitation tactics had spread to Vilna, a Lithuanian border city that was the center for the Jewish socialism that was being channeled into Marxist directions by Alexander Kremer and Yuli Martov. The result was the pamphlet "On Agitation" (1894), which summarized the decision of the Vilna group to forsake the old circle methods and to move directly into worker agitation and strike leading.

This pamphlet had a dramatic impact on circles in Saint Petersburg, Moscow, and other Russian cities. It articulated a new direction for *Russian Social Democracy,* and a more satisfying direction for the newer Marxists who were impatient to get the revolution in motion. Lenin, in Saint Petersburg, was enthusiastically in favor of the new trend.

What Lenin did not know at that time, and what did not become apparent until later, was that a major reason for the publication of the pamphlet had been to explain the position of the Social Democrats to independent advanced workers. A spontaneous worker movement had begun in

Vilna which threatened to leave the Vilna circle high and dry if that circle did not change. "On Agitation" thus stimulated a new direction for the revolutionary intellectuals, but was caused at least in part by the fear that if such changes were not made the workers' movement would pass it by. The pamphlet did not solve this basic problem, however, for assuming the leadership of the strike movement in the 1890s created another dilemma. Police action against the ringleaders of the strikes fell hardest on the circle organization. The intellectuals were usually arrested while the advanced workers were not. The worker groups were often, therefore, left with no Social Democratic leadership, and they found that they could perform rather well on their own. This led directly to the question of the importance of the intellectual to the workers' movement.

Again the responses to this question could be described as soft or hard. Some, insisting that their interests were in a proletarian victory, were content to let the advanced workers lead the struggle—remaining ready with advice and assistance when necessary. Lenin, on the other hand, again opted for a hard response. The revolutionary role of the proletariat could not be maintained, he said, without organization of their localized efforts into a larger, more revolutionary frame of reference. What Lenin sensed was missing from these worker groups, especially after his return from Siberian exile around 1900, was a proletarian revolutionary consciousness. Many of the workers were striking and demonstrating for shorter work days, better wages, improved conditions, and so on. However, Lenin wanted them to see these strikes as steps toward full revolution. The organization must lead *the class struggle* of the proletariat. Coordination was vital, and to achieve this a central newspaper was necessary. The Russian Social Democratic Labor Party (RSDLP) had organized in Minsk in 1898 when Lenin was still in Siberia, and it had established a newspaper, the *Rabochnaya Gazeta (Workers' Gazette)*, but this paper was suppressed by the police. Lenin wanted to begin a new party organ, published outside Russia, which would fight **economism;** bring unity to the movement; and keep these various local events connected with the political struggle for democracy as a means of achieving the further goal of socialism.[11]

Lenin, Martov, and Potresov briefly collaborated in Swiss exile on the development of such a newspaper, **Iskra** *(Spark)*, attempting to steer the RSDLP away from the soft answers which were so close to European revisionism. By 1902, however, Lenin was prepared to go much further. He wrote *What Is to Be Done?* and a few other articles that were clearly the most important of his writings, for the principles he outlined were to guide him until his death in 1924.

Lenin was fully prepared to emphasize one side of Marx's ambiguous position on the relationship between the party and the working masses. The party, Lenin wrote, must be the political **vanguard** of the proletarian struggle. This was necessary because, although the workers had spontaneity, they usually did not possess consciousness. Spontaneity would result in strikes for economic gains, even trade union activity, but it would not, if left alone, result in revolutionary activity. The repository of that revolutionary consciousness was the party. Thus without party organization the proletariat was incapable of bringing about revolutionary change; without the party the proletariat was nothing![12] What did not lead to revolution was "nothing," and what did was thereby good. Thus, whatever tactic, or whatever alliance with other groups that promoted the revolution was what the party should follow.

The party itself was to be controlled from the center. The operating principle would be **democratic centralism,** where debates might take place democratically, prior to a central decision; but once that decision had been made, obedience was the only response. In addition, the party must be small enough to be controllable, secret, and composed of professional revolutionaries. The vanguard of the proletariat was an elite carrying a consciousness that the workers themselves were incapable of sustaining.

Considerable opposition to Lenin developed within the RSDLP, and at the Second Congress in 1903 the party split. After a good deal of maneuvering, two groups emerged: the minority group *(Mensheviks),* led by Martov, and the majority faction *(Bolsheviks),* led by Lenin. For the next fourteen years these two factions struggled as much with each other as they did against the tsarist regime.

In 1903 Lenin emerged as the leader of the Bolshevik party—a hard, small group of professionals, totally dedicated to revolution. However, when a revolution came in 1905 they were almost totally unprepared; other groups were more directly involved. While infighting had been going on in the ranks of the RSDLP, other groups had gathered momentum that provided alternatives and opposition to Bolshevism.

The *Socialist Revolutionary* party (SR) was relatively free of Marxism and had been built on the old populism. The party advocated a socialism based on the village commune and both consumer and producer cooperatives, but a socialism that was compatible with intellectual liberty. The SRs did not completely shun terrorism, for a part of their movement continued to practice selective assassination. The SRs stood for an immediate nationalization of the land without compensation and for industrial socialism as soon as the democratization of the political regime would permit it. They had no desire to see power over industry and trade concentrated in the hands of a ruling bureaucracy.

Another group was the *Union of Liberation,* organized in 1903, forerunners of the later *Cadet* party (or Constitutional Democrats). This was a nonsocialist, liberal movement that began pressing the government for constitutional changes in the direction of freedom of speech, assembly, press, and so on. While this was occurring, the police tried once again to steal the movement away from radicals by organizing their own "revolutionary" group. They put together a *Union of Russian Workers* which called for economic gains for workers and loyalty to Nicholas II, the tsar. A priest, Father Gapon, was made head of the union, but the movement quickly got out of hand.

On Sunday, January 22, 1905, the priest led a massive demonstration of men, women, and children in Saint Petersburg. The purpose was to petition the tsar for desired changes, but they never reached Nicholas. His troops fired on the demonstrators and continued to fire until over seventy persons were killed and many hundreds were wounded.[13] Revulsion over this event swept Russia, and within a very short time the governor general of Moscow, the uncle of Nicholas, was assassinated by the terrorist wing of the SR group. Strikes occurred with great frequency—gradually becoming a paralyzing general strike that was coordinated by a Saint Petersburg group known as the *Soviet* (Council). Within a short time this Soviet was being led by a young non-Bolshevik Social Democrat named Lev Davidovitch Bronstein (1879-1940), who was also called Trotsky.

The Bolsheviks came into the affair late but with great excitement, calling for armed uprisings and a revolutionary dictatorship of the peasants and workers. Lenin's inability to cooperate with slightly less revolutionary groups was successfully utilized by the tsarist government to keep the workers' organizations split. When the *Duma* (legislature) was created as a concession to the populace, the Bolshevik activity provided excuses for Nicholas to reassert his control over the situation, and partly because of this the Duma steadily lost its potential for influence. The armed uprisings called for by the Bolsheviks were failures. Lenin lost many supporters, but his point had been that a revolutionary dictatorship of peasants and workers would quickly be able to establish the bourgeois revolution (the minimum program), on the basis of which the struggle for socialism could proceed.

Trotsky had recently developed a different idea which, in substance, Lenin eventually adopted. Trotsky had maintained that in the struggle for the minimum program the Social Democrats were foolish to forget the peculiar conditions of Russia: a strong proletariat and a weak bourgeoisie. Proletarian activity, initially on behalf of the bourgeoisie, ought to be continued, after the bourgeois success, in a permanent revolutionary spirit to reduce the transition time between the minimum and maximum programs. This worker activity would in turn spark the international proletariat to initiate revolutions in their countries, and worldwide socialism would result. Trotsky's continued effort on behalf of the "permanent revolution" was one of the reasons why he and Stalin later had serious differences.

The 1905 revolution brought modest concessions in the form of Dumas and the more open participation of political parties and unions, but the tsar remained very much in control until 1917. During this lengthy period the Bolsheviks continued their struggle for control of the RSDLP and tried to keep the revolutionary possibilities open in Russia, even though by 1907 it was obvious that the peasants were not going to rise against the government and that the revolutionary energies of the workers had ebbed. Although Lenin changed his mind and permitted the Bolsheviks to support representatives in the Duma, it was too late to accomplish anything—the Dumas had already been denuded of any real counter-tsarist power. Part of the reason was the continuing presence of police spies in the Bolshevik party. This fact provided a pragmatic basis for the later suspiciousness of Stalin.

Thus, the decade from 1907 to 1917 was a depressing time for an activist such as Lenin. He relieved the boredom by ice skating, taking long walks, playing with the children of his friends, and continuing the organizational work in Russia. This was supported by wealthy contributors and occasionally by armed robbery. These funds also helped to underwrite the costs of publishing another newspaper, **Pravda,** which first appeared in May of 1912. To Lenin, perfecting the party organization meant a continual improvement of proletarian hopes, for the party was conceived as the spirit of the advanced working class which led the less conscious workers and peasants. To a great extent, Lenin created the party in his own image, but to think of him as a person able simply to dictate to that party and have it obey confuses dominance with dictatorship.

Although the goal of the party was still the bourgeois revolution, Trotsky's idea was beginning to penetrate. Only the proletariat, Lenin wrote, can achieve a complete victory, and he soon spoke of continual proletarian hegemony in the coming revolution. The minimum and maximum programs were losing their neat separateness, and the proletariat its distinctiveness. Geographical determinism was now beginning to blur the separate phases of historical materialism. "Whoever expects a 'pure' social revolution will *never* live to see it." "The socialist revolution in Europe *cannot be* anything other than an outburst of mass struggle on the part of all sundry oppressed and discontented elements."[14]

What this illustrated was that as revolutionary practice remained at low tide, revolutionary theory continued to develop, providing another example of the way in which European theory and Russian conditions blended. Building on the work of Hobson, Hilferding, and Luxemburg, Lenin constructed a theory of imperialism that also attempted to explain capitalism's astonishing vitality in the face of Marxist predictions of collapse. His theory of imperialism contended that the highest stage of capitalism had now been reached in **finance capital** or **monopoly capitalism.** In order to survive, capitalism had expanded its markets and investments into foreign areas that were more backward or less developed. On the one hand, this caused severe strains in the underdeveloped areas where exploitation was rawest; it also contributed to fewer strains in the home country where super profits could be used to bribe the domestic workers. On the other hand, the export of capital resulted in an uneven development of capitalism in its last phases. Even Russia which had begun to industrialize later than western countries and was only semideveloped was, because of this uneven development, already at this last stage of capitalist development.

Lenin maintained this even though in 1915 small-scale industry employed 67 percent of Russia's industrial labor force and produced a third of its total output. Russian industry had not developed evenly, true—engineering lagged far behind other segments of the industry, for example.[15] However, Lenin meant something different. He was referring to the fact that countries developed capitalism at different rates, and this led him to a surprising conclusion. Because of uneven development, and because the capitalism in Russia was newer and had been developed in the absence of a capitalist superstructure, the revolutionary potential in Russia was higher than elsewhere! Moreover, uneven development resulted in combined development in that in the more backward but capitalized country two struggles had to go on at the same time: the struggle against the autocracy and the struggle for socialism. This gave Lenin the feeling that Russia was the "weakest link" in international capitalism, that Russia's very backwardness provided hope for a Russian proletarian and socialist contribution to the international movement.[16] Thus Russian revolutionary activity would spark an international conflagration and the international revolutionaries would then aid the Russians to shape a socialist society.

This adaptation of theory did not mean that Lenin was now confident of an imminent revolution in Russia. In January of 1917, he described the 1905 revolution as one in which bourgeois goals were sought by proletarian methods, but he did not think that another revolution would occur in his generation.[17] Again he was caught by surprise. A month later, strikes and demonstrations broke out in Saint Petersburg, for the war had exacerbated Russian economic problems, and the government proved incapable of solving them. The demonstrations escalated over a period of days into revolution. Nicholas, who had been at military headquarters near the front lines, was unable to get back to the capital. The railroad workers refused to let the train through. Nicholas abdicated in favor of his brother, but Michael declined the throne. The Romanov dynasty came to an end with scarcely a struggle, seeming to topple of its own dead weight.

A provisional government emerged out of the Duma and attempted to create a democratic order through elections to a constituent assembly, but it acted too slowly and revealed that it insufficiently grasped the rebellious realities of the situation by continuing the war and doing very little to satisfy the land hunger of the peasantry. Inflation grew worse, real wages declined, and strikes and insurrections continued. Failure to alleviate the basic problems resulted in a continuing radicalization of the population, particularly in the major urban centers.

Simultaneously with the emergence of the provisional government, the Saint Petersburg Soviet was recreated and became a forum for deputies from the factories and also from the increasingly democratized army. The Bolsheviks were a minority in this Soviet of Workers' and Soldiers' Deputies, and were therefore quite surprised when Lenin returned to Russia in April demanding that all power be given to the Soviet. What Lenin meant was that the Bolsheviks must take control of the Soviet and, through it, of the many smaller soviets that had sprung up throughout the country. They could then effectively deny power to the provisional government. Because of the increasing radicalism of the population in the capital, the skills of Trotsky in leading the Soviet, and their own organizational capabilities, the Bolsheviks were able to gain a majority by the end of the summer. Lenin's other April slogans helped considerably. Peace, worker control of industry, bread to the worker, land to the peasant— had a very wide appeal and were seriously intended. The autocracy had been overthrown—it was time for the proletarian revolution.

> Doubt is out of the question. We are on the threshold of a world proletarian revolution. And since of all the proletarian internationalists in all countries only we Russian Bolsheviks enjoy a measure of freedom. . . , [more is demanded of us.][18]

Doubt may have been out of the question, but his own party certainly doubted its ability to succeed. Lenin was forced to threaten his resignation if the Bolsheviks did not move, and they finally did. In October (November on the new calendar) the Bolsheviks took advantage of the radicalized situation and seized control of the government. Their success was the result of that situation, very careful planning, and considerable good fortune. Lenin, however, was under no illusion that this act magically brought about socialism. He himself called this coup by a variety of names, such as armed rising or insurrection. This, he wrote, was not a gateway into socialism so much as it was a gateway into the path leading to socialism.[19] At the same time, the Bolshevik insurrection was most definitely not carried out for the purpose of consolidating a bourgeois victory. Lenin said that, in taking power, we are not afraid of stepping beyond the bounds of the bourgeois system; on the contrary we shall fearlessly march towards socialism.[20]

This meant to some of the Bolsheviks that the minimum program had been left so far behind that it could be dropped from the new Bolshevik program that was being formulated. Lenin argued against this because

> We must first carry out the measures of transition to socialism, we must continue our revolution until the world socialist revolution is victorious, and only then, *"returning from battle,"* may we discard the minimum program as of *no further use.* [We have] . . . not yet realized the basic prerequisites for a transition to socialism. . . .[21]

Theory was returning as the dust of revolutionary practice was settling. It seemed evident to Lenin that what the Bolsheviks had been able to do was to establish an international beachhead for socialism. Because of Russian peculiarities, they had temporarily gone ahead of other proletariats in more advanced countries. The Bolsheviks were engaged in a holding action until those other revolutions took place. This international assistance for the Russians was essential, otherwise, capitalist nations would crush the one country that stood for socialism on its own.[22]

With a mixture of Marxism and Russian revolutionary tradition, Lenin's ruthless pursuit of revolutionary power had finally been successful. What that meant for Russia and the world is another story. Marx had provided a partial guide so far, but there were no guides at all for Marxists in actual control of a country. More than they realized, Lenin and the Bolsheviks were on their own.

Suggested Readings

Fischer, Louis. *The Life of Lenin*. New York: Harper & Row, 1964.

Mendelsohn, Ezra. *Class Struggle in the Pale: The Formative Years of the Jewish Workers' Movement in Tsarist Russia*. New York: Cambridge University Press, 1970.

Meyer, Alfred G. *Leninism*. New York: Praeger, 1962.

Valentinov, Nikolai. *The Early Years of Lenin*. Ann Arbor: University of Michigan Press, 1969.

Wildman, Allan K. *The Making of a Workers' Revolution: Russian Social Democracy, 1891-1903*. Chicago: University of Chicago Press, 1967.

Wilson, Edmund. *To the Finland Station*. Garden City: Doubleday Anchor Books, 1953.

NOTES

[1] The adoption of the Julian calendar was an advance, for the former calendar year began on September 1 and dated time from "creation." However, this change only partially met western time standards, for by this time western Europe had been on the improved Gregorian calendar since 1582. The Russian change meant that it was then eleven days behind the west, but by the time of the 1917 revolution she would be thirteen days behind. This leads to confusion of dates for the western observer, at least until February 14, 1918, when the Bolsheviks adopted for Russia the Gregorian calendar. "The Great October Socialist Revolution" actually occurred and is now celebrated in November.

[2] William L. Blackwell, *The Industrialization of Russia—An Historical Perspective* (New York: Thomas Y. Crowell, 1970), pp. 4-5. Reprinted by permission of the publisher.

[3] S. P. Turin, *From Peter the Great to Lenin* (New York: Augustus M. Kelly Reprint, 1968), p. 13. First published in 1935 by Frank Cass & Co., Ltd.

[4] Blackwell, *Industrialization of Russia*, pp. 19-20.

[5] Turin, *From Peter the Great to Lenin*, pp. 36-39, 43.

[6] Karl Marx, "First Draft of the Reply to V. I. Zasulich's Letter, February-March, 1881," *Marx-Engels Selected Works* 3 (Moscow: Progress, 1970), p. 161.

[7] S. V. Utechin, *Russian Political Thought* (New York: Praeger, 1964), p. 197. Plekhanov's transition was made simpler by his living in Switzerland from 1880, and because earlier Russians had tilled the Marxist soil. P. N. Tkachëv (1844-1886) who was living in Geneva and Paris between 1873 and 1886 had already become a serious student of Marx in 1865.

[8] The phrase is Utechin's. See ibid., p. 198.

[9] Plekhanov had also come from noble background. The leaders of the Marxist movement in Russia had similar backgrounds. The origins of the movement came from dis-

affected intellectuals, not the working class. This should not surprise anyone who has seriously thought about these things, but it does partially explain the elitism that would come to characterize Lenin's position in the twentieth century.

[10]Quoted in David Shub, *Lenin* (Baltimore: Penguin Books, 1966), p. 39. Reprinted by permission of Doubleday & Co. Inc.

[11]See Lenin, "Draft and Explanation of a Programme for the Social Democratic Party," *Collected Works* (Moscow: Foreign Languages Publishing House, 1964) 2:93ff, and "Our Immediate Tasks" and "An Urgent Question," ibid., 4:215ff.

[12]Lenin, "Party Discipline and the Fight Against the Pro-Cadet Social Democrats," ibid., 11 (1906): 320.

[13]Similarities and differences between this event and the 1970 Kent and Jackson State shootings in the United States provide interesting material for discussion.

[14]See Lenin, "The Fifth Congress of the RSDLP," *Collected Works* 12 (1907): 457-58; and "The Discussion on Self-Determination Summed Up," ibid., 22 (1916): 356.

[15]See Alec Nove, *An Economic History of the U.S.S.R.* (Middlesex, England: Penguin Books, 1969), p. 17.

[16]Alfred G. Meyer perceptively called this Lenin's "Dialectics of Backwardness." See his thoughtful analysis in *Leninism* (New York: Praeger, 1962), pp. 257-73.

[17]Lenin, "Lecture on the 1905 Revolution," *Collected Works* 23: 238-39, 253.

[18]Lenin, "The Crisis Has Matured," ibid., 26 (September 1917), p. 77.

[19]Lenin, "Speech to the First All Russia Congress of Soviets," ibid., 25 (June 1917): 17-42. Similar references are located in nearly all his writings of this time period surrounding the November coup.

[20]Lenin, "Revision of the Party Programme," ibid., 26 (October 1917): 170.

[21]Ibid., p. 171.

[22]Lenin, "The Principles Involved in the War Issue," ibid., 23 (December 1916): 158.

7

Bolshevism in Practice

The Bolshevization of Marxism was a gradual phenomenon that required several years for its completion. The seeds were there from the beginning. The Civil War struggle against Bolshevik opponents from 1918 to 1921, the death of Lenin in early 1924, the gradual rise of Stalin, and the erasure of all opposition to Stalinism were the stages of its growth. Although this development was separable into domestic and international components, the two were intimately related and should be separated only for analytical purposes. In addition, hindsight must not be allowed to create a patina of inevitability over these developments. Stalinism did not have to evolve out of Leninism—there were other alternatives. Contrariwise, Stalinism was not the complete break with the Leninist past that the followers of Trotsky have for so long maintained. Both the alternatives and the continuity need to be stressed.

In this period from 1917 to 1945 a separation developed between the ideas of socialism and communism that had not existed before, and it would remain until the present as a part of everyday vocabulary. In the nineteenth century the word "communism" was normally interchangeable with socialism. When the two words were occasionally used separately, communism then referred to a higher form of socialism. Marx thought of the future as socialism leading to communism, or communism being the final form of socialism. Although Marx had used the term "Communist party" in the 1848 *Manifesto* (written for the League of

Communists) the parties that emerged in the latter quarter of the nineteenth century normally were named social-democratic rather than communist.

To distinguish the Bolsheviks from this tradition which had become enshrined in the Second International, Lenin urged his followers in his April 1917 speech to change the name of the Bolshevik party to the Communist party. He said that the official leaders of social democracy had betrayed socialism through their advocacy of participation in the imperialist war of 1914. They had, in Lenin's view, deserted to the bourgeoisie.[1] The change of name became gradually accepted after the Seventh Party Congress in March of 1918. Increasingly thereafter, the word communism meant Bolshevism. The distinction became even clearer after the twenty-one conditions of membership in the Third International were promulgated in 1920. These conditions forced those in other countries who were loyal to Moscow to dissociate themselves from other socialists and form groups known as the Communist party of _____. This split the labor movement into "socialism" and "communism" with the word socialism increasingly referring to the social democratic traditions described in chapter 5, and the word communism becoming the prisoner of the Russian Bolsheviks.

However, even in Russia the word had not altered meaning: it still referred to a higher stage of socialism. In changing the name of the party and in forcing partial international adherence to the word, Lenin did not intend to imply that such a form of socialism was now operative in the area under his control—by no means. He even suggested that communism might not arrive. No socialist, he wrote, had ever *promised* that the highest phase of communism would in actuality arrive. The great socialists had had anticipations that it would come, but in those anticipations they did not assume the current low Russian productivity levels nor the present "unthinking man on the street capable of spoiling, without reflection, the stores of social wealth and of demanding the impossible."[2] Nonetheless he led his party to victory in November of 1917 in the name of that communist future.

Part of the problem in comprehending Lenin at this point is the failure to realize that it was his view that Russia in 1918 had not yet even attained socialism, let alone communism. Even though the name of the party was changed, he was aware of the great distance Russia still had to go.

> I have no illusions about our having only just entered the period of *transition* to socialism, about not yet having reached socialism. But if you say that our state is a socialist Republic of Soviets, you will be right. You will be as right as those who call many Western bourgeois republics democratic republics although everybody knows that not one of even the most democratic of these republics is completely democratic.

We are far from having completed even the transitional period from capitalism to socialism. We have never cherished the hope that we could finish it without the aid of the international proletariat. We never had any illusions on that score, and we know how difficult is the road that leads from capitalism to socialism.[3]

Lenin had been willing to describe the future society prior to the seizure of power but was very reluctant afterwards. Before November of 1917 he had referred to Russian socialism as being part of the internationally changed world, wherein the whole of society would have become one office and one factory with equal work and equal pay. The entire society would be governed by factory discipline which eventually would have become so internalized that the observance of simple, fundamental rules of social life would be habitual. Then the door would be wide open for the transition from the first phase of communist society to the second, higher phase—including a complete withering away of the state. This withering away would be possible because no one would any longer need the external coercive apparatus of the state, even of a very democratic one.[4]

Along with this change the distinction between manual and mental work would disappear. Socialism would become extremely productive by removing the retarding influences of capitalism, and through the utilization of new technology. By the "new technology," Lenin had meant things such as the Ramsay method of extracting gas from coal mines, which he felt would release the labor of millions of miners and shorten everyone's work day. Even more advantages would accrue to the society when electric power was applied to the production process.

> The "electrification" of all factories and railways will make working conditions more hygienic, will free millions of workers from smoke, dust and dirt, and accelerate the transformation of dirty, repulsive workshops into clean, bright, laboratories worthy of human beings. The electric lighting and heating of every home will relieve millions of "domestic slaves" of the need to spend three-fourths of their lives in smelly kitchens.[5]

Lenin felt that a new world was coming, an international fresh start where oppression, poverty, privileges, and disunity were gone forever. Socializing the means of production would mean greater production efficiency and shorter working hours. Agriculture and industry would be unified on the basis of collective labor and a redistribution of the population, ending both rural isolation and urban concentration. Every child's education would combine productive labor with instruction and gymnastics, and this would result in more efficient social producers as well as more fully developed human beings. In the new society there would be neither rich nor poor, for all would share the fruits of social labor. The standard of living would increase because people working for themselves would work that much harder. The socialist revolution meant to Lenin, as it had to Marx, the emancipation of the whole, oppressed humanity.[6] After November of 1917 Lenin seemed quite different. He had justified the coup by his theory of imperialism which had permitted a temporary advantage to. the Russian proletariat. Anything permanent in Russia, however, relied on assistance from the expected international socialist revolution, particularly the one in Germany. Without it, he wrote, we are doomed.[7] Two months earlier, however, he had seemed to be saying the opposite when he said:

> It would be a mistake, however, to base the tactics of the Russian so-cialist government on attempts to determine whether or not the Euro-pean, and especially the German, socialist revolution will take place in the next six months (or some such brief period).[8]

Just as the early Christians daily expected the return of Christ, yet in the meantime began to organize a church, so also the Bolsheviks looking forward to international revolution were simultaneously in control of a country. This necessitated operational policy decisions for an interim pe-riod that did not end. The international socialist revolutions simply did not come—Lenin had been wrong. By August 1918, the temporary beach-head of world socialism turned into a holding action that gradually gener-ated a feeling of accomplishment among the Bolshevik leaders.[9] They had stayed in power far longer than the Paris Commune. Not only had they demonstrated that they could defend themselves with the newly created Red Army, but they might also secure the victory of the international rev-olution.[10] The Bolsheviks, they felt, had become the world model—but of what? Because they won power in Russia, called themselves Communists, and named their international the *Communist International,* they became models of communism—a communism they would not have even sixty years later. They did not even have socialism until Stalin decreed in 1936 that socialism had been achieved. The communism that was their goal became a word used to describe their efforts to achieve it.

The absence of international socialist revolutions had another signifi-cant result. It might have been theoretically justifiable to seize power in the name of the proletariat while waiting for advanced countries to follow suit and then take over leadership. When that did not occur, the Bolshe-viks found themselves in power in a semideveloped country that had been further weakened by the First World War. This meant that the wealth that socialism assumed for sharing was not there. Since they were on their own, *that wealth would have to be built.* The historic role of capitalism would have to become the presocialist duty of the Bolshevik Communists. What advanced countries could take more or less for granted, the Bolsheviks had to create self-consciously. Moreover, the first few years in power saw that economic situation worsen.

Civil wars began in mid-1918 and lasted until 1921. During that brief period the Bolsheviks were successful, but the struggle for socialism became the struggle for survival. The problems of the Russian economy had already been made more severe by the First World War, and the three years of civil war made them almost intolerable. In addition, the Bolsheviks lost a considerable amount of rich territory during this time, which only compounded their problems. The *Treaty of Brest-Litovsk* in March 1918, that ended the war with Germany and angered the Allies, was a very costly treaty for the Bolsheviks. They lost the Ukraine, Poland, Lithuania, Latvia, and Estonia to the Germans, even though after the German defeat in November 1918 they received some of this back. They granted independence to Finland, lost Kars, Ardahan and Batum to the Turks, and Bessarabia to Rumania. The lost territory contributed greatly to a real economic crisis, for it represented about 32 percent of their arable land; 26 percent of their railroads; 33 percent of their textile factories; and nearly 75 percent of their coal, iron, and steel industries.

As if this were not enough, the Bolsheviks faced an Allied blockade until 1920—the British landed at Murmansk in March of 1918, and American, British, and French forces landed at Archangel in August. The British and Japanese landed at Vladivostok in the Pacific east in April 1918, and these forces were joined briefly by French, Italian, and American forces. In December 1918 the British occupied Batum, Baku, and Tiflis in the south, and the French tried a landing at Odessa. Great stretches of the trans-Siberian railroad came under the control of Czech Legions (former Austro-Hungarian prisoners of war) whom the Bolsheviks had tried to ship across the Pacific. These interventions, although real enough, were temporary and half-hearted—they accomplished little. Allied troops did not want to occupy Russia or start another war, and there was considerable opposition to these intervention moves by labor groups in the Allied countries.

Allied intervention and financial support, however, did assist the various rival White Army forces that were attempting to destroy the Bolsheviks. This was a real threat, but by 1921 they had all been defeated by the Red Army, skillfully led by Trotsky. The Whites were not united; they often implemented pre-1917 land policies in areas under their control alienating possible peasant support; they had to cover much greater distances; and they had no unified program that appealed to people other than the negative one of getting rid of Bolshevism.

Before this crisis had reached its full magnitude, the Bolsheviks passed legislation that recognized worker control of industry; abolished all classes, distinctions, and privileges; established central planning; abolished all former legal institutions; centralized banking; removed ranks and insignias from the army; made marriage civil rather than religious; made divorce and abortion easier; and destroyed all institutions of the former government in favor of a hierarchy of Soviets. Inheritance and property rights in land were abolished, as were large-scale industrial and commercial enterprises. Some of this legislation proved very temporary.

The Bolsheviks wanted to do more than this if the new program adopted by the Eighth Party Congress, in March of 1919, was any guide. That program called for the liberation of women; the end of all national privileges; full democracy; the right of former colonies to separate; and vast improvements in housing. The program also envisioned the schools as regenerating society. The pupils would receive free food, clothing, shoes, and school supplies. Industry and agriculture would be greatly improved. Workers could count on a six-hour day if productivity were high and if the workers were willing to spend two hours a day studying without remuneration.

The crisis situation made these more positive efforts meaningless. There were tremendous shortages of fuel and raw materials that shut down factories and railroads. There was a terrible food shortage. The urban centers were depleted as people went back to their home villages in search of sustenance. Productivity was down by some 70 percent; inflation was out of control. The ruble in October 1920 bought one percent of what it had purchased in October of 1917. Between 1914 and 1921 Russia lost some 26 million people; 15 million living in Finland, Latvia, Estonia, Lithuania, and Poland; 2 million lost in the First World War; 7 million lost during the civil wars; and another 2 million people emigrated to other countries.

From the beginning, the Bolsheviks had been intolerant of opposition. The crisis situation of the next few years made them even more so. **War communism** was gradually introduced. In November of 1917, they "temporarily" closed rival newspapers. A month later they progressed to the point of prohibiting the liberal Cadet party. By June of 1918 they had expelled the Socialist Revolutionary party members and the Mensheviks from the Soviets. They were even becoming suspicious of the large numbers of people who had recently joined the Bolshevik party. The ranks of loyal workers in Saint Petersburg had been depleted, and Lenin told a conference of trade unions that those who worked in the factories knew very well that many of the workers were not supporting the party.[11] The *Cheka,* the Bolshevik secret police, had been established in December of 1917. Its main purpose was the suppression of dissent and the eradication of opposition which was seen as counterrevolution that must be destroyed.

The precoup optimism expressed in *State and Revolution* had to be quickly replaced, for this early optimism was based on apocalyptic notions of revolution; expectations of European assistance; an overestimation of the consistency of the working class; and on a simplistic view of what this dictatorship involved. In theory, the dictatorship of the proletariat was designed to suppress capitalists, but in practice it became the maintenance of civil order as interpreted by the Bolshevik leadership. To put down crime, hooliganism, corruption, and profiteering, Lenin said, required an iron hand.[12] He was discovering that it was easier to gain power than to hold on to it. By May of 1918 he was saying that a real dictatorship of the proletariat consisted in the pressure of this iron rule being felt in all corners of the country, when

> . . .not a single kulak, not a single rich man, not a single opponent of the grain monopoly remains unpunished, but is found and punished by the iron hand of the disciplined dictators of the working class, the proletarian dictators. *(Applause)*[13]
>
> [Physical force must be used]. . .and we shall cast aside with contempt all who fail to understand this, so as not to waste words in talking about the form of socialism. *(Applause)*[14]
>
> The important thing for us is that Cheka is directly exercising the dictatorship of the proletariat, and in that respect its services are invaluable. There is no way of emancipating the people except by forcibly suppressing the exploiters. That is what Cheka is doing, and therein lies its service to the proletariat.[15]

In other words the dictatorship of the proletariat had quickly become the dictatorship of the party, and counterrevolution was soon described as anything which obstructed the progress of that dictatorship. The same sort of discipline and threats which had helped build the new Red Army also appeared to be necessary on the labor front in order to eliminate inefficiency as well as obstructive subversion. This could be, and sometimes was, very narrowly interpreted. In a telegram to Stalin, for example, Lenin betrayed his impatience with the inefficiency of communications and his solution for inefficient communicators.

> Stalin . . . Today I heard you and all the others very clearly, every word. Threaten to shoot the incompetent person in charge of communications who cannot give you a good amplifier and ensure uninterrupted telephone communication with me.[16]

In this period, therefore, the enormous duality developed which would come to characterize Bolshevism and particularly Stalinism. There was, on one side, brute force and increasing governmental control over the entire society. On the other side, there was a constant stream of words designed to show that these methods would accomplish the emancipation of humanity. These were things which had to be done in order that socialism and communism might come. Marxists who pointed out that the end result of dictatorial policies was an improved dictatorship were summarily dismissed as "sorry revolutionaries" who lacked the understanding and stamina for the ". . . steady advance of the iron battalions of the proletariat."[17]

> Only the development of state capitalism, only the painstaking establishment of accounting and control, only the strictest organisation and labour discipline, will lead us to socialism. Without this there is no socialism.[18]

However, although freely admitting in March of 1918 that the bricks of which socialism would be composed had not yet been made,[19] Lenin spoke optimistically a year later, when things were even more discouraging, to a crowd in Red Square. He told them that the majority of those present who were thirty to thirty-five years of age would live to see the full bloom of communism, even though it was still remote.

> Up to now the story of what our children would see in the future had sounded like a fairy-tale; but today, comrades, you see clearly that the edifice of socialist society, of which we have laid the foundations, is not a utopia.[20]

All one had to do was believe in the emperor's new clothes.

There was one development that gave Lenin great encouragement: the spontaneous emergence of the *subbotniki*. A few railroad workers tried to overcome the great transportation problems by coming back to work without remuneration on their day off. Lenin seized on this as a green shoot of communism or precursor of the future, but he could not leave it alone. He failed to see that its value was in its spontaneity; he began to organize it in order to encourage it. Helping along this beginning of communism, he felt, would mean many things. It would mean, for example, the emancipation of women from the drudgery of petty housework and the establishment of public catering places, nurseries, and kindergartens, all of which would be imbued with this *subbotnik* conscientiousness in working. The castle he built on this straw was perhaps an indication of how frustrated he was. Within months he was *arranging* volunteer labor and defining communism as voluntary, unpaid work, which quickly made it the *sine qua non* of continued membership in the party.[21]

Nonetheless, until the principle of subbotnikism triumphed, communism must be built through organization and technology. The organization was the party. The technology was summed up as electrification.

Political success was assured by Soviet power, economic success by a state-controlled, huge, industrial machine built on a modern technological basis. The party's task was therefore gargantuan even though that party was a small minority of the population.

> This tiny nucleus has set itself the task of remaking everything, and it will do so. We have proved that this is no utopia, but a cause which people live by. . . . We must remake things in such a way that the great majority of the masses . . . will say . . . [well done].[22]

In 1921 events culminated in such a way that a dramatic change of direction was necessary. The forced requisition of grain from the peasantry and the introduction of class war into the countryside, through the creation of "poor committees" which ferreted out the grain hoarders, had resulted in great peasant resistance—both violent and passive. In addition, the Kronstadt garrison, which had been the most important source of Bolshevik support, erupted in a rebellion *against* the Bolsheviks on March 2, 1921. The rebels called for a reelection of the Soviets by secret ballots; freedom of speech, press, and assembly; the release of political prisoners; the end to privileges accruing to party members; the freeing of the peasantry; and an end to food rationing. The rebels felt that other people would join them in their efforts for a socialism without the Bolsheviks, but this did not occur. On March 18 Trotsky and Tukhachevsky led government forces in an attack on Kronstadt. Fifteen thousand Kronstadters were killed. Participating in this bloodbath were some 140 delegates to the Tenth Party Congress, which was then in session.

Kronstadt and the peasantry were not the only problems faced by that Congress. By the end of 1920, as the external threat lessened, conflict grew within the party and challenged leadership positions. This was especially true after Trotsky took over control of industry and trade unions, implementing the dictatorial policies of the Bolsheviks rather unskillfully. Resentment grew among leaders and workers. Dissent movements within the party came to be called the "Workers' Opposition" and the "Democratic Centralists."

The Workers' Opposition resented Lenin's utilization of former capitalists to run factories at high wages; objected to the increasing party practice of ignoring the wishes of the trade union leaders in the selection of local union committees; and strongly felt that control over industry ought to be the province of a central group chosen by the unions. The party program recently adopted had mentioned the goal of concentrating the actual management of the national economy in the hands of the trade unions, but the practice had been to use the unions as a means of maintaining worker discipline and productivity. This was a troubled issue, for the Soviet government was theoretically a proletarian government, feeling compelled to argue against worker control. The Democratic Centralists represented a left-wing movement in the party that sought more decentralization in decision making. They advocated granting more authority to local soviets, and they resisted the growing trend toward the centralization of power in the hands of a very few people at the top. The result of that trend was clearly demonstrated by Lenin a year later when he wrote:

> . . . at the present time the proletarian policy of the Party is not determined by the character of its membership, but by the enormous undivided prestige enjoyed by the small group which might be called the Old Guard of the Party. A slight conflict within this group will be enough, if not to destroy this prestige, at all events to weaken the group to such a degree as to rob it of its power to determine policy.[23]

The Democratic Centralists were not so much bothered by the party dictatorship over the population as they were by the leadership dictatorship over the party.

Just as these two issues were developing adherents in the fairly public debate prior to the Tenth Party Congress, the Kronstadt rising took place. It had likely been encouraged by Zinoviev's attacks on Trotsky's dictatorial policies that were a part of the in-party debate. These problems were considered at the Tenth Congress in a tempestuous atmosphere that seemed far more dangerous than it really was. A resolution on party unity was called for and passed. This was the prohibition of factionalism within the party, adopted while Lenin was still in complete control—adopted in the crisis climate that closely followed Kronstadt, that Stalin would be able to use so effectively within a few years in his drive for total power. The resolution stated that in order to ensure strict discipline and to secure maximum unanimity, all factions within the party must be eliminated. Anyone creating such a faction from this time forward could be reduced in rank or expelled from the party.[24] Since both the Workers' Opposition and the Democratic Centralists were interpreted as factions, they were summarily rejected as such, even by most of their adherents. Party before trade union as interpreter of Marxism, and party unity above every other consideration.

This was a possible development—not a necessary one. Considering Bolshevism as led by Lenin since 1903, and Lenin himself since 1892, the prohibition on factions might easily be construed as a likely possibility in Bolshevik development. However, it was not the only possibility. They did have a choice, but the other option would have been a very difficult one.[25] That alternative was to grant more local power over policy decisions and to yield more authority to workers' organizations, or at least to continue to permit dissent or differing views in the party leadership. This alternative might not have prevented Stalin's rise, but it would have made it much more difficult.

This other option was not that much more liberal—for the dissenting intellectuals and worker leaders were, after all, Bolsheviks who had themselves attained their positions through illiberal methods. It was not a question of liberal against tyrant, just as it would not be in 1956 when Khrushchev made his famous anti-Stalin speech. Rather, in not choosing the alternative, the party hastened the process of the conversion of the Bolsheviks from a group of courageous revolutionaries into a bureaucratic machine. The party narrowed the acceptable definition of communism to whatever the top leaders determined it to be. This killed the Third International as a source of revolutionary energy and was a giant step on the road to Stalinism.[26]

The Tenth Party Congress responded to the crisis in another way. The Congress abolished the previous economic policies, which they had hoped would usher in the new age, in favor of the *New Economic Policy* (NEP) that lasted until the year 1927-28. This was a partial retreat toward capitalism, and a recognition that the Russian economy was in dire straits. Famine once again stalked the land and swollen bellies provided a ghastly mockery of the high ideals of the revolution. The new policies created a free market with private enterprise among the smaller businesses; replaced forced requisition of produce with an ordinary agricultural tax on the peasantry; created loan associations; reintroduced wage systems; removed official sanctions on the use of money; and allowed foreign investment in Russia. Gradually the economic picture began to brighten. By the year 1925-26 the economy was, for the most part, back to 1913 levels, and the question "where do we go from here?" began to assume new importance. However, one voice began to stand out from the rest by this time: Stalin's. Lenin had been ill since 1922, and he died on January 21, 1924. The struggle for the top spot among his subordinates would last until 1928. Stalin won.

Joseph Vissarionovich Djugashvili (1879-1953) was born into a Georgian peasant family. Unlike most of the other leaders, his background was one of poverty and harshness. As the only child who survived, he became his mother's major reason for working as a laundress and maid (his father was an alcoholic and a sporadic factory worker), and by his mother's efforts Joseph attended the church school. When this was finished, the lack of a Georgian university and a small scholarship caused him to attend the Tiflis Theological Seminary, without any serious intention of becoming a priest in the Russian Orthodox Church.

Student protests against the repressive atmosphere of the seminary predated his arrival in 1894—a general strike of students had been threatened unless certain tutors were removed and a chair of Georgian literature was established. This might seem surprising at a seminary. However, in the absence of a university, the Tiflis seminary functioned as the only center for higher learning for a middle group of potential intellectuals—those not wealthy or noble enough to be sent to European Russia for training. Their Georgian nationalism was thus unexposed to the broadening Russian influences, and their rebellious instincts were unaffected by the fact that this was a seminary. Many of the students had no desire for a priestly career. Stalin became involved with this ferment until 1899, when he was expelled for his revolutionary activity. A year earlier he had joined the left wing of a Marxist group called *Messame Dassy,* which had sufficient links with Plekhanov's RSDLP to permit Stalin's easy transition from a vague sort of Marxist socialism, imbued with Georgian nationalism, to an internationalist "Iskra" sort of socialism by 1901. Thus, he was beginning to follow the Lenin line, and he led the May Day demonstrations in Tiflis in 1901. He began a Leninist newspaper and a long life as a Bolshevik underground revolutionary. By 1917 Stalin was an old Bolshevik and one of the very few whom Lenin felt was reliable.[27]

This provides an explanation for the many jobs that Stalin had in the party and the government. There were more jobs than reliable comrades. By 1922, when Lenin had his stroke, Stalin was a member of the *Politburo* (the top-ranking executive committee of the party); a member of the Central Committee; the Commissar of Nationalities (which gave him control over half of Russia's population after 1917); the head of the *Workers' and Peasants' Inspectorate* (in charge of improving efficiency of production, which allowed him complete access to factories and farms); the chief liaison between the Politburo and several other very important party groups; and by 1922 the General Secretary of the party.

The position of General Secretary was not then thought of as the significant post that it quickly became. It was a new position, created to bring some order out of the chaos of the party records of membership, promotions, demotions, and reassignments. Under Stalin's careful control, however, it quickly became a means of ensuring that the delegates whom lower echelons chose for higher-level meetings would be persons acceptable to Stalin. Within a few years he was able to "pack" meetings of the party congresses with persons who owed their present high positions to him, and him alone.

There were other major leaders, but they did not perceive their danger until it was too late to move against Stalin. The period 1922-28 was one in which Stalin maneuvered for total power, but under the umbrella of a conflict with Trotsky, which gave Stalin greater support than he should have otherwise received. His drive to discredit and defeat Kamenev, Zinoviev, **Bukharin**, Rykov, and Tomsky was covert but real. Through a series of skillful finesses Stalin steadily moved toward sole power. It was not a struggle over ideology or interpretations of ideology, even though this was the language in which the conflict took place. It was a struggle for *total* power. However, the words that were used to fight the battles were not entirely meaningless. The issue of permanent revolution versus socialism in one country, or the response to the question of where to go after the New Economic Policy, were real problems that had to be solved, and Stalin utilized them to his advantage.

The issue of permanent revolution was the positive side of Trotsky's criticism of the practice of neglecting international considerations in favor of consolidation at home. The problem with this issue was that the *appearance* of internationalist revolutionary zeal had been created by the formation of the *Third International* (Comintern) in Moscow in March of 1919. The establishment of an organization distinguished from the social-democratic Second International by a dedication to revolutionary socialism was going to lose the majority of socialists who had steadily become addicted to reformism. The *Manifesto* of the Comintern, written by Trotsky, went further. It called for the proletarians to overthrow their existing states and to substitute the new working-class organization—the workers' Soviets. This meant forsaking labor unions and former proletarian parties in favor of the new organizational unit which the Bolsheviks in Russia had already made into an instrument of party, not working-class, control. Trotsky did not mean anything so crude as that international workers should begin speaking Russian. However, this was an effort to export the revolutionary experiences of the Bolsheviks to other countries (particularly the advanced ones), a reversal of the earlier humility that suggested other countries must aid Russia.

Trotsky's position seemed to make sense in March of 1919. Russian success had created an international excitement in the old movement, as noted in chapter 5. Just two months before, a conference of the new communist movement in Germany had come to a close at a very high pitch of revolutionary enthusiasm. The Bolsheviks were represented at this conference by Karl Radek, dressed in a Red Army uniform that drew wild applause from the delegates. From the vantage point of Moscow, Germany seemed on the verge of a revolution sympathetic to Bolshevism, a mistaken equation of the conference's revolutionary ardor with mass support in Germany—and not only in Germany. In France, postwar radicalization ran far ahead of the formal labor organizations, a radicalism carried largely by demobilized soldiers returning to factory jobs. Linking up directly with the Russians was prevented by a French nationalism that refused to cooperate with Russia until such cooperation would not assist Germany, but after the war this obstacle was removed. The fragmentation of the French radical left, however, prevented much Bolshevik penetration until after 1920.

In addition, central Europe was in turmoil after the war, in a "ripe" situation from the revolutionary point of view. Workers' Councils that in some ways resembled the beginnings of Soviets in Russia sprang up everywhere in November of 1918, and new organizations calling themselves communist emerged in many places.[28] From March to August 1919 a Hungarian Soviet Republic shakily maintained itself in power. Everywhere the principal problem was food for hungry people. Had the Red Army been able to supply food, the map of Europe might have developed along different lines than it did, but, as already noted, food was an excruciating problem for the Russians as well.

The Comintern was founded, therefore, at the peak of that revolutionary excitement caused both by Bolshevik success in Russia and the chaos that followed the war's end. Soon after March 1919, however, the situation in various countries began to stabilize, and revolutionary fervor declined. The opportunities for other successful socialist coups lessened, and revolutionary zeal became more centered in Moscow. This encouraged the already existing natural tendency for the Russians to dominate the Comintern. In 1920 the Second Congress' adoption of the twenty-one conditions for Comintern membership sealed this development. It made the Third International a *Bolshevik* instrument of international intrigue, more concerned with protecting Russian national interest than in stimulating indigenous revolutions that might damage that interest.

This was an impressive dilemma. Other revolutions had not come to the aid of the Bolsheviks; they were on their own as leaders of Russia in a world hostile to their continued existence that was made more hostile by Bolshevik propaganda.[29] The Comintern would be one method of handling this dilemma of weakness in the midst of hostility. The Bolsheviks also utilized another, contradictory, method—they began to seek and form alliances with capitalist countries as a means of normalizing their relations with these other countries—a policy to which the interests of the foreign Communist parties were soon subordinated. Bolshevik policy in the 1920s, gradually coming under Stalin's exclusive control, increasingly reflected a desire for normalization of relations that actually began with the Treaty of Brest-Litovsk in 1918. This could be, and was, dressed up in ideological language to make it more palatable. Stalin, in his *Foundations,* published in 1924, described the international proletarian strategy as that of consolidating "the dictatorship of the proletariat in one country, using it as a base for the defeat of imperialism in all countries."[30]

Consolidation of Bolshevik power was seen as progress toward international revolution, yet, that consolidation required friendly relations with supposed enemy governments. Also, Bolshevik power was increasingly coming to mean Stalin's power. This meant that every shift of Stalin's power struggle was faithfully reflected in Comintern shifts of direction.

If Stalin moved to the right or left for his own purposes within Russia, the Comintern followed—often with disastrous results for those who faithfully followed those shifts in other countries. While Stalin was being very cautious in 1923, revolutionary opportunities were lost in Bulgaria and Germany. A modest shift to the left in 1924 came too late. A shift to the right in 1925 meant that the international parties should cooperate with other socialists and liberals—in Poland they helped elect Pilsudski in 1926, who promptly turned on them after his victory. The 1926 communist participation in the British general strike meant a severe loss of members when the strike failed. The required cooperation of Chinese Communists with the Kuomintang (see chapter 9) nearly cost the life of the Communist party in 1927 when Chiang Kai-shek did his best to exterminate it. Stalin's domestic maneuvering was a disaster when it was transposed into the International.

In 1928 Stalin was clearly without important opposition, and it was at this point that he finally felt secure about implementing his own response to the New Economic Policy—forced-draft industrialization, **collectivization of agriculture,** and continuation of the purge of his former colleagues and potential opponents. This shift was actually one to the left, for Stalin was now advocating directions for Russia which he had criticized earlier as being too radical. The Comintern also shifted leftward with the adoption of the Comintern program at the Sixth Congress in September of 1928. This program urged the parties of the Comintern to strive for a violent revolution in their own countries and marked the completion of the Bolshevization of the Third International. This leftward shift meant a policy of noncooperation with other socialists and trade unions, a resplitting of the labor movement that would ease the way in Germany for the rise to power of Adolf Hitler and his National Socialists.

This Comintern policy did not change until the Seventh Congress in 1935, when the successful tactics of the French Communists, tactics of cooperation with noncommunist parties in 1934, were made official policy for the entire movement. This was the **Popular Front,** which urged cooperation and conciliation of old wounds in order to gather opposition to fascism. Once again the purpose was the defense of the Soviet Union, but the new policy had unforeseen consequences. One was the very dramatic shift from antifascism to pacifism after the Russians signed the nonaggression treaty with Hitler in 1939, and the dramatic shift back to antifascism when Russia was invaded by German forces in the summer of 1941. These moves cost communist front organizations many members. Another consequence was more significant in the long run. The Popular Front tactics of cooperation with other leftist groups permitted alliances between communist members of the Comintern and nationalistic movements in underdeveloped countries that were noncommunist but very anti-imperialist. For example, Greek Communists and anti-British Nationalists found common ground. The same was true in Vietnam and Latin America. Although this alliance suffered briefly during the 1939-41 hiatus, many of these parties emerged after World War II leading a much broader movement than would otherwise have been the case had the Comintern again shifted to the left. The Third International was abolished by Stalin in 1943 as a concession to his wartime allies, and the Popular Front was never actually rescinded. Ironically, later communist successes in Vietnam, China, Yugoslavia, and almost in Greece occurred without the Comintern (see chapter 8).

Domestically speaking, Leninism had become Stalinism by 1928, and that meant that communism was whatever Stalin said it was. Because he had won his power struggles, his advocacy of socialism first being consolidated in one country had also triumphed. To protect the Russian island of communism in a sea of capitalism, Stalin determined that Russia must industrialize fully and rapidly. Now in sole control, he implemented the first of many five-year plans—a tremendous push to take giant strides forward in a very short time. As before, under the tsars, this drive was to be financed by the export of agricultural "surpluses." To do this he had to have control of the countryside, hence the drive to collectivize agriculture, reestablishing the old communes under Soviet control. All of this created great strains in the population; caused the death of millions of people; and made Stalin even more suspicious of opposition, both real and imaginary. Failures could be blamed on a Trotsky underground or on White counterrevolutionary groups, and later on fascist groups. These labels provided his subordinate secret police with convenient scapegoats for a pattern of arrests and executions that did not know how to stop. The "Great Purges" snowballed. In a climate of near hysteria, rapid industrialization proceeded as did collectivization, but tens of millions were killed and many more millions mindlessly built roads and settlements as forced labor components of prison camps.

This was a vicious distortion of the humanism of Marxism, a fundamental tarnishing of communism that exceeded the worst predictions of its enemies. It can be understood but not forgiven. Stalinism was a continuation of policies already set in motion by Lenin, and only partially mitigated by liberalization attempts after his death in 1953. The stigma and the paranoic fear of dissent remains a dust cloud swirling around the Soviet Union, obscuring the successes and advances that have been made. People receive free medical and hospital care, subsidized transportation and housing, and plentiful food. Almost everyone can find employment. However, this is true of many capitalist countries as well. The super rich of those other countries are more than matched by the privileged caste of party leaders. Likewise, the class structures of those countries are balanced by the stratified Russian society. Hindsight agrees with Stalin that rapid industrialization was vital for Russia; that undoubtedly the grain crisis of 1926-27 caused the government grave difficulties that required either capitulation to the kulaks or a firm response; and that there was opposition to Stalin within the top levels of the party. However, what justified the enormous slaughter of people? Millions of eggs broken for what kind of an omelet? A liberal constitution promulgated in the late thirties while orphaned children hunted like wolves for garbage to eat, and some ten millions of people barely existed in labor camps.

Bolshevism became a model of tyranny artfully concealed from millions of international Communists. Bolshevism also became a model for the rapid industrialization of a backward society that other undeveloped countries would soon see as a vital need of their own. As a model of communism it had become a travesty of Marxism, a tarnished communism, a **state capitalism** that was far more despicable than those against which Marx had reacted with such intensity. *Theoretical* Bolshevism began as a passion for revolution that nestled in an ideology seeking the emancipation of people to full, free, humanized lives. *Practical* Bolshevism, however, established a beachhead that became a holding action and then a prolonged defense of the earlier coup that sacrificed its original ideology. Moreover, the Second World War gave it opportunities to expand.

Suggested Readings

Daniels, Robert V. *The Conscience of the Revolution.* Harvard University Press, 1960; New York: Simon & Schuster Clarion Books, 1969.

Deutscher, Isaac. *Stalin: A Political Biography.* Oxford University Press, 1949; New York: Random House Vintage Books, 1960.

Dmytryshyn, Basil. *U.S.S.R. A Concise History.* New York: Scribner, 1965.

McKenzie, Kermit E. *Comintern and World Revolution, 1928-1943.* London: Columbia University Press, 1964.

Rosenberg, Arthur. *A History of Bolshevism, From Marx to the First Five Years' Plan.* Oxford University Press, 1934; Garden City: Doubleday Anchor Books, 1967.

Ulam, Adam B. *Stalin: The Man and His Era.* New York: Viking, 1973.

NOTES

[1]See Robert V. Daniels, ed., *A Documentary History of Communism* (New York: Vintage Books, 1960) 1: 91.

[2]Lenin, *State and Revolution* (New York: Vanguard, 1929), p. 201. This was written a little over a month before taking power in 1917.

[3]Lenin, "Third All Russia Congress of Soviets," *Collected Works* 26 (January 24, 1918): 464-65.

[4]Lenin, *State and Revolution,* pp. 205-206; also see pp. 155, 189, 193, 194.

[5]Lenin, "A Great Technical Achievement," *Collected Works* 19 (April 1913): 62.

[6]See Lenin, "The Working Class and the National Question," ibid., 19 (May 1913): 92; "Karl Marx," ibid., 21 (November 1914): 71-72; "To our Comrades in War-Prison Camps," ibid., 23 (March 1917): 348; "To the Rural Poor," ibid., 6 (March 1903): 366, 376; "What the Friends of the People Are and How They Fight the Social Democrats," ibid., 1 (1894): 184; and "Revision of the Party Programme," ibid., 24 (May 1917): 468.

[7]Lenin, "Extraordinary Seventh Congress of the Russian Communist Party (Bolshevik)," ibid., 27 (March 6-9, 1918): 98.

[8]Lenin, "Theses on the Question of a Separate Peace," ibid., 26 (January 1918): 443-44.

[9]Lenin, "Speech at a Meeting in Sokolniki District," ibid., 28 (August 1918): 53.

[10]Lenin, "Resolution of the Joint Session of the All Russia CEC," ibid., 28 (October 1918): 130.

[11]Lenin, "Fourth Conference of Trade Unions," ibid., 27 (June 1918): 466.

[12]Lenin, "The Immediate Tasks of the Soviet Government," ibid., 27 (March-April 1918): 264.

[13]Lenin, "Report on Foreign Policy," ibid., 27 (May 1918): 379.

[14]Lenin, "Session of the Central Executive Council, Moscow Soviet, Red Army, and the Trade Unions," ibid., 27 (June 1918): 435.

[15]Lenin, "Speech at a Rally and Concert for the All Russia Extraordinary Commission Staff," ibid., 28 (November 1918): 170. See also, "Plenary Meeting of the Moscow Soviet," ibid., 29 (April 1919): 264; "Plenum of the All Russia CCTU, Speech Closing the Session," ibid., 29 (April 1919): 300; and "Foreword to 'Deception of the People with Slogans,' " ibid., 29 (July 1919): 377-81.

[16]Lenin, "Telegram to J. V. Stalin," ibid., 30 (February 1920): 363.

[17]Lenin, "Left-Wing Childishness and the Petty-Bourgeois Mentality," ibid., 27 (May 1918): 276-77.

[18]Lenin, "Session of the All Russia CEC," ibid., 27 (April 1918): 297.

[19]Lenin, "Extraordinary Seventh Congress of the RCP (B)," ibid., 27 (March 1918): 148.

[20]Lenin, "Three Speeches Delivered in Red Square," ibid., 29 (May 1919): 330.

[21]See Lenin, "A Great Beginning," ibid., 29 (July 1919): 427, 429; "The Fight to Overcome the Fuel Crisis," ibid., 30 (November 1919): 141; and "Political Report of the Central Committee," ibid., 30 (December 1919): 186.

[22]Lenin, "Speech at a Plenary Session of the Moscow Soviet," ibid., 33 (November 1922): 442.

[23]Lenin, "The Conditions for Admitting New Members to the Party," ibid., 33 (March 1922): 257.

[24]See Lenin, "Tenth Congress of the RCP (B), Preliminary Draft Resolution of the Tenth Congress of the RCP on Party Unity," ibid., 32 (March 1921): 244; and Robert V. Daniels, ed., A Documentary History of Communism (New York: Random House Vintage Books, 1960) 1: 206-16.

[25]For a view stressing the lack of choice, see Isaac Deutscher, The Unfinished Revolution—Russia 1917-1967 (New York: Oxford University Press, 1967), p. 31. He maintained that the survival of the revolution depended on the single-party system.

[26]A Yugoslav view that blames the rise of a monolithic party on "Stalinism," thus exonerating Lenin, can be found in Svetozar Stojanović, Between Ideals and Reality, A Critique of Socialism and Its Future, trans. Gerson Sher (New York: Oxford University Press, 1973), pp. 55-56. An informative discussion of the opposition problem in 1921 can be found in Leonard Schapiro, The Communist Party of the Soviet Union (New York: Random House Vintage Books, 1971), pp. 201 ff.

[27]The designation "old Bolshevik" most definitely could not belong to Trotsky, who only joined the party in July 1917, but whom Lenin elevated above many of the old guard. This, as well as Trotsky's arrogant personality, created an intense dislike of him which Stalin used in the 1920s to his own advantage. Lenin began to have distinct reservations about Trotsky, and especially about Stalin near the end—reservations which Trotsky knew about but did not publicize (party unity) until too late to stop Stalin's climb to total power. See Daniels, A Documentary History of Communism 1: 223-35, for Lenin's Testament.

[28]F. L. Carsten, Revolution in Central Europe, 1918-1919 (Berkeley: University of California Press, 1972), p. 108.

[29]See John H. Kautsky, Communism and the Politics of Development (New York: John Wiley, 1968), p. 131. See also p. 130 for a discussion of the "self-fulfilling prophecy" in regard to the actual Comintern threat to capitalist countries.

[30]J. V. Stalin, The Foundations of Leninism, in The Essential Stalin, ed. Bruce Franklin (New York: Doubleday Anchor Books, 1972), p. 157. Reprinted by permission of Doubleday & Company, Inc. See also Daniels, A Documentary History of Communism 1: 257-61.

The Expansion of Bolshevism

Between the two world wars, the countries of East Central Europe were a hodgepodge of democratic experimentation yielding to dictatorships, and of divisive nationalism, both within and between countries, over disputed territory. It was a weak area of the world in more ways than one, where the old ideas and methods of life met the new—with the old often winning. As in earlier times, this area maintained a precarious existence between two giants—Germany and Russia. The latter behemoth, feverishly industrializing, watched with nervous eyes as Germany annexed more and more territory between them. Subsequent to the Munich collapse of France's dream of containing Germany in 1938, Stalin bought more time for the Soviet Union by agreeing to a nonaggression pact with the Nazis, which had the pleasurable bonus of ceding some of this in-between territory to Russia. In the *Molotov-Ribbentrop Pact* of 1939 Russia received over half of Poland and one-third of its population. The newly acquired population was composed of a minority of Poles—many were Jewish, Ukrainian, and White Russian.

Germany moved into its half of Poland on September 1, 1939, an action that finally convinced a reluctant Britain that nothing short of war would stop the territorial ambitions of the *Third Reich*. Russia moved into her new area on September 17. Poland once again disappeared. Also leaving the map as independent countries were the Baltic republics of Lithuania, Latvia, and Estonia. They once again became part of Russia; the old tsarist empire had been regained. In the summer of 1941, however,

Russia was attacked by Germany and suffered heavy losses while Stalin tried to make up his mind as to what to do. The eventual Russian defense was both costly and valiant, but it was not until the winter of 1942-43 at Stalingrad that the tide of battle finally turned in Russia's favor. By this time the United States was also fighting Germany, and both British and American ships were beginning to supply Russian war needs along the very cold and dangerous northern shipping lanes. This alliance was a temporary truce in the hostility between America and Russia that had been only partially mitigated by mutual diplomatic recognition in 1933. There was a basic distrust of the other country's intentions, coupled with a recognition of a joint need for the other's power during the battle against the Germans and Japanese.

Japan was fully occupied in defending its expanded Pacific territory against American forces and did not violate its nonaggression treaty with the Soviet Union. The military unpreparedness of Great Britain and the United States, and their geographic separation from the European continent left the main European battle against the Germans to Russia, at least until the Normandy invasion in 1944. The decision to open a second European front against Germany took so long to implement that Stalin became suspicious that the West had ulterior motives in delaying. When it came in 1944, the tide of the war had already turned against Germany. In addition, the decision to attack through France, rather than a militarily untenable route through the Balkans, reflected Roosevelt's feeling, expressed as early as 1943, that postwar East Central Europe would be difficult to regain from the advancing Red Army as it began pushing Hitler's forces westward toward Germany. The armies of the Western allies met the armies of Russia at the Elbe River in May of 1945. At that time it would have been nearly impossible to contemplate reversing the process of the Russian occupation of Eastern Europe.

Essentially the European war had been against Germany. That nation was now defeated and lying in ruins, its territory occupied by victorious armies and its prison camps providing horror tales for months and years to come. The roundup of Nazi leaders, imperfect at best, provided visible defendants at Nuremberg. This war was over. To have suggested another against Russia, so recently an American ally, would have been political suicide in the democratic countries.

Second, America was still fighting the Japanese in the Pacific. Their tenacious defense of various islands had convinced American planners that an invasion of the home islands would be necessary. One such invasion was planned for late 1945 with a second to follow in early 1946. In February 1945, therefore, the United States sought and received assurances from Russia, at the Yalta Conference, that she would enter the Pacific conflict within ninety days of the cessation of European hostilities. In May of 1945, when Germany surrendered, American planning was still counting on Russian help.

Third, the pragmatic decision to recognize the inevitability of a Soviet occupation of East Europe had already been made, and this was reflected in decisions such as permitting the Russians to take Berlin. More specifically, the United States had agreed the year before to honor the percentages arrangement that Churchill had worked out with Stalin in October 1944. This agreement recognized a predominant Russian interest in Bulgaria and Rumania; a fifty-fifty arrangement for Hungary between British and Russian interests; and British predominance in Greece. This was in a sense a *quid pro quo* that followed the earlier American and British decision not to allow Russia to participate in the Italian surrender and occupation. Nonetheless this was a recognition of a Russian sphere of influence in East Europe. The thinking at that time becomes more understandable if one recalls that Bulgaria, Rumania, and Hungary were allies of Nazi Germany during the early years of the war, and that both Rumania and Hungary had participated in the 1941 invasion of Russia. Greece had been under British influence for some time before the war.

German territory was parcelled out in four zones of occupation to Britain, France, the United States, and Russia. What would later be called East Germany was the Soviet zone of occupation immediately after the war. Theoretically, Germany was to be reunified by a peace treaty officially ending the war; this was not seen as a problem in 1945. What did become a problem that exacerbated everything else was the resumption of hostility between the United States (assisted by Britain) and Russia that began to be visible after American atomic bombs had made that earlier dependence on Soviet Pacific intervention totally unnecessary.

The Cold War, as it came to be known, developed with apparent inevitability in 1945-48 as it became obvious that the postwar world contained only two powerful countries—Russia and the United States. In 1945 the hostility latent between them quickly began to corrode cooperative ventures and soon resulted in outright competition between them. One area where cooperation was important was Germany. Korea was also important because it had been divided between Russian and American zones in a five-year trusteeship prior to a projected Korean unification. A third vital component, designed in 1945 to keep the postwar peace, was the United Nations, where expected cooperation soon degenerated into bitter wrangling between the rival powers and their satellites.

There were reasons on both sides for the resumption of these aggressive attitudes, and the international scene quickly became a giant chessboard in a game dangerously played for high stakes by the plucky Missourian,

Harry S Truman, and the crafty Georgian, Joseph Stalin. What occurred in East Central Europe between 1945 and 1948 must be seen against that international conflict.[1]

Poland provided a good example of what happened. After the German invasion of Russia in 1941, Poland ceased to be a partial Russian prize and became instead an ally against Germany. The Russian government recognized the Polish government-in-exile and agreed to train a Polish army on Russian soil. Stalin did do this, but he dulled its potential impact on postwar Soviet-Polish relations by assigning the Polish units in 1942 to the Middle East and later to the Italian operations. In 1943 German soldiers discovered the corpses of thousands of former Polish officers buried in the Katyn Forest. The Germans blamed the Russians and the Russians blamed the Germans. When the Polish government-in-exile asked for a neutral investigation, this provided an excuse for Stalin to break off relations and gave him an opportunity to create a new Polish government that would be in exile in Moscow rather than in London. This was the *Lublin Committee,* a Polish government much more in the Bolshevik image than the London group. In 1944, when the Red Army pushed across Poland on its way to Berlin, it rather quietly installed this Lublin Committee in power and treated it as though it were the new Polish postwar government. During August of 1944 the Red Army under Marshal Rokossovsky stood by and watched the Germans decimate the Warsaw Polish underground, which had risen in an attempt to free Warsaw before the Russians arrived. This deliberate Russian delay, alleged to be necessary because of supply problems, further weakened resistance inside Poland to the Lublin Committee.

In addition Stalin saw no reason to give up the territory Russia had gained in the 1939 pact with Germany. However, he sought to compensate Poland for this loss by giving it territory on the Polish western flank carved from former German areas. This moved Poland westward, actually creating a Poland some thirty thousand square miles smaller. However, the western addition included more seaports and coastline, more fertile farm lands, and some heavy industry. The territory Russia kept was less valuable. The move also created a more homogeneous Polish population and gave it a better balance between industry and agriculture, but Russia had acted on its own, without agreement from the other allies.

Therefore, the Polish problem was a big topic at the Yalta Conference in February of 1945. The border question could not be resolved; it was left for the Potsdam Conference in July, and in turn left to be determined by the final peace treaty, which was never completed because of the Cold War. In short, the Polish border question remained a thorny issue for over twenty-five years, interfering with possible recognition of the

German Democratic Republic (East Germany) by the West as well as cooperation between the two Germanies after 1949. However, the issue of the Lublin Committee versus the Polish government-in-exile was "settled" to the satisfaction of the Yalta conferees: Stalin agreed to broaden the new Polish government by adding some members from the London group.

This broadened Polish government was still essentially the Lublin Committee, headed not so much by old Polish Socialists as by new Bolshevized Communists. In the next three years, from 1945 to 1948, the government of Poland became more rigidly Bolshevik. First, the noncommunist opposition was isolated and politically destroyed through a variety of methods (including the formation of **National Fronts**); second, the socialist movement was increasingly Bolshevized until by 1948 the Socialists and the Communists merged; and third, the Polish Communist party was purged of all members and leaders who betrayed too much Polishness and too little subservience to Moscow. Hindsight makes this appear inevitable, as a type of master plan of conquest. In one sense it was a conquest by Stalin, occurring not only in Poland but throughout East Central Europe. In another sense the heightening tensions of the Cold War made Stalin feel that these steps were a necessary defense against possible Western attacks on the Soviet Union—providing a plausible excuse for the increasing rigidity of his control.

In this time period there were many areas of international tension. One, of course, was in the heart of Europe where the Russian and American armies uncertainly faced each other. Joint conferences became more and more difficult. This was also true of the joint administration of Korea. It had disintegrated so much by 1947 that when a United Nations mission went to Korea to attempt the beginning of unification elections, the team was not permitted to enter the Russian-controlled north. Russia did not trust the United Nations, for that organization was dominated by the West, particularly in the Security Council. The result of not allowing the UN team into the north of Korea, however, was that the team went back to the United Nations recommending that elections be held in the areas that it *had* surveyed—in the south alone. When this was done and the very anticommunist Sigmund Rhee was elected the leader of South Korea, the Russians followed by organizing a separate North. This formalized the division that the Cold War had created, making it much more rigid and more difficult to dismantle.

Another tension area lay to the south. By the end of 1945, Ho Chi Minh was in undisputed control of the north of Vietnam, except for remnants of the Chinese, who had officially received Japan's surrender in the north. British forces had landed in the south to do the same thing, but they quickly released the French from confinement and reinstated them in administrative control. This was possible in the south because the *Viet Minh* (a combination of Nationalists and Communists under Ho) were much weaker in the south, had much more political competition than in the north, and therefore were unable to prevent the French coup from succeeding. This began the French effort at reestablishing its colony in Indo-China which it had seized in the mid-1870s, but now some forty thousand French troops had great difficulty keeping order just in the south. In 1946 open hostilities broke out between the French and the Viet Minh, and by 1947 the United States was assisting the French in Vietnam with economic aid.

In Greece the communist-led ELAS was driven out of Athens by the British in 1945. This struggle revolved around the question of what group should rule postwar Greece. The communist-led nationalist coalition resented the right-wing government that Britain installed, and civil hostilities broke out again. This became so difficult for Britain to handle that in the winter of 1946-47 a request was made to the United States to take over this "anticommunist" struggle. By February of 1947 the American government was ready to do so. The 1946 elections had gone to the Republicans, and one charge against President Truman that had been made was that he was soft on communism. Not only did he go out of his way to disprove this allegation, but he and his aides discovered that this fairly tight-fisted Congress was quite susceptible to a plea for funds made in the name of anticommunism. This fact plus the international developments sketched above resulted in the *Truman Doctrine,* pledging aid to Greece and Turkey (which had been threatened by Russia in 1946), but also insisting that the United States was prepared to defend any government that appeared threatened by a totalitarian-minded armed minority. This was widely taken as an official throwing down of the gauntlet to the Soviet Union, an effort to contain Russia and prevent further expansion.[2] Containing Russia was one thing, but being ready to suppress indigenous communist or leftist revolutions wherever they occurred was quite another. The Truman Doctrine established an equation between Russian expansion and international communist activity even though Russia was not directly involved in the Greek, Chinese, or Vietnamese problems. The Truman Doctrine provided a precedent for later American military activity in Korea, Vietnam, Lebanon, Guatemala, the Dominican Republic, and military aid to Chinese opponents of Mao.

This message was not lost on Stalin. His response was to tighten his control over the countries within his sphere of influence. By 1948 this was complete in Poland, Hungary, Rumania, Bulgaria, and the Soviet zone of Germany. Three countries varied from this pattern: Czechoslovakia, Yugoslavia, and Albania.

Czechoslovakia in the interwar years had been more industrialized than its Eastern European neighbors. More industry was added during the war, as the Germans sought safer places for their factories because of heavy allied bombing. In the postwar situation the Czech government, recalling the Western betrayal previous to the war (Munich, 1938), felt as though Russia were her patron, not the West. Czechoslovakia attempted, therefore, to bridge the gap between East and West. The Communist party of Czechoslovakia was quite strong and had solid labor support. The attitude of the government, plus the strength of the party, encouraged a Soviet belief that an electoral pursuit of power in this country might succeed. In the elections of May 1946 the Czechoslovak Communist party received some 38 percent of the popular vote and became the largest single party, even though strongly opposed by the Czech Socialist and the Catholic Populist parties. The Communists were strongly represented in the new cabinet. When the next years saw a gradual erosion of their popularity and a protest resignation of twelve democratic cabinet ministers created a golden opportunity in February 1948, the Communists staged a coup. By June of that year they were in control of the entire government, and immediately began to impose Stalinist Bolshevization on Czechoslovak society—somewhat irrational considering previous Czechoslovak industrialization.

This appeared to the United States as proof of the truth underlying the Truman Doctrine, and hostility increased, manifesting itself particularly in Germany where the three Western powers introduced a monetary reform which Russia had long opposed. Stalin responded to this with the blockade of Berlin, and America answered with a year-long airlift of supplies to the western sectors of Berlin that lay within the Soviet zone.

In postwar Russia Stalin had reimposed very tight controls on the population. Returning Russians who had been German prisoners of war were very often reinterned in Russian prison camps because of their surrender and alleged exposure to Western ideas. The Fourth Five Year Plan demanded considerable belt-tightening again, as Russia sought to rebuild shattered industries and farms and develop atomic weapons as quickly as it could, to balance those possessed by the United States. Russian requests for aid to replace the abruptly cancelled lend-lease in 1945 were conveniently "lost" by the U.S. Department of State —once again the Russians had to do it on their own. This helped to explain their suspicions of the 1947 *Marshall Plan*. However generous it might have been, it was specifically anticommunist in nature and a part of Cold War politics. Russia created the **Council for Mutual Economic Assistance** in response. The very tight controls in Russia were gradually introduced in East Central Europe, and this was complete by 1948 with one glaring exception—Yugoslavia.

The problem with Yugoslavia was that Tito had for a long time been a maverick from Moscow's point of view, consistently listening to a Yugoslav rather than a Russian tune. In the confused war period when Stalin was playing a very cautious game with his Allies, Tito refused to go along with this caution. He fought against the Germans which pleased Stalin, but he also fought against the forces of Mihajlović, who was linked with the exiled former government of Yugoslavia. This did not please Stalin at all. Tito's assumption of power in 1945, almost entirely without the aid of the Red Army, encouraged an immediate implementation of Yugoslav dictatorial communism that resembled the Soviet or Stalin model. While other East European countries were moving through the step-by-step program of the assumption of total power, Tito was already there. While Russia attempted to discourage activity by Greek Communists against Britain, Tito encouraged the rebels, supported them, and also shot down American planes flying over Yugoslavia. While other countries meekly accepted the exploitative trade deals with Moscow, Tito objected. Attempts by Stalin to penetrate Tito's organization through spying or bribery were failures. Yugoslav assistance to Albania, involving integration of five-year plans; considerable economic and technical assistance; and talk of an eventual union of the two countries stimulated some Albanians to fear a Yugoslav take-over. All this gave Stalin the feeling that Tito was a potentially dangerous in-house rival who had to be stopped.

In 1947 with the organization of the Communist Information Bureau (**Cominform**), Stalin had a structure for the general supervision of the East European countries. In retrospect the group's major purpose appeared to be bringing Yugoslavia into line. Its headquarters were initially in Belgrade, and until 1956, when it was quietly disbanded, the only significant thing it did was to expel Tito's Yugoslavia from the group. This was in 1948—the high point of Stalin's demand for conformity. Other members of the group were instructed not to trade with or aid Yugoslavia in any way, and the expectation was that Yugoslavia would be forced rather quickly to concede to Stalin's terms.

The context of this event was the peculiar thinking that had arisen in these early years of the Cold War, a kind of thinking that would reappear in surprising ways in the 1950s and 1960s. The hardening of hostilities had created the notion on both sides that there were just two camps in the world—Russia and the United States—locked in a struggle between good and evil. There was no middle ground. If a country did not fully belong to one side, a strong suspicion arose that it secretly belonged or wanted to belong to the other side. Neutralism was impossible in this context. The conformity demanded on either side was extensive.[3] Yugoslavia, although conforming in nearly every important way, was simply not something that Stalin could easily control. Therefore, Yugoslavia had to change—even if that meant a destruction of the Yugoslav Communist party.

This period saw not an expansion of communism so much as the extension of Stalinist Bolshevism. Stalin had no concern about Yugoslav communism as such—only whether he could control it. He actually had little or no concern about his own party—the Great Purge had fallen just as heavily on party members as it had on other groups in the population. One of Khrushchev's later charges would be that Stalin ruled through a personal secretariat that in fact voided the party, nearly destroying it. This was still true after World War II. The expansion into Eastern Europe, creating a "buffer zone" between Russia and possible future German militarism, was an extension of the Russian sphere of influence which became an area of direct Russian manipulation and control, particularly between 1948 and 1956. This could also be called a wider scope for Stalinist Bolshevism, but not for communism or socialism. Stalin exercised his control through puppet parties that were restructured versions of the previous socialist or communist movements in those countries. The crisis atmosphere provided by the Cold War created a convenient rationale.

The dispute with Yugoslavia was not ideological but personal—a dispute over timing and methods and who should control whom that was instantly cast into nationalistic terms by Tito. When the members of the Yugoslav Central Committee gathered on April 12, 1948, Tito said:

> This is not a matter here of any theoretical discussion. . . . Comrades, the point here, first and foremost, is the relations between one state and another.
> No matter how much each of us loves the land of socialism, the USSR, he can, in no case, love his own country less.[4]

This gained Tito more popularity in Yugoslavia, and during the next two years he demonstrated to his party that he had not become a "soft" communist by increasing the pressure for industrialization and collectivization. It quickly became obvious, however, that without external aid the Yugoslavs were going to have a very difficult time. The decision to accept American aid was as surprising as the American decision to offer it. This was both economic assistance and military aid.

The United States' decision to grant aid negated the recently adopted conclusions about the two rival camps in the world. To many, of course, it did not—Yugoslavia would simply be counted on the side of the West—a net loss to Russia. However, this was a country still ruled by a Communist party. While American (and other nations') soldiers fought against the devilish possibilities of a communist rule in Korea, America's other hand granted some $600 million in economic aid and $588 million in military aid to Yugoslavia between 1949 and 1955.[5] This should have resulted in a fundamental alteration in American foreign policy—a flexible policy that had as its goal the creation and sustenance of other "Titos." However, events in Asia and McCarthyism at home maintained the myopia of only two camps, which the Yugoslav assistance program only temporarily improved.

The Yugoslav decision to accept American assistance was also a decision to break completely with the Stalin pattern. Forced first into the position of nationalists, by 1950 the Yugoslavs were pushed in the direction of being the first of the liberalizers of the so-called communist world. This, in turn, pushed the development of a more distinctive Yugoslav communist ideology which made it an alternative to Bolshevism (see chapter 10).

Although Stalin had failed in his attempt to bring Tito to heel, the 1948 policy toward areas that were under his sole control became increasingly anti-Titoist or extremely suspicious of even the possibility of nationalist deviations from the Bolshevik line. Leaders in the Eastern European countries whom Stalin suspected of such leanings were purged from their positions. In Poland, Wladyslaw Gomulka had sought to buttress his fairly weak party strength by an appeal to Polish nationalism. He had to go but his reputation in Poland was sufficient to make his punishment merely one of arrest and confinement; other leaders were not so fortunate. In March of 1950 some eleven Czechoslovak "Nationalist" leaders were hanged and the Czech party came under the control of the Stalinist, Antonin Novotny. Leaders were also executed in Hungary in 1949. The purges swept the boards of potential opposition to the smooth implementation of Stalinism.

This suited many Albanian leaders very well. Albania had been occupied by the Italians in 1939, and resistance to Italian and then to German occupation had been led by Tito's Yugoslav Partisans. However, anti-Yugoslav feeling was so high that, when the Germans came in 1943, some nationalist leaders began a policy of cooperating with the Germans against the Partisans. This gave Tito an excuse for the civil conflict which the combined Albanian (under Hoxe) and Yugoslav Partisans won in November of 1944, right after the Germans left. Just as in Yugoslavia, the postwar pace of the communist takeover was far more rapid in Albania than in the rest of Eastern Europe, and it seemed to some Albanians that larger Yugoslavia would swallow the smaller country. The 1948 dispute between Stalin and Tito gave Albania the lever to distinguish itself from Yugoslavia. The pro-Tito elements of the party were purged, and Albania became rigidly Stalinist. Anti-Yugoslav feeling was the principle underlying this development, not love of Russia. When the pendulum swung back to a more favorable Russian policy toward Tito in 1955-56, the Albanians refused to go along, and in 1960 Khrushchev's open dispute with the Chinese gave Albania a new ally even though its policies remained Stalinist.

There were also purges in Bulgaria in 1949 directed against Titoist elements, but here again anti-Yugoslav feelings did not require much of a push. Macedonia, a part of which had been given to the Yugoslavs, remained a sore point with the Bulgarians, and they too resisted the move in 1955-56 to bring Tito back into what Khrushchev euphemistically called "the world socialist movement."

Therefore, because of the coexisting factors of Russian fears of German military resurgence; Stalin's mania for control; and the Cold War pressure; Eastern Europe between 1948 and 1956 was frozen into a rigidly Bolshevized area. The Western response was to defensively unify the Western European countries. In 1949 the three Western occupation zones of Germany were united into the *German Federal Republic*. The Soviet zone followed in a few months with the organization of the *German Democratic Republic*. The split in Europe was frozen at the Elbe. Also in 1949 the Western European countries were organized into NATO for the purposes of defense against Soviet attack. This defensive maneuver was seen as even more necessary when it was learned that the Soviet Union had successfully developed atomic bomb capacity. The hysteria increased.

In addition, United States assisted military activity against the Greek rebels was finally successful in 1949. Yugoslavia's defection from the ranks of the rebel supporters was a significant factor. Russian unwillingness to enter this conflict, even remotely, contributed greatly to the rebels' defeat.[6] Nonetheless, the mistake made by the Truman Doctrine in equating indigenous communist-led risings with Russian expansion went unrecognized, and the results in Greece convinced American planners that military resistance was a successful way of containing that "expansion." This policy was implemented a year later when trouble developed in Korea.

The triumph of Chinese communism in 1949 and the military struggle in Korea in 1950-51, against both North Korean forces and Chinese volunteers when MacArthur came too close to the Yalu River, drew attention away from Europe and focused it on Asia at just the time when policies might have been changed. American leaders assumed that what was developing in Asia was simply more "communist aggression," which had come to mean Russian expansionism. The containment policy which had evidently worked so well in Europe was applied with vigor in Asia. The American navy patrolled the waters off China's coast, and the American military dominated the United Nations' anticommunist efforts in South Korea. In addition, the United States began to carry almost the entire burden of supporting the French struggle against the Viet Minh in Vietnam, as well as underwriting the costs of maintaining Chiang Kai-shek's military domination of Formosa. Domestically, this crusade against communism was fed by the hysterical charges of Senator Joseph McCarthy, a Republican from Wisconsin, and the activities of the China lobby led by such luminaries as John Foster Dulles, Richard Milhouse Nixon, and Cardinal Spellman. The timing, however, was unfortunate. In 1949 Stalin had begun to alter his aggressive anti-Western policies. He spoke of the possibility of peaceful coexistence. This might have been due to the apparent strength of the NATO alliance or to the sudden successful emergence of Maoist communism in China, which presented Stalin with a new Tito potential.[7] However, it may also have resulted from the successful testing of the atomic bomb in Russia.[8] Whatever the reason, the hint that relations might be substantially altered was ignored by the West. Americans became so preoccupied with the all-out struggle against communism that, after Stalin's death in March of 1953, the American Secretary of State, John Foster Dulles, viewed the obvious attempts by Stalin's heirs to reduce tensions in Europe and Asia as a trap into which American policy must not fall.

In one sense this was correct. Georgi Malenkov, the brief successor to Stalin, made clear in a speech to the Russian legislature that if Western Europe were unable to agree on the specifics of the European Defense Community in the present crisis situation, a Russian easing of the international tension might lead to an even greater disintegration of that anti-Soviet alliance.[9] Also, the recently successful Russian testing of a hydrogen bomb meant that Russia was now able to deal from strength. One Soviet purpose in the reduction of tension was to weaken the defensive alliance threatened against them. To that extent Dulles was correct.

In another sense the Dulles-Eisenhower response to this new development, which by 1954 included the possibility of rearming the Germans with nuclear weapons, artificially preserved the hostility at a very high level long after it would otherwise have begun to dissipate. If there were less need for a defensive alliance and military saber-rattling and brinkmanship, then their continued existence was in fact counterproductive—unless the purpose of these activities was less anti-Soviet maneuvering and a more pro-American dominance of European affairs. At any rate, the aggressive hostility from America continued. Not even containment was pleasing to Dulles—this was too passive. He began calling instead for the liberation of the captive peoples in Eastern Europe, but this was quickly proven to be a slender reed for the aspirations of populations within the Soviet orbit. In June of 1953 workers in East Berlin staged a general strike and demonstrations protesting higher work demands for the same wages, culminating in demands for free elections. When Soviet tanks arrived to crush this proletarian outburst with proletarian force, Dulles did nothing. Wisely so, perhaps, considering that war with Russia now meant a thermonuclear holocaust—but unwisely in the sense that an obvious distinction became visible between American deeds and American words. This distinction was true in other ways as well. Dictatorships were upheld in many parts of the world in the name of anticommunism, revealing clearly that American goals were not the liberation of "captive peoples," but winning the rivalry with the Soviet Union. From a neutral observation point the sheep had come to resemble the wolf.

Malenkov's control of the party apparatus in the Soviet Union quickly gave way to that of Nikita S. Khrushchev, who soon began to "out-liberal" the man he had replaced. Rule by terror was reduced and tensions generally eased, both domestically and internationally. Eastern Europe had new freedoms. To accomplish this and to create a platform of power for himself, Khrushchev shocked the delegates at the Twentieth Party Congress in February of 1956 with a speech directly attacking Stalin. He accused Stalin of having been brutal, capricious, and despotic. Khrushchev said that Stalin had violated revolutionary legality and had executed many honest Communists. He alleged that Stalin had been a very distrustful, sickly suspicious man, possessed with unlimited power, who had acted shamefully not only in the domestic situation but also internationally in his dispute with Yugoslavia. Therefore, he concluded, the party must make every effort to prevent the **"personality cult"** (the glorification of the leader) from returning by insisting on collegial leadership in the future.[10]

This attack on Stalin was supposed to be kept within the Soviet party, but it quickly became common knowledge. What was also highly visible at this time was a dramatic improvement in relations between Russia and Yugoslavia that had begun the year before. Soviet leaders evidently forgot that the power of other East European party leaders was based on anti-Titoism, pro-Stalinism, and a slavish imitation of Soviet practices. An article in *Pravda* in July of 1955, describing the new Russian foreign policy as solidly based on Leninist principles, opened the door wide for the previously condemned "nationalistic" communism by stating:

> All nations will arrive at socialism, Lenin pointed out; that is inevitable, but not all will arrive there in exactly the same way. Each one will introduce its own features into this or that form of democracy, into this or that form of dictatorship of the proletariat, into this or that rate of socialist transformation of different aspects of social life.
>
> The historical experience of the Soviet Union and of the peoples' democracies shows that, given unity in the chief fundamental matter of ensuring the victory of socialism, various ways and means may be used in different countries to solve the specific problems of socialist construction, depending upon historical and national features.[11]

Different roads to socialism that were not possible before, suddenly became quite proper. In addition, Stalin was branded as a despotic criminal. The basis of power for the leaders of Eastern Europe was quickly eroded. Even the organization that bound them together (Cominform) was disbanded. The announcement of the demise of the organization came in April of 1956, stating in part that each party and group would continue the struggle for working-class interests, peace, democracy, and socialism, within the common framework of **Marxism-Leninism.** Within that framework, however, ". . . the specific national features and conditions of their countries . . ." would be allowed to shape policy decisions.[12] What was expected in this looser arrangement was *cooperation* toward the common goal, theoretically replacing the lock-step conformity that had previously been required. However, careful reading of the manner in which this looser arrangement was expressed would have resulted in greater caution. *Pravda* carried a lengthy editorial on July 16, 1956, that contained several clues for the future.

One such hint was that the scope of permissible divergence was narrower than one might have imagined. In an italicized paragraph, the *Pravda* editor wrote: "The communist construction in the Soviet Union and the socialist construction in the people's democracies form a unified process of the movement of peoples toward a new life."[13] This not only indicated a unified progress, but it also placed the people's democracies in a subordinate position to the Soviet Union by describing their activity as the construction of socialism, whereas the Soviets were now constructing communism. The Soviet Union was the model, and although some national differences were being conceded, this principle remained in Russian minds.

A second clue to the future lay in the way this editorial described socialism—and by extension—communism. First, the East European parties were leading the people. The role of party over people was undiminished. Second, the development of socialism in these countries had very little to do with a liberation of people. Soviet experience was still being "exported."

> The construction of socialism gave these countries, and other people's democracies as well, the opportunity to do away once and for all with the economic backwardness of the past, to build up heavy industry, and to secure the growth of national culture.
>
> It is significant that the once backward countries of Eastern Europe, having entered the path of socialism, are almost completely catching up with the advanced states of Western Europe in the development of the most important branches of heavy industry.[14]

Thus, socialism was understood as a construction process, an industrialization which was led by the party. Success would be determined by the fulfillment of plan quotas, continued party dominance, and continued subservience to the Soviet model.

A third interesting hint of future developments was the reference to China. Socialist construction in China, it was said, was proceeding at a "roaring tempo." This was interpreted as the fulfillment of industrialization plans and the plans of the agricultural cooperatives.[15] However, later in the editorial Mao Tse-tung was quoted in support of the firm togetherness of the socialist nations, in words that would soon compel Khrushchev himself to be the one to break this so-called unity of the socialist world. Mao was quoted as saying:

> At present the Soviet Union has achieved such power, the Chinese People's revolution won such a great victory, the governments of the people's democratic countries have scored such great successes, the movement of the countries of peace against oppression and aggression has attained such scope, and our front of friendship and solidarity has become strengthened to such an extent, that it is possible to say in full confidence that we are not afraid of any kind of imperialist aggression.[16]

In 1957, when the successful launching of Sputnik was added to the thermonuclear power of the Soviet Union, the Chinese expected that this power would protect them in their struggle against the American Seventh Fleet over the offshore islands of Quemoy and Matsu. This was much further than Khrushchev wanted to go, for, as with John Foster Dulles, his ideological bark never confused his pragmatic bite. Russian communism was communism in the national interests of the Soviet Union. This difference in attitude about the use of Russian power became one of the major reasons for the 1960 break with China (see chapter 9).

Nonetheless, the 1956 developments created an *appearance* of opening up the scope of permissible discussion within an individual party about its past, present, and future, and doing so in the context of a condemnation of Stalinism and terrorism as methods of control. Party members learned that ". . . the path of socialist development differs in various countries and conditions, that the multiplicity of forms of socialist development tends to strengthen socialism. . . ."[17] Ten days after that was published riots broke out in Poznan, Poland, demonstrations by workers that turned into battles with the police which the Polish authorities were quickly able to put down. Although very brief, these riots were a turning point for Eastern Europe. Even though the workers' demonstrations were condemned in Poland and in Russia as the work of enemy agents that was completely repudiated by the entire Polish people, the riots in Poznan represented the beginnings of the outward movement that any constrained system makes when the external pressure appears to have been removed.

Beginning in 1953, in the deliberately relaxed Malenkov period, reforms had been made in the Polish economy without loosening the political terror methodology of the past. However, after the execution of Beria in Russia and the Western defection of a Polish secret policeman named J. Swiatlo, whose revelations were repeatedly broadcasted into Poland by Radio Free Europe in 1954, there was a cautious attempt to lessen the significance of the Polish secret police. This relatively freer atmosphere provided a climate for a dialogue *within the party* that became increasingly hostile to the old methods and the old leaders. Adding fuel to the fire was the quiet release of Gomulka from confinement in December of 1954. In 1955 there existed in Poland a growing challenge within the party that previously would have been easily suppressed but that was now not only permitted but reluctantly encouraged. When Khrushchev replaced Malenkov in 1955, and the liberalizing line soon continued as part of the rapprochement with Tito, the Polish party committed itself to a more relaxed policy. This quickly spread beyond the limits of party membership, and in 1955 discussion clubs developed, grew rapidly, and increasingly began to debate issues formerly decided only by top leaders in secret. All of this grew more intense after Khrushchev's anti-Stalin speech in February of 1956. That speech undercut the party ideologues' pro-Bolshevik line by forcing them back to Leninism and Marxism as well as Polish nationalism. The nonhumanist, dogmatic approach was condemned as Stalinism. The revised, more humanized ideology began to attract people who had had socialist commitments before the war, and the debate and discussion spread widely.

Party leaders fought a rear-guard action, not really condemning, merely warning against excesses, but backing up while doing so. This party dilemma was exacerbated by the death of the Polish party leader, Boleslaw Bierut, in March of 1956. His replacement was a Stalinist, but the relaxation was not halted. Former political prisoners were amnestied; Gomulka's release was made public; and the press began to modestly criticize some of the former sacred cows, such as the notion that life was continually getting better under socialism. The Soviet Union was apprehensive but did nothing that might interfere with getting Tito back into the socialist family of nations.

This balance was dramatically altered by the Poznan worker riots that were suppressed by the Polish army. This firm response was painful for Polish soldiers, but saved Poland from direct Soviet intervention. The Polish party appeared to be in control. Actually, it was split in a variety of complex ways, although the leading protagonists were the usual hard dogmatists opposed by the softer evolutionists or revisionists. This unresolved conflict within the party festered until October, when the Stalinists attempted a coup. It failed, but it brought the Soviet leaders to Warsaw for frantic negotiations. In a face-to-face confrontation, Gomulka was able to convince them that the relaxed domestic policies which he advocated in no way endangered unity with the Soviet Union and the socialist bloc, and Soviet intervention was again forestalled. Gomulka would remain in power until December of 1970. His regime was less liberal than expected and was finally terminated by striking workers in 1970.

Gomulka's successor, Edward Gierek, appears to be less ideological and more pragmatic, more oriented toward workers and less toward intellectuals. He has purged the party of some of the more conservative elements and seems to be successful in leading a Polish revision of Bolshevism that sees the country as an ally but not a satellite of the Soviet Union. The key to his long-range success, however, lies in the thorny field of economic reform, of which the most difficult aspect for any authoritarian party is the decentralization of economic decision making.[18]

In 1956 Hungary presented an even clearer deviation than did Poland. The new post-Stalin relaxations were inaugurated by a divided party. Feeling very uneasy about the weakened secret police; the relaxation of the collectivization drive; the new emphasis on consumer goods production; and planned economic decentralization; the Stalinist wing opposed the more moderate policies of the Nagy group. While superficially agreeing at conferences and congresses, the two wings of the party were very hostile to each other. In 1955 when Khrushchev replaced Malenkov in the Soviet Union, the new Russian line initially appeared to harden in the direction of reemphasizing the importance of heavy industry over consumer industries. Such a temporary position strengthened the hand of the Stalinist Rakosi in Hungary, and he replaced Nagy as leader. This was a temporary shift in Soviet policy which Khrushchev felt was necessary until his own position was more secure, but it had dire consequences for Hungary. Nagy was gradually eased out. The rise of Rakosi in 1955 occurred after two years of the more relaxed policies, making the return of the old methods a bitter pill for some to swallow. When Rakosi returned to the tactics of secret police terror in the latter part of 1955, Stalinism was reimposed on Hungary with vigor.

This, in turn, made the deposed Nagy much more self-consciously anti-Stalinist and more aware of the necessity of a specific *Hungarian* path to socialism and communism in cooperation with, but not dominated by, the Soviet Union as under Stalin. Nagy matched this possibility of diversity within socialism with a concept of diversity within capitalism—in other words, he was exploding Stalin and Dulles' concept of two hostile camps in the world. It was possible, Nagy felt, to be internationally neutral and still be a socialist or communist nation coexisting with other socialist as well as capitalist countries. These and other ideas, similar to those in Poland, began to be debated by groups of intellectuals in the Petofi clubs, still very much an in-party debate but one increasingly uncomfortable to

Rakosi after the February 1956 anti-Stalin speech in Russia. By July the divisions within Hungary were open and very noticeable. Soviet diplomatic intervention resulted in a new compromise leader that the increasingly revolutionary situation would not tolerate, especially when Polish events became common knowledge in Hungary. When the October news of Gomulka's reinstatement came, the opposition no longer feared Soviet intervention. Crowds demanded the resignation of Gerö (the compromise candidate), the secret police fired on them, and wider revolts resulted. The protest movement was concentrated in Budapest and coincided with Nagy's return to the premiership, but Soviet troops intervened anyway. Order was quickly restored and, as the Soviet troops were allegedly planning to withdraw, Nagy was made head of the party. In this tense situation that was made even more precarious by divided opinions in Russia about what ought to be done in Hungary, Nagy acted far more courageously than wisely. On October 30 he declared the formation of a multi-party government. The next day he declared that he had not been the one to request Soviet intervention, and he officially proclaimed Hungary's withdrawal from the **Warsaw Pact** to a position of neutrality.[19] This, however laudable, gave ammunition to the hard-liners in the Soviet Union and weakened the strength of the more liberal Russian leaders. This new development went too far too fast. Soviet troops returned to the struggle and suppressed a wide rebellion with great force. Different roads to socialism meant *slightly* different roads—and were only permitted when the indigenous Communist party remained loyal to Moscow and demonstrated its ability to keep domestic reform under party control.

Even though post-Stalin developments in the Soviet Union, the new line to accommodate Tito, and the anti-Stalin drive gave the appearance of liberality, this was nonetheless a liberality still heavily conditioned by the strict ideological past out of which it had come. The Russian innovators were cautious. Against strong opposition, which nearly unseated Khrushchev in 1957, they were making changes that should have been viewed by others (such as Nagy) as political moves which had as yet no secure base. These liberalizers were prepared to see changes take place, but only changes under their control that would not rock the quivering boat they were rowing. The weak position of the liberals was further undercut by British and French military intervention in the Middle East to protect the Suez Canal from being nationalized by Egypt. While Nagy was proclaiming Hungarian neutrality, French and British planes were bombing Egyptian positions; the international situation was very tense, and unity rather than diversity seemed vital in the Warsaw Pact. Nagy's failure to grasp Hungary's position in this wider context and his misunderstanding of the nature of the ideological changes taking place in Russia made him a hero—but also a failure. The subsequent regime imposed on Hungary by Soviet arms set Hungarian development back for many years. Only in the last decade has it begun to improve.

In other East European countries the impact of changes within Russia and in Soviet policies was much milder and occurred over a longer period of time. Both Rumania and Bulgaria developed a semblance of national communism that remained well within the limits of Soviet tolerance. The German Democratic Republic, under Walter Ulbricht until 1971, remained more Stalinist than the Soviet Union for a considerable period. Its later reforms, particularly economic, were from the top down and have been quite successful, without dismantling the police-state apparatus.

Twelve years after the events in Poland and Hungary, East Europe again witnessed an attempt to probe the limits of permissible change within Bolshevik ideology in Czechoslovakia. The turmoil of the middle fifties had barely touched this country; it remained quite Stalinist under Novotny until well into the 1960s. However, the imposition of a command economy on the already existing healthy economy in 1948 was finally beginning to show ragged edges; economic reforms such as more decentralization and more rational pricing were vital. The reforms made were enough to stimulate expectations of more essential reforms, but too modest to do any good. The stable situation that party leaders had enjoyed gradually deteriorated, opposition developed within the party, especially visible from Slovakia. As artists and writers began to work under less controlled supervision, they produced a culture in the large cities that went well beyond the limits of "socialist realism." In January 1968, when Novotny was replaced with Alexander Dubcek, a younger, much less rigid Slovak, a gradual but fairly complete erosion of Stalinism took place.

This was most visible in the party's changing view of itself. The April Action Program denied that the Communist party was a monolithic entity able to dictate to the population. It should lead, not by authoritarian direction, but by service, by example, by earning the right to lead. In addition, the old notion of prohibiting factions was completely discarded in favor of an honest confrontation of ideas. The program called for a more complete democracy than that available in bourgeois societies, and for the free flow of information. As a result, a much freer atmosphere began to prevail, workers began thinking along the lines of workers' councils, censors were removed from newspapers, and a real alternative to Bolshevism appeared to be developing.

However, these events in Czechoslovakia were alarming the new leaders of Russia. Although the enforced retirement of Khrushchev in 1964 was followed by a year of relative uncertainty exhibited by Leonid Brezhnev, the new party secretary, and Aleksei Kosygin, the new premier, by 1966 they were beginning to take steps backward toward Stalinist repressiveness. Dissident Baptists were arrested and imprisoned. Writers who had published satirical accounts of Soviet life were publicly tried and sentenced to long terms in prison camps. When the uncensored press in Czechoslovakia began to criticize, however gently, the Soviet Union in 1968, Russian opposition mounted.

These developments in Czechoslovakia could not help spilling over from the party to the general population. Already in May demonstrations were demanding opposition parties and the recognition of Israel—just one year after the Six-Day War of 1967. These developments alarmed Brezhnev so much that he summoned Alexander Dubcek and a few others to Moscow to explain what was going on. When Dubcek returned from Moscow he had an opportunity to place controls on these developments, to create a facade of conformity that might have staved off the August invasion of Soviet and Warsaw Pact forces. However, he did not, and they came. Czechoslovakia was re-Bolshevized. Once again an effort to liberalize Bolshevism had crashed on the rock of Russian fear of dissent and divergence. In a fervor of anti-Stalinism in Russia in 1961, the body of Joseph Vissarionovich (Stalin) was removed from the mausoleum it shared with the body of Lenin in Red Square. It was quietly buried alongside Lenin's tomb and hardly marked. His ghost, however, was far more difficult to bury. Alternative models of communism could and did develop—not within that European sphere of Russian influence, but in other parts of the world.

Suggested Readings

Alperovitz, Gar. *Cold War Essays.* Cambridge: Schenkman, 1970.

Barnet, Richard J. *Intervention and Revolution, America's Confrontation with Insurgent Movements Around the World.* New York: World, 1968.

Bernstein, Barton J., ed. *Politics and Policies of the Truman Administration.* Chicago: Quadrangle Books, 1970.

Brzezinski, Zbigniew K. *The Soviet Bloc: Unity and Conflict.* New York: Praeger, 1961.

Compton, James V. *America and the Origins of the Cold War.* Boston: Houghton Mifflin, 1972.

Ionescu, Ghita. *The Politics of the European Communist States.* New York: Praeger, 1967.

Kirkendall, Richard S. *The Global Power: The United States Since 1941.* Boston: Allyn and Bacon, 1973.

Lettis, Richard, and Morris, William E. *The Hungarian Revolt.* New York: Charles Scribner's, 1961.

Paterson, Thomas G., ed. *The Origins of the Cold War.* Lexington, Mass.: D. C. Heath, 1970.

Rothschild, Joseph. *Communist Eastern Europe.* New York: Walker, 1964.

Schlesinger, Arthur M., Jr. "Origins of the Cold War," *Foreign Affairs* 46, no. 1 (October 1967): 23-51.

Schwartz, Harry. *Prague's 200 Days: The Struggle for Democracy in Czechoslovakia.* New York: Praeger, 1969.

Starobin, Joseph R. "Origins of the Cold War: The Communist Dimension," *Foreign Affairs* 47, no. 4 (July 1969): 681-96.

Steel, Ronald. *Pax Americana.* New York: Viking Compass Books, 1967.

Tatu, Michael. *Power in the Kremlin: From Khrushchev to Kosygin.* New York: Viking Compass Books, 1967.

NOTES

[1]Although the Cold War concentrated on Europe between 1945-49, the other participants in the conflict must not be ignored. China, Vietnam, Turkey, Iran—each became a part of the overall conflict and influenced it.

[2]Containment became a popular word in 1947. George Kennan's perceptive "X" article in *Foreign Affairs*, based on his February 1946 dispatch from Moscow, gave intellectual respectability to the doctrine, but subsequent American policy went far beyond Kennan's frame of reference, as in "containing China." See George F. Kennan, "The Sources of Soviet Conduct," *Foreign Affairs* 25 (July 1947): 566-82. Also see John L. Gaddis, *The United States and the Origins of the Cold War, 1941-1947* (New York: Columbia University Press, 1972), esp. pp. 316-52.

[3]As far as John Foster Dulles was concerned, the fact that Italian and French Communists participated in some of the postwar governments of those countries made them very unreliable allies in the 1950s. America had to carry the brunt of the burden, especially after Britain had to give up the struggle in the Mediterranean area. This helps to explain the American drive for the European Defense Community in 1953-54, when it was unnecessary. The ideological struggle also had payoffs in the expansion of American power and influence, especially in the Pacific, as well as the expansion of American business interests, as in Iran or Guatemala. See, for example, Walter LaFeber, *America, Russia, and the Cold War, 1945-1971* (New York: John Wiley, 1972), esp. pp. 147-72.

[4]R. Bass and E. Marbury, eds., *The Soviet Yugoslav Controversy, 1948-1958: A Documentary Record* (New York: Prospect Books, 1959), p. 15; cited in Paul Lendvai, *Eagles in Cobwebs, Nationalism and Communism in the Balkans* (Garden City: Doubleday Anchor Books, 1969), p. 93. Reprinted by permission of Doubleday & Company, Inc.

[5]Lendvai, *Eagles in Cobwebs*, p. 107.

[6]Soviet willingness to play a militarily active role in the internal affairs of other countries has so far been limited to those countries which are along potential invasion routes from Germany to Russia. This persistent fear of German militaristic resurgence is a key factor in assessing the difference in Russian behavior between active involvement in the German Democratic Republic (1953), Poland and Hungary (1956), and Czechoslovakia (1968); and the very different response to Yugoslavia (1948), Greece (1949), Austria (1955), and Albania and China (1960).

[7]This possibility did not so much derive from Mao's declared preferences for a Tito-like independence, nor yet from hindsight's vision of later Sino-Soviet disagreements; rather from the fact that similar to Tito's rise to power, Stalin had had very little to do with Mao's success. As a matter of fact, it was only by ignoring the advice of the Comintern and because of Stalin's caution in the immediate postwar years that Mao was successful. Hence the fear on Stalin's part, a fear he seemed to have about anyone who did not owe his position to Stalin alone.

[8]This suggested the possibility that Stalin's aggressiveness from 1945-49 was in fact a large bluff to protect a weak Russia. An interesting possibility.

[9]See Robert V. Daniels, *A Documentary History of Communism* 2: 215-18.

[10]Ibid., pp. 224-31.

[11]From *Pravda*, 16 July 1955, trans. in *The Current Digest of the Soviet Press* 7 no. 26 (August 10, 1955): 3; and cited in Paul E. Zinner, ed., *National Communism and Popular Revolt in Eastern Europe: A Selection of Documents on Events in Poland and Hungary, February-November 1956* (New York: Columbia University Press, 1956), p. 8. Reprinted by permission of the publisher.

[12]From "Announcement of the Dissolution of the Information Bureau of the Communist and Workers Parties, April 17, 1956," *Pravda*, 18 April 1956; cited in ibid., p. 11.

[13]From "The International Forces of Peace, Democracy, and Socialism Are Growing and Gaining in Strength," *Pravda*, 16 July 1956; cited in ibid., p. 20. Reprinted by permission of the publisher.

[14]Ibid., p. 19. Reprinted by permission of the publisher.

[15]Ibid.

[16]Ibid., p. 24. Reprinted by permission of the publisher.

[17]From "Declaration of Relations Between the Yugoslav League of Communists and the Communist Party of the Soviet Union, June 20, 1956," cited in ibid., p. 13.

[18]For a recent discussion of Gierek's Poland, see Adam Bromke, "Poland Under Gierek," *Problems of Communism* 21, no. 5 (September-October 1972): 1-19; and Michael Gamarnikow, "A New Economic Approach," ibid., pp. 20-30. See also *New York Times*, 10 October 1974, p. 10.

[19]The Warsaw Pact was a Soviet-sponsored defensive alliance similar to NATO that had only been organized the year before, in 1955, in response to the rearmament of West Germany and its inclusion in NATO.

PART III

Alternatives to Bolshevism

PART III

China:
Theory and
Practice

China is a very ancient country. It was already older than the United States is today when Kung Fu-tzu, or Confucius, took on disciples and attempted to spread his ideas on moderation, virtue, and moral conduct. This was between 551 and 479 B.C. By contrast, the time period characterized by the rule of the Chinese Communist party has been very short indeed. Any discussion of modern China must grasp that fact first of all, for Mao Tse-tung and Chinese communism built on that past and gave it fresh impetus by infusing Marxism-Leninism into the Chinese tradition.

Much of that long history has been characterized by attempts to follow the precepts of an evolving Confucianism, adapted from feudalism to imperial rule. It lasted through some twenty-five dynasties. In the process Confucianism became eclectic; in order to survive so long it absorbed new ideas and different eras into itself. It was a very useful set of doctrines, for it tended to maintain the status quo as a part of the cosmic and eternal order, and to justify the hierarchy within China as well as China's inherent superiority over the barbarian cultures that lay outside her borders. That long history was not a peaceful one: frequent dynastic convolutions and wars of conquest checker that lengthy period.

Although Confucianism endured an incredible length of time, this did not mean that it solved all problems. There was a considerable gap between theory and practice, just as there would later be a similar gap in the Christianity of the Western societies. Peasants, who ranked second in the

Confucian class structure, found that the landlord was the one who normally profited. In theory the monarch was supposed to be the most moral of humans, but in practice he very often fell far short of the mark. At times when this became obvious, when the portents of famine and corruption suggested a loss of the mandate of heaven, an overthrow of that monarch might be necessary. This would be revolution, but in the Chinese language the concept connoted a change to the proper path, in order that the harmony between heaven and earth might be regained.

By the nineteenth century it was obvious that Confucianism had lost its dynamic force. The system gave evidence of continuing practices which had lost all functional meaning. The examinations of students, which had originally served the purpose of providing opportunities for all to achieve intellectual status regardless of their origins, had become a means of perpetuating an intellectual elite whose status prohibited manual labor. The examinations themselves became ritual exercises stressing rote learning and formal, flowery essays. This memorization of the classics and the ideographic character of the written language stifled creativity, tended to downgrade technical competence, and in time led to intellectual sterility and the ossification of the Chinese bureaucracy. This was exacerbated by China's sense of superiority and isolation from potential stimulation. Confucian values had no impact on the growth and decline of the overwhelmingly rural population as it fluctuated at the limits of the altering food supply. The justification of the hierarchy preserved a glittering capital with a well-fed elite who, contrary to original Confucianism, ruled over the often starving masses. It is understandable, therefore, that the present Chinese regime does not encourage an adulation of Confucius. He represents much that is now rejected. A commentary broadcast from the southwestern province of Kweichow in 1974 sharply criticized his teaching, stating that although Confucius had been dead for more than two millennia, his corpse continued to emit a stench that was an extensively influential poison.[1]

All aspects of that Confucian past were not eradicated, however. The justification of the status quo in the past had included the doctrine of individual submissiveness to a larger whole, the family, and by extension, the state; a reminder that the much later teaching of Georg Hegel might well have had an Asian foundation. This teaching contributed to imperial order in ancient China. The word for freedom in Chinese actually connoted a negative concept, an acting for oneself, independently of the group—thereby acting against the interests of the larger entity. This part of the old tradition was very much something that Chinese Marxism could build on. The individualism that had characterized the bourgeois society of Marx's day, which the new socialized environment would in theory overcome, was not a significant factor in China. In that old tradition the social individual, manifest in so many different ways in the new China, had had a very long history. Much of the success attributed to Maoism in this regard is therefore unwarranted.

Traditional China, believing itself to be superior to all other peoples and the center of civilization (as did Europe for a time) found it very difficult to deal with aliens who did not share these beliefs.[2] The Mongols in the thirteenth century briefly ruled the Chinese, and both the Portuguese sailors in the sixteenth century and the Russian cossacks in the seventeenth caused an apprehensive China to close its borders against these unknown and unwelcome barbarians. Increasingly, however, the Western world was able to break down those barriers: sea merchants who sought profits and missionaries who sought souls often came on the same vessel to a China that welcomed neither. This was a very difficult problem for a country whose concept of foreign relations was that of a bureaucracy in charge of administering the tribute paid by subordinate societies. However, the West had not come to pay tribute to China but to extract one.

This became particularly painful for the Chinese in the nineteenth century. Industrializing nations found it simple to force unequal treaties on China, which had the effect of ruining the small domestic industry that existed, and of widening the already large gap between the rich and the poor. Competition between the Western powers for trade deals encouraged both the breakdown of the weak central government and the development of regional warlords. One of the goods that Westerners wanted to sell in Chinese ports was prohibited by law—opium. High profits from such sales, however, encouraged the West to insist on the right to bring it in from Turkey and India. The resulting *Opium War* lasted a very short time, 1840-42, and the West won. Britain won the port city of Hong Kong as a result, and before long the powerless Chinese government was compelled to legalize the importation of opium in some sixteen ports. Along with this, the Western nations had not forgotten the Chinese soul, for with the right to sell opium came the right to establish Christian churches on Chinese soil, an irony that no one seemed to notice.

The obvious weakness of the Chinese government had a predictable result. From 1850-64, the country witnessed another Chinese attempt to overthrow its weak central government—the *Taiping Rebellion,* led by a man who claimed that he was the younger brother of Jesus and who developed a revolutionary theory based on a Chinese version of Protestant Christianity.

> The T'aip'ings proposed not only to overthrow the Manchu rule; they intended also to achieve a social revolution. Driven by Hung's messianic

creed, the rebels aimed at improving the status of women, opposed the opium traffic, and introduced communal economic organization. They also embarked upon a reform of land tenure in order to achieve a better balance between the agricultural population and available arable lands and thus won support from the discontented Chinese peasantry.[3]

This revolutionary attempt failed, partly because the Western powers had a vested interest in defending the central government. The result was even more concessions for the West.

The last part of the nineteenth century saw other nations such as Russia and Japan follow the exploitative patterns established by Britain, France, and to some extent the United States. Tsarist Russia received the territory northeast of the Amur River and east of the Ussuri and built the city of Vladivostok on the new land. This explains why this area is presently claimed by the Chinese. Japan defeated China in an 1894 war that gave Japan the Korean peninsula, the Pescadores, and Formosa. The evident weakness of the Chinese encouraged other nations to join in the rape. Thousands of peasants were seized and placed in labor pools that were a form of legalized slavery. The term "Shanghaied" became everyday parlance. By 1898, when the Americans gained control of the nearby Philippines from Spain, they became much more interested in China than they had been before. In 1899 the Americans proposed an internationalization of Chinese ports, Chinese "independence," and governmental reforms. Some of this was implemented, but the *Boxer Rebellion* was already underway. This was a Chinese attempt to drive the foreigners, whether in legation or in church, back into the sea from which they had come. Once again the "barbarians" won, and only competition among the victors saved China from extinction.

Later rebellions finally forced the abdication of the Manchu dynasty in 1911, but the new government that resulted in 1912 was republican in name only. China remained very factionalized, and new governments were heavily dependent on Western aid and loans. The American-educated Sun Yat-sen was behind the scenes, but his group was declared illegal in late 1913. He quickly reorganized it into a conspiratorial party called the *Kuomintang* (Revolutionary party), loyal to himself alone. By 1917 Sun had declared himself Generalissimo, but his power was actually limited to the Canton area. The continuing factions, internal dissension, and problems relating to the First World War prevented the emergence of any real unity for China. It remained a very weak country.

This helps to explain why so much was dependent upon a favorable outcome in the postwar peace negotiations taking place in Paris. China's contribution to the First World War (labor battalions) was minimal, but her expectations were very high. These expectations were related to the previous century of exploitation that had created great frustration among intellectuals who sought an answer to the question of what China had to do in order to recover her destiny. Any attempt by post-1912 governments to further westernize China had only increased frustrations—for the attempts made Chinese inferiority to the West all the more obvious. Western-trained intellectuals found it quite difficult to meaningfully use their new skills in China for a variety of reasons. Because of these frustrations a new Chinese nationalism was developing into a strong force—a combination of pride in being Chinese coupled with the contradiction of China's backwardness in relation to the industrialized countries of the West.

One obvious answer was for China to industrialize, but the previous activities of Western nations had made this nationalism anti-West. As a result, two non-Western but industrializing countries competed with each other as possible models for China: tsarist Russia and tiny Japan. By 1900 Russia had clearly become the favorite, for after the 1894 war with Japan that country lost in attractiveness. Marxism was known by a few of the intellectuals, but it was not understood as meaningful for China—the Marxist system appeared to require full capitalist relations of production before it became meaningful. That made it inapplicable to China, even though it was a revolutionary ideology. However, Lenin's success of November 1917 in fairly backward Russia had a tremendous impact on Chinese intellectuals, for he had demonstrated that Marxism could be applicable to a backward society hungry for a non-Western model of modernization. As a result a *Society for the Study of Marxism* was begun in 1918 by Li Ta-chao. The Bolshevik seizure of power in Russia aroused an interest in Marxism that could be applied to China. This would be a revolution in the name of a man (Marx) who was anticapital, which meant anti-West to the new, small group of Chinese Marxists. If the pro-Western European ethnocentrism of Marx were ignored, the Chinese possessed, as in the Bolshevik demonstration, a revolutionary ideology that did not have as its goal the humiliating imitation of the West but the transcendence of Western civilization—a concept that fit into Chinese traditions of superiority very well.

Perhaps this early development would have come to little if frustrations in China had not peaked in 1919. The *Versailles Treaty* that came out of Paris in that year sanctioned Japan's takeover of former German holdings in China, even though China had entered the war on the Allied side in the expectation of regaining these holdings. This strong sense of betrayal by the West led to a massive demonstration of feeling by students, intellectuals, merchants, and workers. It was not simply anti-West, but also directed against the weak Chinese government that had permitted this to occur. The demonstrations on May 4 began a movement that was anti-West, antiwarlords, and increasingly pro-Russian, as Russia then represented that same beleaguered spirit that was driving the Chinese. This encouraged a growth in socialist thinking that had an additional appeal because of Lenin's use of imperialism as an explanation for the conduct of Western nations. Imperialism fit the recent Chinese experience very well. Moreover, the Bolshevik government seemed, in the Karakhan Proposal, to be willing to give up some of the tsarist claims on Chinese territory. In such a climate Chinese Marxism-Leninism grew, and when the Comintern was established in 1919, the Chinese responded. A Communist party of China was formed in 1921.

The new party fit into the old tradition in a number of ways. The Chinese intellectual tended toward deductive rather than inductive thinking, predisposed to see things as a whole rather than as parts. This created a desire for a programmatic approach aimed at solving all the problems of China at once, and a resistance to the piecemeal reformist approaches that had become so common in Western Europe. Also fitting into the past habits was the way that Marxism-Leninism used the past to explain the present and predict the future. The dialectic of Marxism-Leninism appeared to fit the traditional Chinese (Taoist) belief in a negative *yin* and a positive *yang* that characterized everything. In addition, Marxism-Leninism created the possibility of breaking out of the traditional cycle of history and moving to a new and higher plateau. The lack of a proletariat in China was counterbalanced by Lenin's teaching that even if such a force developed it would not by itself be sufficiently class conscious. The party was vitally necessary in order to raise that consciousness to its proper level—a bridge between the intellectual and the masses which Confucianism had not provided but which their frustrations now demanded.[4]

The fact of the party developing ahead of the proletariat, not merely ahead of unions, as was noted in chapter 5, increased the revolutionary side of the balance between reform and revolution in the party. In China, however, this potential was masked by Comintern policies in the 1920s. As was noted in chapter 7, the Communist International was an organization that quickly became a sponsor of the national interest of Russia under Stalin. His needs became Comintern needs, regardless of what was needed in the country where these policies were being applied. Stalin's attention was preoccupied with the more industrialized countries; areas such as India and China, in his view, still had to go through the bourgeois stage of the revolution, a curious theoretical position for a post-1917 Bolshevik to maintain. Chinese communism was considered a very weak reed indeed, compared to the German or the French party. As a result, Comintern policy as regards the Chinese party seemed offhanded and quite ill-advised.

The dilemma of diplomatic negotiation with a government while at the same time appearing to subvert it (which characterized Russian relations with European and other Western countries) did not develop in China until after 1927. Because the next step in Chinese history must be the bourgeois revolution, the Russians felt that they ought to encourage that event. They saw their best opportunity to do this through backing Sun Yat-sen against his other rivals for power in chaotic China. He saw an opportunity for himself in aligning his group with the new Soviet government. In 1923 he sent a young assistant, Chiang Kai-shek, to Moscow as liaison, and in January 1924 Sun (aided by Michael Borodin—a Russian advisor) established a new Kuomintang that was set up on the model of the Russian Communist party. A new platform called for an alliance with the Soviet Union; cooperation with the small (about 500) Chinese Communist party; and the creation of support among the workers and peasants. In the Canton area which Sun controlled, a military academy was established under the direction of Chiang Kai-shek, assisted by the young Communist, Chou En-lai. Soviet advisors and arms arrived to give substance to the Soviet promises of assistance. Most of China lay to the north, the domain of squabbling warlords. In 1924 Sun left Canton when there appeared to be a chance of sharing power in Peking, but he died in Peking a few months later.

The time appeared to be ripe for revolutionary activity. A British officer ordered Shanghai police to fire on demonstrating students and twelve were killed. Anti-foreign nationalism grew rapidly, but the Kuomintang was beset by internal quarrels over who should inherit Sun's leadership. In the middle of this dispute, the military government at Canton declared itself the *Nationalist* government of China, and by 1926 Chiang Kai-shek had declared himself the leader. This new group was deeply divided between right and left factions, with Chiang increasingly leaning toward the right. His communist left wing, now some fifty-eight thousand strong, was becoming a dangerous liability. Partially in 1926, and fully in 1927, Chiang turned against the Communists and very nearly destroyed them. The government that declared itself the *Republic of China* in 1928, therefore, was heavily conservative or right wing, although apparently adhering to Sun Yat-sen's Nationalist and anti-imperialist ideology. Nonetheless, from the beginning, Chiang's government was a dictatorship dedicated to maintaining the old stratifications of Chinese society.[5]

Comintern policy in China had backfired. Although in 1928 the Sixth Congress of the Comintern passed a very revolutionary program for international parties, the Russian government, preoccupied with industrialization and collectivization at home, continued to court the favor of the Nationalist government of Chiang Kai-shek, and paid only minimal attention to the problems of the Chinese Communist party. This attitude, contradictory only if one believed the Russians' revolutionary rhetoric, resulted in support of the Chiang government up to 1949, when the agrarian, peasant movement led by the Chinese Communist party was successful in driving Chiang off the mainland of China.

In May of 1926 an early "victim" of the KMT's first anticommunist purge was a thirty-two-year-old deputy chief of the Kuomintang propaganda department named Mao Tse-tung. He had been born on December 26, 1893, to a peasant family that was locally distinguished by the success his father had in raising himself to the status of middle peasant. The family, in other words, was reasonably well off. This provided the basis for Mao's good education in which he was exposed to the Confucian classics as well as to Western ideas such as those of Adam Smith, Charles Darwin, and Jean Jacques Rousseau. After his graduation from school Mao drifted, as many others were doing, in the direction of some sort of social revolution that would rid China of foreigners and competing warlords.

In 1919 Mao attended summer classes at the University of Peking and became an assistant to the librarian, Li Ta-chao, already a Marxist-Leninist. Mao now read the *Communist Manifesto* and other Marxist literature. In May of 1920 he went to Shanghai to coordinate student activities there against the government, and he met another Marxist, Chen Tu-hsiu, who assisted him in concluding that only political power secured by violent mass action could bring social justice to China. The Marxism provided a general, ideological frame of reference for the almost Leninist preoccupation with political revolution and the necessity of a strong elite party to bring it about. Therefore, in July of 1921 Mao had no reservations about joining the new Communist party of China.

His political career began with the party and, through the party, also with the Kuomintang. However, his preferences from the beginning were for organizing peasants rather than urban workers. His job with the Kuomintang was to train peasant supporters, and by 1926 Mao was the head of the Party Committee on Peasants. When Chiang moved against the party, Mao and Chu Teh set up an organization in the southeast, still attempting to follow Comintern directives, which called for their gaining a proletarian base for the party. They therefore attacked the cities of Wuhan and Changsa in 1930, but their lack of success, coupled with the unavailability of any unified direction in the scattered, now clandestine party, pushed Mao in the direction which had shown him some success—the organization of rural soviets and the creation of peasant support for protracted **guerrilla warfare.**

What Mao was doing was basically altering Marxism-Leninism to fit the specific conditions and needs of China. This made the revolutionary ideology sensible in China. The fact that Mao was not particularly learned about Marxism at this stage probably helped rather than hindered him, for he was freer to create a Maoist Marxism than he might have been if he had been steeped in the Marxist classics. By the time of the *Long March* from the southeast (1934-35) made untenable by Chiang's armies, to the more easily defended northwest (Yenan), opposition to Mao's adaptations from the more traditional elements in the party had diminished to the point where Mao could be elected chairman of the Politburo in 1935. He very quickly appointed others who agreed with him to top party positions, and the Chinese Communist party became peasant-oriented. This remaking of the party in Mao's image did not result from a Comintern or Stalin directive. Soviet attention was increasingly directed to the potential dangers of Adolf Hitler. This created a wider scope for Mao's own further independent development in a peasant-oriented direction, and the gap between the Comintern and Mao widened. Actually, the success of Mao came from ignoring Comintern advice rather than accepting and implementing it. This helps to explain Stalin's lack of enthusiasm for Mao's revolutionary potential right up to 1949.

Maoism, therefore, although conditioned by Marxism-Leninism, developed out of the Chinese revolutionary, guerrilla experience. This was soon generalized into a concept of the necessity of *practice* conditioning theory, first published in 1950, but alleged to be based on a 1937 or earlier concept. The idea of testing theory by means of experience was quite Marxist and Leninist. Lenin, for example, was the one who had insisted that Marxism was but a guide to action, not a dogma to be slavishly followed. Marx himself, although proceeding more from a theoretical plane, wrote about actualizing that theory in practice.

In the late 1930s and early 1940s, the concept in Mao's hands became a defense against those who disagreed with him, and whom he accused of literally following the scriptures of Marx without reference to revolutionary experience. Theoretical conclusions, he felt, were not to be accepted as valid simply because they seem to be logical to the theorist sitting in his library—they must be tested experientially. He was not suggesting that a person proceed inductively; that would have been shallow empiricism. There was also no suggestion that the truth of Marxism-Leninism was in doubt. The revolutionary principles derived from that truth were, however, to be purified in the fire of actual experience, and adaptations of those derived principles were to be made if necessary. Mao did not intend to imply that every person had the right or ability to do this. He was not arguing for a secular priesthood of all believers. In the small things that are a part of an individual's immediate environment, the person can test theory in the light of practice and quite possibly come up with suggestions about how his machine might be improved or how more crops can be grown. For larger questions, involving the forest rather than the trees, the party reserved the right to synthesize that experience.[6]

When these ideas were coupled with Mao's concept of *contradictions*, a novelty or at least a distinctiveness of Maoism began to emerge. As early as 1949 Mao informed his Central Committee that their struggle was far from over.

> After the enemies with guns have been wiped out, there will still be enemies without guns; they are bound to struggle desperately against us, and we must never regard these enemies lightly.[7]

It was as though Mao were unwilling to end the long guerrilla war that had brought the party into power in 1949. He was extending that protracted war into the period after the revolutionary seizure of political power and, in so doing, justifying the continuation of the revolutionary struggle. In one sense this was natural, for China was a very poor country with an enormous population to feed. Any group which sought not only to maintain that society but also to dramatically increase its productive output in order to construct the socialist base, would be compelled to see this as a struggle. In another sense, of course, the perpetuation of the revolutionary struggle preserved Mao's role as revolutionary leader into that construction period.

His theory of contradictions was published in 1952. This answered the question of whether dialectics ceased to operate subsequent to the proletarian revolution in the same way that Lenin and Stalin had answered it—no, dialectics continued. Stalin particularly had added the idea that the intensity of the class struggle increased as socialism was approached—less a theoretical innovation and more a doctrinal justification for his coercive methods. Mao added interesting variations on this theme. The contradictions present in society did not obscure the unity of the system. This was, after all, conflict within unity, a permanent condition of contradiction within the ongoing unity of the system. Additionally, of the two conflicting elements, one could be called primary and the other secondary (as with the traditional notions of yin-yang) with the quality of the developing system mainly determined by the principal aspect of the contradiction. Changes in quality took place when the principal aspect of the contradiction altered.[8] In other words, if the two contending aspects of the relationship were the proletarian forces and the nonproletarian or bourgeois forces, and the time period in question was the postrevolutionary era, then the principal or dominant part of the relationship would be the proletarian; and changes *in it* would result in the qualitative changes in the whole. The changes sought in 1951-52 were both extensive and intensive. This was the theoretical underpinning not only for the campaigns of 1951-52, which became thoroughgoing attacks on bourgeois attitudes and practices, but also the justification for the attempted cleansing of the party apparatus to rid it of bureaucratism—to put it another way, to rid the party of self-seeking individuals who had failed to understand or maintain the goals of the party.[9]

The timing of these moves was no accident. Chinese soldiers were fighting American soldiers in Korea, and bourgeois attitudes were easily seen as American attitudes. University production of technically competent people became less important than their production of people with the correct social attitudes. The First Five Year Plan was already in the advanced planning stage. It would begin in 1953, and it would be ambitious in the setting of industrial and agricultural targets. The overwhelmingly agricultural base, where land had been redistributed to peasants in 1949, had to face the necessity of the extension of the cooperative principle which would make labor-intensive methods possible and rationalize the production of surpluses to support the industrialization. This would result in a definite swing to collectivization in 1954-55.

Thus, Mao's ideas of the permanence of contradictions seemed less a doctrinal innovation and more a theoretical justification for a very ambitious construction of socialism in the climate of hostility emanating from the Korean War. It had to be accomplished quickly, and the proletarian party had to become the instrument of that change.[10] It could not effectively perform this role if it were itself infected with a new kind of "bourgeois" attitude. The bureaucratic attitude created a separation between the bureaucrat and the masses, just as effectively as the older bourgeois consciousness had done. The army had to be ideologically renovated as well, to make it a companion to the party as the principal aspect of the contradiction, so as to ensure the proper changes in social quality. This period became, therefore, one of intense ideological mobilization of the entire society. To make this less abstract to the general population, as well as to shore up his own weakening position within the party, the cult of Mao Tse-tung seriously began to mushroom. This had begun earlier, but in a smaller way. The contrast within just ten years was remarkable and can be illustrated by a song very popular in 1949, compared with another that was popular in 1959.

1949: The East is Red
       The Sun Rises
       On the Horizon of China
       Appears the Great Hero Mao Tse-tung . . .
       He is the Great Savior of the People.

1959: Chairman Mao is infinitely kind,
       Ten thousand songs are not enough to praise him.
       With trees as pens, the sky as paper
       And an ocean of ink,
       Much would still be left unwritten.[11]

Mao's thought became the correct line, the authoritative word on every-thing—no matter how mundane; the unity underlying the conflicting ele-ments in the contradictory relationship; and the vitalizing force of the principal, proletarian, or socialistic aspect of that relationship.

Just as this was seriously under way, however, Khrushchev gave his so-called Secret Speech against Stalin (February 1956). In that speech he condemned the Stalinist notibn of the intensification of the class struggle as the society approached its goals. The dictatorship of the proletariat be-came the state of the whole people in this Soviet development, creating problems in China for the simple reason that this contradicted Mao's con-cept of the permanence of contradictions, while at the same time reaffirm-ing the leadership position of the Soviet Union in the world socialist movement. At this time in China there had been sufficient success from the First Five Year Plan to allow Mao to claim that socialism had been accomplished, but there was also a dependence on Russia for economic aid and a promise of nuclear weapons in the near future. Thus, although Khrushchev's attacks on Stalin were received rather coolly in China, the Chinese response was muted by their dependency. Nonetheless, the seeds of future conflict were present. Khrushchev, according to Mao, in at-tempting reapproachment with Yugoslavia, was moving in the wrong di-rection even though differences between Moscow and Peking were pa-pered over in the 1957 *Unity Declaration* that came out of Moscow in conjunction with the celebration of the fortieth anniversary of Bolshe-vism.

When events in Poland, and especially in Hungary, did not essentially change the Soviet anti-Stalin, anti-contradiction direction, China began to reemploy the idea of contradictions on its own. The fact that con-tradictions still existed was made quite obvious by the disastrous amount of criticism that the regime received in the brief *Hundred Flowers* period, when criticism was encouraged from the general population. The party knew that it still had a long way to go before the population could be said to be properly socialized.

Soon the Chinese began to act more independently in other ways. In 1958 they began the *Great Leap Forward* which included an intensive ef-fort to build agricultural communes. This was more than simply another Five Year Plan. It was an attempt to leap across stages of productive growth by a massive mobilization of the population. In December of

1957, Liu Shao-chi announced the Chinese intention of overtaking Britain in gross heavy industry output by 1972.[12] Claims made with reference to the new communes in the countryside stressed the possibility of bypassing the socialist phase, which meant the Soviet experience as well. Although the first commune was named Sputnik, the claims made for it easily surpassed the Soviet frame of reference. The new commune was a prototype of others, whose task it would be to manage all industrial and agricultural production, cultural and educational work, and trade, as well as political affairs within its borders. This would consolidate the social system and energetically create the conditions for the gradual transition to communism, as well as the gradual eradication of all differences between town and country and between mental and manual labor.

> As the social products become abundant and the people have high political consciousness, so will the transition from the principle of "from each according to his ability, to each according to his work" to the principle of "from each according to his ability, to each according to his needs" be gradually effected.[13]

The Soviet response to this was generally cautious, but also fairly negative. China was attempting to build on the basis of Marx and Lenin without travelling the same road as the Russians. This greater independence was caused by several factors besides the ones already mentioned. Russia was being very friendly with India—a country China had territorial disputes with—and Khrushchev had not given the Chinese the nuclear weapons or nuclear reactor he had promised. As a matter of fact, he was beginning to talk about the cessation of atmospheric testing as a means of preventing the diffusion of nuclear weapons into more hands than presently controlled them. Although Khrushchev was not moving fast enough for an alarmed Andrei Sakharov, he was moving away from the direction Chinese leaders wanted.[14] They needed the nuclear umbrella to cover their acquisitive attitudes in regard to the offshore islands of Quemoy and Matsu, then controlled by Chiang who was protected by a nuclear power—the United States. In the following year Khrushchev moved even further away from Chinese interests by travelling to the United States and establishing his "Spirit of Camp David" detente with President Eisenhower. And finally, at the Twenty-First Party Congress (CPSU) in 1959, Khrushchev declared that there could be no sudden leaps to communism, even though by this time the Chinese had toned down their claims about the communes because of the difficulties they were having with them.

When the Soviet-American friendship appeared to collapse over the U-2 spy plane incident in May 1960, Chinese hopes were raised by the harsh anti-American criticism that began appearing in the Soviet press. However, at the socialist unity meeting in Bucharest in June 1960, where Chinese delegates attempted to push Khrushchev into expressing a unity against the West, he responded with a blistering attack on China and, a month later, called back all Soviet technicians in China and ended Russian economic aid. The gap that had existed in theory now became a crevasse into which sank not only Soviet-Chinese togetherness but also the ambitious and optimistic Great Leap Forward. This lost political support for Mao within his own party, and it put China completely on its own. Things looked bleak for a time.

The Chinese response that eventually triumphed, however, was Mao's resurrection of the continuing presence of contradictions that required an endless struggle against revisionism. What was revisionism in this context? It was Khrushchev's denial of the necessity of the dictatorship of the proletariat, and the state of the whole people.

> Throughout the stage of socialism, there is inevitable struggle between Marxism-Leninism and various kinds of opportunism—mainly revisionism—in the Communist Parties of socialist countries. The characteristic of this revisionism is that, denying the existence of classes and class struggle, it sides with the bourgeoisie in attacking the proletariat and turns the dictatorship of the proletariat into the dictatorship of the bourgeoisie.[15]

This was an assertion of *Chinese* leadership of the *real* world socialist movement, the one which the Soviet Union, according to Mao, had deserted. This assumption of the Marxist-Leninist-Stalinist mantle by Mao accounted for the sense of superiority he displayed, which visitors from other socialist countries found rather difficult to accept. This too was in line with ancient Chinese traditions of superiority, and Mao appeared to be much more interested in exporting the Chinese experience abroad. However pleasant that mantle must have felt, it was probably an even greater pleasure to no longer play poor relation to Soviet bounty. That freed Mao to return to what was of greatest importance to him: the remolding of people in the sense of their internalization of the revolutionary spirit. This was much more important than sustaining a growth rate in industry or agriculture. It was as though Mao said to himself that however important those criteria of success might be, they paled into nothingness compared with the loss of the revolutionary vision. Nostalgically recalled from the Yenan period, the spirit of self-sacrifice; revolutionary togetherness; and the sense of *serving* the masses of people all seemed to him to be in danger, the victims of the very success of the revolution.

In order to regain control over Chinese policies and directions, Mao significantly departed from the Stalinist pattern of purges by terror. The *Cultural Revolution* that began in 1966 was a massive effort by Mao to regain control, not so much through a secret police that became a law unto itself, but through the army and the massive utilization of adolescents organized into detachments of Red Guards. News reports coming out of Hong Kong stated that some of the most enthusiastic supporters of Mao and the sharpest critics of his opponents were children under the age of twelve. The "revolutionary tiger cubs" that were being trained were between the ages of three and seven years.[16] When the Red Guards appeared to be getting out of control from Mao's point of view, he called in the more ideologically secure army to restore order. The extensive turmoil thoroughly shook the system with the deliberate goal of creating what Benjamin Schwartz called a revival atmosphere[17]—like turning the Youth for Christ loose on politicians in Washington, D.C.

Much of the criticism of the Cultural Revolution was directed against the party itself, as a group that contained far too many "revisionists"—a group that had become to a considerable degree a bureaucratic machine. As Mao saw it, the Cultural Revolution represented a revolutionary evangelical approach to the problem of the revolution not being carried through to the end. This had been endangered by the party bureaucratism that divorced officials from the masses, and by educational policies in the universities that seemed to be recreating the old class attitudes. As a result, the school system was made much more ideological than it was previously, and there is now a great emphasis on physical work accompanying the study of academic subjects. In addition, the production group to which the student belongs decides whether he or she will be educated at a university, and it is usually to that group that a student will return. The practical significance of the education supplements the ideological climate in the hope that equal opportunities will prevent the emergence of an educated elite cut off from the general population. The leaders seek to completely change that part of the Chinese tradition.

The same principle applies to the party. The attack on bureaucracy was a charge of separation from the masses. Party members are now frequently urged to leave their offices and go out into the field, into the "May Seventh **Cadre** schools," for a renewal of their revolutionary spirit through contact with the masses. In order to lessen the possibility of a redevelopment of this problem, China has been reorganized into nearly autonomous units of production. The more autonomy the units have, the less necessity for the growth of a massive administrative machine. There is still central planning and centralized manipulation, but this is done as much as possible through the use of the nearly autonomous units. Because some of these ideas are difficult to implement continually, periodic up-surges of renewal and revival can be expected or threatened, at least as long as Mao is alive, but probably not to the extent of the movement in 1966-67. The upsurge of criticism (mainly by wall posters) that developed in the late fall of 1973 and continued sporadically through 1974 appeared to be under party control. Nonetheless, the wall posters exhibited a fair amount of freedom of expression.

Another such gigantic revival does not appear visible on the Chinese horizon. This may be due to opposition to Mao within the party, but it is also true that such a serious disruption of the country may no longer be necessary. There are still many problems, such as dislocated young people who have left their communes and are living in the cities, without the nec-essary group identification that is so essential in modern China even to buy a bicycle or a watch on the open market. There still is crime to cause concern for Chinese authorities. The majority of those criticized and hu-miliated in the Cultural Revolution have been rehabilitated (party mem-bers, factory managers, and university professors), and they declare themselves to be reformed people in touch with the masses and no longer seeking separation as proof of status. A great many among the masses talk as though they have just come from an ideological lecture; many have internalized social goals to a great extent. Once again, this phenomenon is not universal. There are still peasants who seek to avoid state controls on produce grown on their private plots, for example. However, if a young man on the city street is asked for his opinion of a young lady, his first re-sponse may well be a reference to her state of socialist consciousness.

Everywhere that Western travellers have visited in China during the more relaxed Sino-American relations of recent years, they have found people who are well-fed, decently clothed, and display, in their personally owned bikes, watches, radios, and sewing machines, a much higher degree of wealth than ever before in China. The feet of women are no longer bound. Families no longer sell their daughters as brides to the highest bidder, and illiteracy has been greatly reduced. Travellers to cities re-port the absence of prostitution, begging, and the formerly ubiquitous coolie. They also report of vast reclamation projects in the rural com-munes that have restored to use formerly unarable land, through in-tensive irrigation and fertilization. Agricultural production continues to stay ahead of population growth. Part of the reason for this may well be the continuing presence of the peasant's private plot, but it is also due to the great diversification on the communes—a result of in-creased autonomy. The commune is likely to grow its own vegetables; very intelligently use labor-intensive methods; raise fish in an artificially made pond; and engage in small-scale industry to provide communal and social needs.

There may be much more to lose than to gain by another momentous revival. This has evidently encouraged the growth of moderation in the party policy in regard to the sensitive issue of income equalization. In 1972 this policy underwent revision. Formerly it was felt that everyone should get the same wage, regardless of how hard he or she worked. However, in the interest of achieving higher outputs, the earning system on the communes was revised so as to remunerate the more diligent workers who produce more, above the level of those who do not. The same pattern is discernible in the industrial sector.[18] That this is being done indicates a preoccupation with production goals that again suggests a moderation—a blending of revolutionary and pragmatic goals. A part of this effort is agitation for more equal rights for women in China. The new incentives would still be a great distance from the income differentials obtaining, for example, in the Soviet Union. The wages paid at the top of the Chinese scale are normally no more than three times those at the bottom, with professional and managerial remuneration roughly at the top of the workers' scale.[19] The point is that, both in agriculture and in industry, production continues to grow, even in the extensively decentralized industries such as iron and steel production or the production of chemical fertilizers. In 1971, for example, nearly 60 percent of the total chemical fertilizer output in China was produced in small rural plants.[20]

A major alternative to the Bolshevization of Marxism has been the implementation of a moderated Marxist ideology in China, giving the appearance of having been responsible for a new, vastly improved society. Yet, how Marxist are its actual goals?

First Mao's vision of the future sounds quite similar to that of Marx, but since Marx was fairly vague this might not really mean much. For example, Mao has written that, in communism, classes, state power, and political parties would die out naturally. People would then develop more harmonious relationships made even more attractive by great material abundance, the disappearance of private possessions, and the distribution of social wealth according to need.[21] There should be no difficulty in calling this Marxist.

Second, the differences that do exist between Mao and Marx appear to be a reflection of the necessity of applying Marxism *in China*. Marxism was developed in Western Europe and came out of the developments noted in chapter 1, namely the coexistence of great poverty and great wealth that the industrial revolution created; the frustrations emerging from the French Revolution; and the leftist, critical direction of post-Hegelian philosophy as it developed in Germany. In applying these concepts to China, Mao has been able to pick and choose. Historical materialism, for example, did not apply well, but Engels' expanded idea of **dialectical materialism** did. The central place that alienation played in

Marxism also did not make great sense in China. The preoccupation with alienation reflected the values and concerns of societies steeped in liberalism, capitalism, and Christianity. However, traditional China had always been a group-oriented society, and the overcoming of alienation, which was such a giant step in Marxism, was a very small one in China. Thus, the vision of communism as the *dramatic* flowering of the social human was also lost to the Chinese Marxists, and the distinction between socialism and communism became less visible.

In addition, the vagueness of both Marx and Engels in referring to the kind of authority necessary in the future society left an opening for Mao to stress within the Marxist framework a continuing necessity of correct leadership even in communism. This could be another reflection of his Confucian past, but it need not be. It could also be an imitation of that part of the Soviet Third Party Program adopted in 1961 which created a dominant role for the party well into the future Russian communist period. However, Mao's image of the continued need for correct leadership was far more likely derived from his own view on the continuing contradictions even in socialism and communism.

. Socialist society also develops through contradictions between the productive forces and the conditions of production. In a socialist or communist society, technical innovations and improvement in the social system inevitably continue to take place; otherwise the development of society would come to a standstill and society could no longer advance. Humanity is still in its youth. The road it has yet to traverse will be no one knows how many times longer than the road it has already travelled. . . .

It is obviously incorrect to maintain, as some people do, that the contradiction between idealism and materialism can be eliminated in a socialist or communist society. . . .

Therefore, not everybody will be perfect, even when a communist society is established. By then there will still be contradictions among people, and there will still be good people and bad. . . .[22]

This is a less utopian view of the future, and one in which correct leadership provides the unity and positive direction for future development. This fits in very well with the traditional (Taoist) *yin* and *yang*.[23] This fact that *yin-yang* opposition is not between absolute opposites seeking synthetic resolution, but between contradictory moments of the same thing, may be a partial explanation for the ease with which Mao sees this as continuing into the future.

That correct leadership represents constancy of revolutionary spirit to Mao, distinguishing it from the Soviet experience but not necessarily from Marxism. The revolution seems to have been a one-time event to

Marx, with the expected benefits more or less automatically flowing from the socialization of the means of production. However, no one can be sure. Mao, as Lenin, carved out new territory—there are no stop signs on such frontiers.

In China the social wealth that is being created is in fact being shared by an enormous population. This is truly a monumental achievement. That China nonetheless appears to be as moralistic and **totalitarian** as Calvin's Geneva in the 1540s may be only the fault of an observer's Western orientation.

Suggested Readings

Bodde, Derk. *China's Cultural Tradition.* New York: Rinehart, 1957.

Brandt, Conrad; Schwartz, Benjamin; and Fairbank, John K. *A Documentary History of Chinese Communism.* New York: Atheneum, 1966.

Compton, Boyd. *Mao's China, Party Reform Documents, 1942-1944.* Seattle: University of Washington Press, 1952.

Creel, H. G. *Confucius and the Chinese Way.* New York: Harper Torchbooks, 1960.

Fairbank, John K. *The United States and China.* Cambridge: Harvard University Press, 1959.

Gray, Jack, and Cavendish, Patrick. *Chinese Communism in Crisis—Maoism and the Cultural Revolution.* New York: Praeger, 1968.

Lewis, John Wilson. *Major Doctrines of Communist China.* New York: W. W. Norton, 1964.

Rue, John. *Mao Tse-tung in Opposition: 1927-1935.* Stanford: Stanford University Press, 1966.

Schram, Stuart. *Mao Tse-tung.* New York: Penguin Books, 1966.

NOTES

[1] *New York Times,* 12 February 1974, p. 12 "Confucian" also means antirevolutionary attitudes.

[2] This is a very common phenomenon that is encouraged by great power or great isolation. For example, the United States in the third quarter of the twentieth century found not only communism difficult to comprehend, but also the French desire for an independent position vis-à-vis the United States.

[3] O. Edmund Clubb, *Twentieth Century China* (New York: Columbia University Press, 1972), p. 13. Reprinted by permission of the publisher.

[4] See a fuller description of this relationship between tradition and Marxism-Leninism in James Chieh Hsiung, *Ideology and Practice, The Evolution of Chinese Communism* (New York: Praeger, 1970), pp. 34-37. Also see John K. Fairbank, *The United States and China* (Cambridge, Mass.: Harvard University Press, 1959) pp. 294-96; Edward E. Rice, "A Radical Break With the Past," *Problems of Communism* 23, no. 5. (September-October 1974): pp. 16-20; Krishna P. Gupta, "Continuities in Change," ibid., pp. 33-38; and W. Dobson's "China as a World Power," an unpublished Centennial Lecture delivered by the University of Toronto's Professor Dobson on March 6, 1973.

[5] See Clubb, *Twentieth Century China,* pp. 114-45, for a more lengthy description of the events from 1923-28.

[6]See Benjamin Schwartz, "Thoughts of Mao Tse-tung," *New York Review of Books* 20, no. 1 (February 8, 1973): 27.

[7]Mao Tse-tung, *Selected Works* (New York: International Publishers, n.d.) 5: 364; cited in David E. Powell, "Mao and Stalin's Mantle," *Problems of Communism* 17, no. 2 (March-April 1968): 25. Reprinted by permission of *Problems of Communism.*

[8]Mao Tse-tung, cited in Arthur A. Cohen, *The Communism of Mao Tse-tung* (Chicago: University of Chicago Press, 1964), p. 21.

[9]The campaigns referred to are the 1951 "Three Anti Campaign" against waste, corruption, and bureaucracy; and the 1952 "Five Anti Campaign" against bribery, tax evasion, fraud, theft of state assets, and leakage of state economic secrets.

[10]It is not often recalled that many American leaders were advocating a preemptive strike against China during the Korean War—a sort of preventive "medicine" to be applied before the "enemy" became too strong. This contributed to the disagreement between General Douglas MacArthur, who saw wisdom in the preemptive approach, and President Harry Truman, who most definitely did not want an extension of the war into China.

[11]Songs quoted from James T. Myers, "The Political Dynamics of the Cult of Mao Tse-tung," in *Communist China: A System-Functional Reader,* ed. Yung Wei (Columbus, Ohio: Charles E. Merrill, 1972), pp. 83 and 89. The second song suggests both an American love ballad and the last verse of the Gospel of John. Even fighter pilots alleged the authoritativeness of Mao's thought to be superior to compasses and radar. The level of adulation is particularly intriguing in the 1959 period, when Mao's political strength appeared to be very low.

[12]Cited in Harold C. Hinton, *Communist China in World Politics* (Boston: Houghton Mifflin, 1966), p. 36.

[13]"Tentative Regulations (Draft) of the Weihsung (Sputnik) People's Commune," *Jen Min Jih Pao,* 4 September 1958; cited in Theodore H. E. Chen, *The Chinese Communist Regime, Documents and Commentary* (New York: Praeger, 1967), p. 240. Reprinted by permission of the publisher.

[14]Andrei D. Sakharov, "How I Came to Dissent," *New York Review of Books* 21, no. 4 (March 21, 1974): 11. Sakharov has been called the father of the Russian hydrogen bomb. He began dissenting in 1957 over the issue of nuclear testing in the atmosphere. His dissent has steadily expanded to include defense of the literary intelligentsia as well as demands for a more liberal Soviet regime.

[15]"On Khrushchev's Phoney Communism and Its Historical Lessons for the World" (Peking, 14 July 1964); published in A. Doak Barnett, *China After Mao* (Princeton: Princeton University Press, 1967), p. 131.

[16]*New York Times,* 5 February 1967, p. 6.

[17]Schwartz, "Thoughts of Mao Tse-tung," p. 31.

[18]See *New York Times,* 7 May 1972, article by Tillman Durdin.

[19]Dwight H. Perkins, "An Economic Reappraisal," *Problems of Communism* 22, no. 3 (May-June 1973): 12.

[20]Ibid., p. 7. See also *New York Times,* 7 October 1974, p. 1, in regard to the "backyard production" of ammonium bicarbonate for fertilizer.

[21]Mao Tse-tung, "On People's Democratic Dictatorship," *Selected Works of Mao Tse-tung* (Peking: Foreign Language Press, 1961) 4: 412.

[22]These three statements are quoted from editorial in *Jen Min Jih Pao,* 5 April 1956; reprinted in Stuart R. Schram, *The Political Thought of Mao Tse-tung* (New York: Praeger, 1963), p. 236. Reprinted by permission of the publisher.

[23]See Hsiung, *Ideology and Practice,* pp. 102-103.

10

Minor Chords

In the last half of the twentieth century, the ideas of Marx and Lenin have been applied in several areas of the world that are sufficiently distant from the Soviet Union so that Russian troops have not dictated their communism, and sufficiently different in tradition from China that their attempts to implement the ideology make up a minor chord of communist pluralism in the international composition. The countries selected to exemplify this feature of international communism are Yugoslavia, Cuba, Chile, and Italy, but the list could easily be longer. French Communist development is also very interesting because the party in France is strong and because, in league with the Socialists, the party came close to legitimate political power in 1974. African socialism, especially in a country such as Tanzania or in the "recovered" territories in Angola, suggests a socialism-communism variant that is a Marxist patina over traditional tribal communism in a modernizing framework. The evolution of the Finnish Communist party is fascinating for its independence as well as for its necessary dependence on the Soviet model.

All of these areas manifest differences that are a reflection of geography; time; past historical traditions; whether the party is in power or striving to gain it; and the interplay of international and domestic relations, such as the Cold War or the later detente between America and Russia. These differences are often obscured by the similarity of the ideological language or by the vague generalities of declarations that follow unity conferences, but the differences are real. Just as a study of capitalism should be more extensive than a survey of General Motors in Detroit or of International Telephone and Telegraph in New York, so also a study of communism cannot ignore the minor chords. Just as there is no real unity in capitalism or the Christian church, so there is no monolith in world communism. Despite periodic ecumenical movements, these differences persist. However, the value of such diversity, in an ideological movement is difficult to acknowledge—whether inside or outside the movement. Proponents of communism as often vainly seek unity as opponents of communism myopically fail to note the diversity. The differences are there to stay.

In Yugoslavia communism has been in power since 1945, and its distinctiveness emerged out of its relations with the Soviet Union. Cuban communism has been in control of Cuba since 1959 or 1961, depending on how one views Fidel Castro's development. Cuban differences were a function of the peculiarity of Cuban proximity to the United States, its great distance from Russia, and its partisanship of revolutionary developments in other Latin American countries. In Chile the Communist party was much less radical than the Socialist party. Communist participation in a ruling coalition from 1970-73, led by Marxist socialist Salvadore Allende, moved the Communist party from a previous position of electoral strength to one of impotence in the mid-1970s. In Italy the Communist party (PCI) has never ruled the country, but continues to be a major opposition party in the Italian political system.

Yugoslavia

In the years immediately following Stalin's expulsion of Yugoslavia from the Cominform (1948), the Yugoslav leaders tightened up their regime—as though seeking to prove Stalin incorrect by revealing how conformist they really were. However, the prolongation of the dispute, as well as aid from the West which reduced their dependence on the socialist bloc of nations, created a pressure to distinguish Yugoslavia ideologically from Stalinism. Their attempt to accomplish this makes Tito appear to be a liberal and Yugoslavia a liberalized communist country because they came to understand the ideology, against which they tried to redefine their own position, as a bureaucratic and centralized elevation of the state above society.[1] Thus their own tentative, groping, and sometimes contradictory ideological developments moved in the other direction.

The two major innovations introduced in the 1950s were the notions of workers' control of industry, which required substantial decentralization of economic decision making, and the establishment of nearly autonomous communes as the form of local government, a form of political decentralization. This did not mean that the central government or the party no longer had any role to play, but it did mean a great deal more local autonomy. In 1952, at the Sixth Party Congress, the Yugoslavs even changed their name to the *League of Communists of Yugoslavia.* Coinciding as this did with the loosening of central controls, the name change clearly went beyond mere semantics.

The implementation of this decentralization has resulted in a very different sort of communist society. One of the major features of Titoism, as Adam Ulam has pointed out, lies in the substantial depoliticization of society; an increase in the amount of an average person's life that is not viewed in a political frame of reference.[2] In the Soviet Union, for example, it appears as though the attempt to politicize all of the social relations of the population constitutes one of its chief characteristics. In Yugoslavia the scope of nonpoliticized activity became much greater. This sort of liberalization, however, carried with it a considerable problem for an ideological party which saw its major function as that of unifying culturally divided Yugoslavia.[3] How can unity be achieved when the scope of the political has been reduced and substantial decentralization has taken place? If more and more decisions are made on pragmatic or rational rather than on ideological grounds, what happens to the socialist or communist goals that the leaders originally advanced? These problems cause pendular swings between centralized and decentralized decision making.

> The distinctive and exciting feature of the Yugoslav political scene is the continual flux and evolution of an unfinished system and a doctrine built piece by piece. Experiments of all kinds, from industrial reorganization to the revamping of the delicate mechanism regulating relations between nations and republics, are freely tried out and discarded. The official doctrine is still, on the face of it, the Holy Script, Marxism-Leninism. But by drawing on bits and pieces from the scattered statements of Marxist thinkers and at the same time borrowing freely from the economic theories of the bourgeois West, the Yugoslavs have devised many sets of constantly changing institutions, adapting them with uninhibited daring to practical needs.[4]

The desire for unity and a degree of ideological conformity remains constant, but this comes into periodic conflict with the decentralized economic and political life.

The workers' councils have been given real decision-making power, even though this reform has come from the top down. The councils are found in factories, commerce, transportation, schools, hospitals, and civil service, as well as in other areas. The members of each council are elected by a secret ballot, and the number of council members is related to the size of the enterprise work force—it can have from fifteen to seventy members. Each council has half of its members renewed each year through elections. Majority votes make decisions, and the decisions are significant ones. The council chooses a director and management board of at least five people who are then responsible for the day-to-day administration of the enterprise. The council members, who must meet approximately once every month, receive no remuneration for this extra activity, and a member can be reelected only once. Besides the authority to fire the director, the council has power over the distribution of the net profit. The overhead items paid out of gross profits resemble the sort of thing Marx imagined in the *Critique of the Gotha Program,* such as amounts for equipment depreciation, new investments, and the social funding of various important programs. Through the workers' councils, therefore, the worker has a limited ability to influence his or her own wages. The councils function well so long as worker interest and participation remain high.

The communes in Yugoslavia began as an attempt to create grassroots democracy on the local level. They were small enough so that decisions could be made at town-meeting gatherings, but over the years they have been consolidated with other communes to such an extent that they are now too large to permit such direct democracy to function effectively. They resemble a combination of county and urban government in the West. Communes have considerable powers, nonetheless, and at times this interferes with the republic's decision-making freedom. At other times a commune and a workers' council, in an enterprise within the commune, might easily differ over an issue. With a dash of good will on both sides, this works well—but the opposite is also true.

One of the issues that periodically interferes with the smooth functioning of this system is the interference from the central government. In the decentralized economy, decisions are theoretically based on rational, pragmatic criteria. Very often, however, a factory will be constructed that is not justifiable on these rational economic grounds; instead, the reason for its construction and operation is political or ideological. Area X has such a factory, therefore area Y wants one too. This will continue as long as the central government makes many of the investment decisions, or backs the occasionally irrational decisions of local banking institutions.

A related ideological problem lies in agriculture. When the forced collectivization of farming was abolished (1950-53) nearly all the farmers went back to private holdings, but in a socialist society it was not ideologically possible to free agriculture completely. Hence, a limitation was imposed on the amount of land a family could own—about twenty-five acres. This is large enough to support a family, but it is insufficient for the production of the surpluses that Yugoslavia needs. Governmental decisions relating to the provision of farm machinery and fertilizers deliberately favor the voluntary collectives, attempting in this way to encourage farmer cooperation—working against the peasant resistance to cooperative farming.

Although government policy seeks to prevent the rise of a capitalist agriculture at the expense of potential production, ironically it does not prevent the rise of capitalist relations of production from developing the contracting subunits *within the collectives.* Another illustration of the problem would be the individual who wants to erect a small motel on the coast to attract the tourist trade—an important part of the Yugoslav economy. Almost immediately many people in the commune and workers' councils of the area begin to debate whether such private enterprise is compatible with a socialist society, and the result is often discouraging to the new entrepreneur.

A second related issue that quickly becomes tinged with nationalism is the matter of the socioeconomic gap between the developed republics, such as Croatia and Serbia, and the undeveloped ones, such as Macedonia or Montenegro. If the gap appears too large to the central planners, steps are often taken to equalize the differences or at least to reduce the size of the gap. This is attractive to the less developed area, and it comforts those in the country who have a strong ideological commitment to the equalization of incomes, but the developed republic often feels that its profits are being unnecessarily drained to assist a less efficient and less work-oriented set of people. The same result is visible when envy arises in Croatia over central investment decisions that apparently overly benefit the capital city of Belgrade, which is in Serbia. Ideological desire for national equality thus sharpens nationalist divisiveness.

Just as there are problems in a capitalist system that alleges to be a free market system, or problems in a bureaucratized system that operates from central direction with a controlled market, so also there appear to be problems in the Yugoslav combination of the two. There is enough of a free market to make competition meaningful, yet, enough controls so that ideology appears to hinder development rather than help. Nonetheless this combination has resulted in a higher standard of living for Yugoslav citizens than for most other "communist" societies. Many more consumer goods are available, even though they are expensive. The decentralization of decision making has also resulted in a great deal more intellectual and artistic freedom than in any other communist society: more possibilities for the average citizen to travel freely in other countries; and even the possibility of living and working in another country such as West Germany.

Even so, this liberalized environment has definite limits. In 1954, when Milovan Djilas wrote that the League of Communists ought to wither away along with the state, his views were called anarcho-liberalism and rejected. He was eventually imprisoned and not released until December 1966, when Tito was courting liberal support against a conservative challenge to his power. However, that liberalized atmosphere of 1966 did not prevent Mihajlo Mihajlov from getting into trouble. He wanted to start an anti-League magazine called *Free Voice,* based on democratic socialism rather than on communism. Mihajlov considered the Belgrade government totalitarian because it sought to inhibit discussion. "It is this anti-constitutional monopoly that is the enemy of socialism, not I," he said. "The paradoxical fact is that Marx's ideas are more alive today in the West than here in the East because of the lack of discussion."[5]

There were (and continue to be) attempts at critical intellectual discussion in, for example, the Zagreb journal *Praxis.* This journal promulgates a critical, humanistic Marxism, but this has often resulted in governmental interference. Another example of frustrated discussion began in June 1968. Students at Belgrade University occupied all university buildings for a week, demanding, among other reforms, the abolition of bureaucratic privileges. Tito at first sided with the students, but when the crisis was past he blamed the professors of the philosophy department for corrupting the students. Attempts to dismiss these professors, however, crashed on the rock of university autonomy. Consequently the government sought and obtained changes in the self-management laws that permitted an enlargement of the Faculty Council which has hiring and firing authority over individual professors. Non-faculty people were added to the council, and janitors now had a voice in who should teach. This sounded very democratic, but since the purpose was the dismissal of critical faculty it was a case of democracy backfiring on liberalism.[6]

In the early 1970s Croatian nationalism threatened the unity of Yugoslavia and the unity of the League. In a way this had resulted from increased decentralization emanating from the Ninth Congress of the League in 1969. By December of 1971 Tito had made it very clear, by purging the Croatian wing of the League of Communists, that the increased republican freedoms most definitely did not include the freedom to secede from Yugoslavia. This has made Croatian nationalism less visible but has not made it disappear.

The depoliticization of life in Yugoslavia has had another impact as well—one having an effect on the League itself. The party has increasingly become an organization of clerks, administrators, officials, and officers. Workers and young people, unable to see the significance of the League in their daily lives, have left it in large numbers. The result is that the party is increasingly older and more bureaucratically inclined, less leavened by worker influence—the very thing Yugoslav leaders felt they saw in the Soviet Union.

Yugoslavia is therefore a liberalized communist country with problems of unity compounded by divisive nationalism and decentralization of authority. Pendular swings of centralism and decentralism are to be expected. It remains a delightful paradox among communist countries. Attempting to solve its unemployment problems, for example, workers were allowed to take jobs in the Federal Republic of Germany. This in turn has meant that a possible recession in Germany creates the novelty of a communist country anxiously concerned about the economic health of a capitalist one. This, however, may prove to be a harbinger of future global interdependence rather than an ironic erosion of ideology. If so, Yugoslavia may be more model than stepchild.

Cuba

Prior to the Russian revolution of 1917, the ideas of Marx and socialism came to Latin America through books, immigrants, and travel contacts, creating an intellectual leftism that fit into the emerging nationalism and anti-imperialism of the nineteenth century. The socialist groups were simply more radical than the other liberal groups that arose, and often the radicalism was more of an anarchistic than a Marxist socialism. However, after the Bolshevik seizure of power in Russia in 1917 and the establishment of the Comintern, communist parties began forming in Latin America. The Cuban Communist party organized in 1925 in Havana, some years after other parties had already formed—such as Mexico's in 1919, Argentina's in 1920, and parties in Chile, Brazil, and Uruguay in 1921. These were small groups that were often deeply divided on ideological interpretations, and they attempted to work in countries that had very small and uneducated labor forces.

The Cuban group only showed signs of strength when it was allowed to cooperate with other groups on the left during the Popular Front periods of 1935-39 and 1941-45. During these periods the Communist party of Cuba advocated a democratic government; honesty in politics; the extension of social services; and economic advancement of both urban and rural workers—goals that won it many followers. After World War II, when Cuba's overwhelmingly dominant neighbor, the United States, became so preoccupied with anticommunism, Cuban political leaders gained favor in Washington by repressing the Cuban communists, and the party gradually lost what strength it had so recently gained. In 1952 when Batista decided not to wait for an election and seized power instead, he began to crush all political parties, among them the quite small Communist party. It was actually an insignificant threat to any government.

Russian diplomatic relations with other Latin American governments, in what Stalin saw as the American sphere of influence, put great pressure on Latin American communist parties to prohibit any attempts to seize power by violence. This anti-insurrectionary attitude became an ideological position of some magnitude. However, Batista could justify his dictatorship in Washington's eyes by the alleged necessity of suppressing Communists. They therefore became even smaller and more insignificant.

Batista soon had opposition from a new source, namely Fidel Castro. This was basically a liberal opposition, forced into guerrilla warfare by the nature of the Batista regime. Fidel's struggle began with an abortive attack on the Moncada Barracks on July 26, 1953. When he came back to renew the struggle in 1956, he called his group the "26th of July Movement." A manifesto of the group put out the year before called for a restoration of political democracy; social justice; a return to the 1940 constitution which Batista's coup had violated; and the redistribution of land among the peasants. He did not proclaim specifically socialist or communist aspirations until over two years after he had won political power from the defeated Batista forces. During the time of the struggle there was little or no cooperation between the Cuban Communist party and Castro's guerrillas. The party was officially against insurrections such as Fidel's, and many of the liberals in Castro's group were quite definitely anticommunist. The Communist party was not instrumental in Fidel's success.

Yet on December 1, 1961, Fidel Castro said: "I am a Marxist-Leninist." What had happened? He had started his rule of Cuba in a moderate position between what he described as the capitalism that starves people and the communism that deprives people of their freedom. Communism, he had said, was a solution to an economic problem at the expense of human liberty. This new humanism of Fidel's with reference to Cuban needs required financing. Failing to gain sufficient economic assistance from the United States, Castro discovered he could expect it from the Soviet Union, much as Egypt found that it could gain funds for the Aswan dam from Russia when the United States refused to grant it. However, this was an insufficient reason for his adoption of Marxism-Leninism.

His new ideology appeared to develop gradually for several reasons. Fidel first and foremost was a revolutionary humanist who, through his guerrilla activities, gained a broad popular support which eventually placed him in a position to accomplish his social goals for Cubans. Reform laws promulgated in 1959 reduced rents and redistributed land—and opposition grew from a middle class which was damaged by those laws. Fidel's desire to battle the enormous illiteracy of Cuba and the endemically poor health standards, and to raise the standard of Cuban living—all required mobilization of the masses as well as public financing of some magnitude. There was a militant, revolutionary ideology available that was cast in a humanistic spirit: the Marxism of the *Communist Manifesto*. Communism had become a model for modernization *on one's own*, and this appealed to his anti-American feelings. Leninism could be thought of as radical anti-imperialism, and Cuban history had been replete with examples of the United States' imperialism towards Cuba. Making the transition even easier was the fact that in 1960-61 the Marxist-Leninist ideology was certainly viewed in Washington as anti-American, and Castro's February 1960 trade agreement with Russia gave him non-American external support. A final reason came in April of 1961 with the abortive *Bay of Pigs* invasion that was manned by Cuban exiles but planned by the American CIA.

In addition, internal disputes within Cuba pushed him toward a communist ideology. Many of the 26th of July Movement people resented the radicalism of Castro's initial programs, his failure to immediately restore civil liberties, and his acceptance of help from the formerly despised Communist party. In moving against the moderates in his own group, Fidel was painting himself further and further into a leftist corner where the adoption of a radical ideology was easier. Using the party gave Castro organizational advantages—at a time when his programs needed a cohering mechanism. At any rate, by December 1, 1961, Fidel declared himself to be a Marxist-Leninist.

However, Cuba was not to be an extension of the Communist party of Cuba. Almost immediately in 1962, Fidel began moving *against* that party in order to consolidate his own control. What he sought in both 1962 and again in 1968 in purging the Anibel Escalente faction was the merger of the radicalized 26th of July Movement with a Castroized Communist party into an instrument of personal power which he could use for the transformation of Cuba. As a result, neither the 26th of July Movement nor the old Communist party survived intact—both changed into more radical movements, made easier by the departure from Cuba of thousands of moderates or opponents; the Bay of Pigs fiasco which seemed to demand revolutionary vigilance; and by obvious Cuban needs which demanded a total effort by the Cuban population.

While this was going on, Khrushchev was playing a game of his own that involved Cuba. It is possible that in order to gain support for a less expensive military budget in Russia, he sought to demonstrate the lessened need for enormous land forces by placing intermediate range ballistic missiles in Cuba aimed at targets in the United States. President Kennedy, however, dramatically forced Khrushchev to begin withdrawing the missiles in October of 1962. Castro found himself in the middle, not consulted by either side, even though he allegedly gained an American promise of no more invasions. Although heavily dependent on continued Russian economic assistance, Castro appears to have set his mind on an independent Cuban path to socialism. That independence manifested itself particularly in the support and encouragement of guerrilla insurrections in Latin America, which conflicted with Russia's diplomatic and profitable relations with established Latin American governments.

This Cuban-Soviet difference was quite obvious at the January 1966 Tri-Continental Solidarity Conference in Havana, where Fidel attacked those revolutionaries who spent their time theorizing rather than acting, and urged the recognition of a new Venezuelan revolutionary group that was distinct from and an opponent of the Venezuelan Communist party. The call for violent insurrectionary movements in Latin America angered the Russians. It seemed to infuriate the Yugoslavs, who attacked the militant line in an article in *Borba* in January. It delighted the Chinese, who were right in the midst of advocating revolutionary militancy both at home and abroad. According to a speech made by Castro in February 1966, however, the Chinese were trying to infiltrate Fidel's organization with the thought of Mao Tse-tung. Castro reacted very negatively to this attempt, which must have pleased the Russians.[7] Support for Castro's allegations of attempted Maoist infiltration came in 1967 when a commentary from Hsinhua, the Chinese press agency, stated with reference to revolutionary activity in the Dominican Republic, a close neighbor of Cuba in the Caribbean:

> More and more revolutionaries are studying Chairman Mao's works assiduously and beginning to use Mao Tse-tung's thought to guide their revolutionary struggle.
> Carrying their weapons, they moved into the hills, rousing and organizing the peasants, and educated the masses with Chairman Mao's idea of the people's war.[8]

The call for insurrectionary violence was also splitting the Latin American Communist parties, creating a new *Fidelista* faction on top of the already existing Moscow-Peking divisions, and at times erecting a new leftist movement that disregarded the more conservative Communists. This made organized communism in Latin America even more unlikely as a threat to established governments. The August 1967 Solidarity Conference in Havana continued this attempt to export Fidelismo into other areas, and for a brief time activity by revolutionaries captured headlines far in excess of their real potential. In October of 1967 Fidel's close associate in Cuba and the hero of many American leftist youths, Ernesto Che Guevara, was killed after having been captured by Bolivian authorities. Che had been trying to export Cuban insurrectionary success to Bolivia, but the Bolivian rebels had failed to gain the support of the Indian peasants. The rebels' defeat in 1967 seemed to take the steam out of the insurrectionary movement throughout Latin America. Fidel began to concentrate on domestic problems in Cuba. It was well that he did. There are undoubted achievements of Castroism in Cuba. Medical care on a nationwide basis is probably the best in Latin America. The massive attack on illiteracy is still continuing, but it has already had a profound influence on the new Cuban generation. Child labor has been abolished, and an eight-hour work day introduced, although workers are often encouraged to work longer hours for no remuneration, just as Lenin did in an attempt to encourage the subbotnik "shoot of communism." Agriculture has been diversified to some extent, and certainly expanded; industrialization is considerably above the pre-Castro period; and women have been granted a much more vital role in the economy. The Cuban government is also a likely candidate for the honor of being the least corrupt Latin American government.

However, there are still problems. Continued shortages and crop failures force a continuation of a rationing system that few admire.[9] Unwise economic decisions and practices, such as sending urban workers, who are unfamiliar with farming, to the country to cut sugar cane, harm more than help the slowly growing Cuban economy. The practice of "storming" (sporadic, great effort), in other words, partially solves the problem of seasonal labor needs but at the expense of the crop. Continued dependence on Soviet aid for a wide variety of merchandise mortgages the Cuban future to an enormous degree. Juvenile delinquency, crime, truancy, hoarding, and a working class that is quite capable of resisting revolutionary motivations for greater labor efforts continue to plague the Cuban leaders.

By far a more serious criticism of Cuban communism is the charge that it is actually a benevolent paternalism which, because the masses of the people are not involved in choosing the decision makers, faces the very real prospect of becoming as bureaucratized and, therefore, as rigid and possibly Stalinistic as Russia in the 1930s. Cuba in the 1970s had more problems than solutions in her economy although the high sugar prices masked the problems. The main crop, sugar, had failed to yield the expected tonnage, and other areas of the economy showed similar weaknesses. The weak performance by the economy encourages a radicalization of the paternalism, leading to greater militarization of the party's efforts. In March 1971, for example, a law was passed against parasites in the society—the vagrants, malingerers, and those who had too many absences from school or work.These parasites could receive from six months to two years of forced labor in rehabilitation centers. In other words the drive to create the material basis of socialism, a basis assumed by Marx, is far more likely in the absence of success to destroy the humanism of Marx as well as that with which Fidel apparently began his struggle. The end would then be lost in the pursuit of the means.

Continued boycotting of the Cuban economy by the United States contributes to this problem and encourages the rigidly bureaucratic potential in Cuban communism. While this may provide some short-run satisfaction to a few Americans, the long-term foolishness of prolonging hostile anti-American feeling in an island ninety miles from Florida may yet bring about a change in American policy toward Cuba.[10] Such a change toward normal relations would be a benefit not only to the United States, but also to the Cuban people by assisting the development of a more distinctive alternative to Bolshevism.

Chile

On the eve of the Solidarity Conference held in Havana in August 1967, where Castro hoped to consolidate an insurrectionary direction for Latin American Communists, an article appeared in *Pravda,* the official newspaper of the CPSU, denouncing in advance Castro's attempts to interfere in the revolutionary affairs of other Latin American nations. The article was not written by a Russian, but by a Chilean; not by a businessman who feared communist activity, but by the secretary general of Chile's Communist party, Luis Corvalan Lopez. Corvalan's point was that Castro's attempts to impose his view of proper revolutionary procedures on other Latin American groups was adventuristic, and would be so divisive that enemies of communism would be given an easy victory.[11]

Corvalan's article demonstrated more than that "solidarity" was a hope rather than a realization. It demonstrated that in attempting to export Cuban revolutionary experiences, Fidel Castro was being extremely annoying to the large, well-organized and disciplined, Moscow-oriented and conservative Chilean Communist party. It was an old party (established in 1921) that had gone through considerable difficulties to get to the position it then held: real electoral strength in Chilean politics if it could work in an alliance with the far more militant Chilean Socialist party. The Chilean Communists were not simply demonstrating the caution of the earlier Popular Front, nor simply remembering the frustrations of the years from 1948 to 1958 when the party was illegal. The Chilean party was more conservative in relation to the insurrectionary demands of the Cubans, for the main reason that it had a great deal to lose by such openly revolutionary activity. Chile was also a highly urbanized and relatively industrialized society—which contrasted with Cuba and many other Latin American countries more suitable for peasant guerrilla warfare. The party had over forty thousand members in 1968; strong union strength;

successful organizational work among peasants; eighteen out of 147 seats in the lower legislative chamber and five out of forty-five in the upper chamber. The more leftist Socialists had a similar political strength even though they were far less organized and disciplined. The potential of alliance with the Socialists created the possibility of legitimate electoral success, causing the Chilean Communists to walk a careful line. This was frustrating to Fidelista "adventurists" as well as to other revolutionaries, including some Catholic priests. The priests had come to revolutionary Marxism out of Christian idealism that stood in stark contrast to existing Latin American property relations, which the Church had declared itself unable to alter. Communists also valued the status quo, which ironically led the revolutionary Marxists to reject both Church and communist policies as being too conservative.

This was the party and these were the circumstances which brought Salvador Allende to the office of President of Chile in September of 1970. Allende was a Socialist who had run for office on the basis of a unity coalition between the Communists; Socialists; elements of the radical party (which was middle-class reformist); and leftist Catholics. This new coalition won the election by a slim margin of thirty-nine thousand votes (36.3 percent of the total vote), which meant that Allende's government, however dedicated to the campaign promises of socialism, liberty, and pluralism, had to operate with the handicap of all minority coalition governments: the constant necessity of maintaining a legislative majority through cooperation with other parties, including the left wing of the Christian Democrats. The deep divisions between right and left in the unity coalition that backed Allende originally would have been cause enough for him to move slowly, but the additional restraints resulting from his minority status created even more reasons.

The ideological excitement of having a Marxist, however moderate, at the helm in Chilean politics contributed to the heightening of the politicization of the Chilean electorate, which—given economic problems—accelerated the pace of electoral dissatisfaction with the new government. CIA involvement did not help either.

> Instead of the pattern of three years of success followed by three years of relative failure, which characterized the Alessandri and Frei administrations, Allende's brilliant first year in office had been followed by a dismal and increasingly disastrous second year—raising questions about what is likely to occur during the remaining four years of his presidential term.[12]

In addition, the unity coalition in the 1970 elections began to break up in 1972 along right and left lines. The split was an ideological confrontation between those who were convinced that Allende was moving too slowly and that socialism would never come this way, and those who saw the necessity of remaining within the constitutional limits to avoid a takeover by the armed forces in the name of that constitution. President Allende tried to hold the coalition together, believing that he would be able to lead Chile into socialism through peaceful and essentially legitimate channels. In November of 1970 he quoted Engels in support of a

> . . . peaceful evolution from the old society to the new in countries where the representatives of the people have all power and, in accord with the constitution, can do what they desire when they have the majority of the nation behind them.
> This is our Chile. Here at last the anticipation of Engels is fulfilled.[13]

This would be a slow, steady process but within the law.

Allende's group began to nationalize certain factories and banks; the Bethlehem Steel iron mines; the cement, nitrate, and coal industries; formerly private shares of Pacific Steel; and most importantly the copper mines, by mid-1971. Compensations for nationalized industries were a part of the takeover procedure, but the amount of compensation and the rate of payment were not always satisfactory to the former owners. Anaconda and Kennecot, American-based former owners of the major copper mines, ended up owing Chile money, a result of a penalty levied on those companies for excessive profit-taking during 1955-71. In agriculture, the government gradually took over all estates in excess of 200 acres (80 hectares) between September 1970 and mid-1972. Although all this was done legally, there were elements in the nationalization process that suggested illegality, such as workers deliberately striking a factory so as to provide justification for the government's intervention. Of course, it might easily be pointed out that in former times similar questionable practices had also been utilized in the private acquisition of economic power; nonetheless, illegal methods in certain cases gave ammunition to the opponents of Allende and encouraged resistance.

Income redistribution was accomplished by granting large wage boosts to the poorer work force; increasing the tax burden for the wealthy; increasing pensions; and increasing the tax exemptions for the poorer elements of the society. Public works such as housing construction were expanded tremendously. The initial result was gratifying to Allende's government, but the production boom did not last. Governmental deficit spending produced a rapidly expanding inflation in late 1971, and particularly in 1972-73, an inflation that blended with rising consumer goods' prices to rob the average worker of the gains achieved only the year before. Also, popular fears of potential totalitarian or undemocratic rule were enlarged when Allende sought a legislative reform that would have made the Chilean legislature unicameral and a judicial reform that sought neighborhood tribunals, staffed by individuals from social and labor institutions, which could mete out punishments of up to a year of rehabilitative labor.

These two reform efforts and the worsening economic situation became the preoccupation of the opposition press in Chile. The result was a severe erosion of the popular support for Allende's government. Demonstrations against the government had already occurred in late 1971, such as the December protest by housewives against high food costs. Strikes in government-owned industries created an embarrassing dilemma for a socialist-communist government that had agreed to operate within the bounds of legality. Lack of new investment caused by economic uncertainty began to create a severe shortage of vital commodities.

Nonetheless, President Allende's early successes were considerable. He had nationalized key industries in Chile, undoubtedly a necessity if Chile were to survive independently. He had quite drastically redistributed income; reorganized the agricultural sector; increasingly involved workers in decision making; and maintained a very high level of personal freedom for the Chilean people while doing this. However, he had not been able to control inflation and rising costs, a situation that worsened in 1973—exacerbated by serious shortages. The result was a rapid polarization of the Chilean electorate, coupled with an erosion of support for what was increasingly called the "socialist experiment." In the midst of the deepening political and economic crises, the military carried out a coup (September 11, 1973), and Allende was apparently killed while defending his constitutional regime in the only way that appeared possible on that date—with a machine gun.

The military government that replaced Allende in the fall of 1973 ruled without much regard for the constitutional rules and rights that had restrained the pace of Allende's socialism. Leftist newspapers were shut down; allegedly Marxist professors at universities were fired; labor unions were forbidden to strike or have unauthorized meetings; and the number of political prisoners held by the new government without benefit of either charges made or dates set for trial was estimated at between three and ten thousand persons. The one area where the military junta was somewhat successful was in the economic area, where an austerity program encouraged foreign and domestic investment but allowed prices to seek their natural level. This hit the poor particularly hard, but it had the counter-revolutionary impact of making people worry more about food than about the recovery of lost civil liberties.[14]

The Marxian advocacy of a possible peaceful transition to socialism, therefore, faced a severe test in Chile. Is the authoritarianism of Lenin a necessary ingredient, even though it appears to contradict the humanistic foundation of the socialist movement? Should Allende have picked up a machine gun (figuratively) in 1971 rather than in 1973? Allende's basic problem was his *minority* election. He never had a legislative majority in the Chilean Senate. To institute major socioeconomic reforms, however, Allende needed the support of an extraordinary majority of the people. Considering his slim electoral base, Allende moved too far too fast, while simultaneously being accused of footdragging by leftist factions in his own coalition. It also seems evident from the Chilean example that socialist intentions are insufficient—the economy has to be carefully controlled in the transition period, a situation foreseen more by Bernstein than by Marx.

Italy

Conversely, the Italian Communist party (PCI) did not seize power when the opportunity appeared in 1945. It might have failed miserably in such an attempt, but that is not the point. This is quite a different party from the usual stereotype of a small band of dedicated revolutionaries whose fanaticism has made them excessively narrow in their understanding of what needs to be done. From the beginning, the PCI was a blend of various elements. The party split off from the Italian socialist movement to form a splinter that joined with the Cominform in 1921, but the PCI carried into that organization a considerable amount of syndicalism and idealism. The rapid emergence of Mussolini's anticommunist fascism prevented extensive growth and stimulated intensive theoretical development, particularly in the person of the PCI leader from 1924-27, Antonio Gramsci (1891-1937).

Born in Sardinia, Gramsci was well acquainted with the poverty of peasant life in Italy. Educated in northern, industrial Turin, he was also familiar with the intellectual life of Italy. He became the foremost Italian Communist intellectual. Imprisoned by Mussolini from 1927 until just before his death in 1937, Gramsci was isolated both from Comintern control and the Stalinism developing in the Soviet Union. He was free in the sense of being able to independently develop a Marxist theory that drew as much from Italian sources, including Machiavelli and Benedetto Croce, as it did from Marx and Lenin.

While in prison Gramsci developed a theory of the future state that included coercion as well as proletarian hegemony. The coercive aspects were designed to coordinate and direct the society toward desired goals, to transcend the extreme differences in life styles that Italy demonstrated so vividly. The hegemonic aspect of the new state referred to the role played in the society by the intellectuals—who by virtue of their association with the necessary party had developed a living, organic relationship with the society that they served. The ruling intellectuals would not serve the older, traditional interests of the past, but the entire society of the present in a democratic rather than a bureaucratic centralism.

> Parties come into existence and are constituted organisationally in order to lead the situation in historically vital moments for their classes; but they are not always able to adapt themselves to new tasks and new periods, they are not always able to develop according to the development of the complex relations of force (and hence relative position of their classes) in the particular country or in the international field. In analysing this party development it is necessary to distinguish: the social group; the mass of the party; the bureaucracy and High Command of the party. The bureaucracy is the most dangerously habitual and conservative force; if it ends up by constituting a solid body, standing by itself and feeling independent from the masses, the party ends by becoming anachronistic, and in moments of acute crisis becomes emptied of all its social content, like an empty shell.[15]

An organic and democratic centralism was not bureaucratic or dictatorial, therefore, but a centralism that coordinated and returned the dynamic pressures from below. To achieve this sort of hegemony, Communists ought to form a "historic bloc" composed of workers and intellectuals who would strive for the new culture where human freedom could flower.[16] Non-violent political action was vital to achieve this. Gramsci called his ideas a philosophy of "praxis."[17] An early example of the implementation of the historic bloc was the formation of workers' councils in northern Italy in the early 1920s, an idea revived in the 1940s, and again from the radical left in the late 1960s.

The PCI has not always been loyal to these ideas. It was, after all, a member of the Cominform and was pulled in a Bolshevik direction as well. However, over the years, as Gramsci's prison writings have become more available and the party has continued to operate as a powerful opposition group in Italian political life, a distinctiveness has emerged that makes this party noteworthy. It is a blend of Leninist revolutionary attitudes about the vital necessity of a party, combined with a broad, reformist approach that seems to be characteristic of social-democratic parties in other countries, parties which would shudder at the idea of being called communist.

There is in the PCI an independence from the Soviet Union that was clearly manifested in the Italian opposition to the Soviet occupation of Czechoslovakia in 1968. There is a consistent attempt to mobilize the masses of Italy behind the party, not simply the industrial proletariat.

Those masses include peasants as well as middle-class segments that are considered productive rather than parasitical, such as the smaller shop-keepers, white collar workers, technicians, and small to medium industrialists. Even though these groups might well belong to other organized political groups, the party counts them as part of the masses with which it seeks an organic relationship—so it courts unity with the other organized groups on the left as well, such as the Socialists or the left-wing Catholic groups. When the radicals erupted in Italy in 1967 and 1968, and the workers in many areas spontaneously created the workers' councils again in 1969, the Italian Communist party worked to absorb these new influences and make them a part of itself.

The pursuit of power in Italy, thus, is accomplished by a method of broad, electorally oriented alliances, a search for unity on the left that has meant substantial compromises. For example, in the late 1960s there was a strong movement for union independence of the political parties. The PCI decided not to oppose this movement even though it created substantial problems for the party—problems such as having the unions develop strategies and methods that might be narrowly economic, or having the unions go out on strike just when the PCI wanted them to hold things down in order to increase the possibility of getting a major reform approved by the legislature. Nonetheless, since 1969, union officials have been barred from holding elective office or from serving on the executive committees of the political parties. This union autonomy, although not complete, is very different from the Soviet notion of the unions functioning as transmission belts for party policy decisions. The PCI now has to be quite cautious in its factory organizational work, for it seeks to lead what could easily become competition—the unions and the workers' councils which have been absorbed by the unions.[18]

The Italian Communist party thus pursues political as well as social alliances and continues to grow in strength as the major opposition force in Italian politics. In 1968 it received nearly 30 percent of the votes in the general election. As a party of reform, however, it is an easy target for extreme left radicals in Italy. The sight of party leaders driving expensive cars easily leads radicals to the conclusion that the PCI has lost its revolutionary aspirations and has, in fact, become bourgeois. The party responds by maintaining that this is not true, that its strategy of alliance seeking will bring about an eventual and peaceful revolution. The radicals can also be partially silenced by quoting excerpts from the writings of Georg Lukács (1885-1971), the Hungarian Marxist theorist, who is popular among Italian intellectuals. Revolutionary impatience can result, Lukács said, from too narrow a view of strategy that results from an overpreoccupation with "enemies." A movement that becomes too sectarian feels that there are only two groups in the society, the working class and its enemies. It can therefore not see the necessary mediations in the class struggle and perpetuates a siege mentality that distorts the facts in order to fit them within a theoretical framework.[19] The PCI patiently works with its radical left wing, for it too is a part of the historic front and hegemony that the PCI seeks.

What the question really amounts to is what one means by revolution, and whether that definition allows for incremental development or only for a dramatic and complete alteration of the existing society. The Italian Communists prefer the former to the latter.

The differences between various parties and areas of the world raise many questions that have no easy answers. Is there such a thing as a Communist party? Does that concept make sense if the only thing that unifies these various parties is a selective adherence to Marxism and/or Leninism? Is communism really left-of-center politically? Perhaps by analyzing communist and New Left developments in the United States some answers may be found.

Suggested Readings

Fagen, Richard R. *The Transformation of Political Culture in Cuba.* Stanford: Stanford University Press, 1969.

Hoare, Quintin, and Smith, Geoffrey Nowell, eds. *Selections from the Prison Notebooks of Antonio Gramsci.* New York: International, 1971.

Matthews, Herbert L. *Fidel Castro.* New York: Simon & Schuster Clarion Books, 1970.

Petrović, Gajo. *Marx in the Mid-Twentieth Century.* Garden City: Doubleday Anchor Books, 1967.

Schapiro, Leonard, ed. *Political Opposition in One-Party States.* New York: John Wiley, 1972.

NOTES

[1]See the speeches by Milovan Djilas and Tito in 1950, cited in Robert V. Daniels, *A Documentary History of Communism* 2: 189-96; and the discussion in Wolfgang Leonhard, *Three Faces of Marxism* (New York: Holt, Rinehart, and Winston, 1974) pp. 267-74.

[2]Adam B. Ulam, "Titoism," in *Marxism in the Modern World,* ed. Milorad M. Drachkovitch (Stanford: Stanford University Press, 1965), p. 152.

[3]Yugoslavia is divided into six quite different republics, which often introduces a divisive nationalism into its political life, severely threatening the unity of the country. At the Tenth Congress of the League, in May 1974, President Tito urged the party to extend its control in order to unify the country more securely.

[4]Paul Lendvai, *Eagles in Cobwebs. Nationalism and Communism in the Balkans* (Garden City: Doubleday Anchor Books, 1969), p. 111. Reprinted by permission of Doubleday & Company, Inc.

[5]*New York Times,* 19 April 1967, p. 14. One discussion he may have been referring to was the International Marxism Conference held in 1965, interestingly enough, at Notre Dame University, a conference in which Yugoslav philosophers such as Gajo Petrović, an editor of *Praxis,* participated. Mihajlov was again in trouble in 1974. See Milovan Djilas' article in *New York Times,* 14 November 1974, p. 47.

[6]See the discussion of the issue in "The Repression at Belgrade University," *New York Review of Books* 21, no. 1 (February 7, 1974): 32-33.

[7]See excerpts from Castro's speech, *New York Times,* 7 February 1966, p. 12.

[8]Cited in *New York Times,* 13 May 1967, p. 9.

[9]This began to improve in 1972. See *New York Times,* 15 May 1972, p. 12.

[10]A small step in this direction was the decision by the Nixon administration in 1974 to permit United States companies (General Motors and Chrysler) based in Argentina to sell their products to Cuba. *New York Times,* 19 April 1974, p. 1. See also ibid., 29 April 1974, p. 33, "Washington's Futile Policy Towards Havana," and ibid., 13 July 1974, p. 1, "U.S. Believed Losing Control Over Its Policy of Isolating Cuba."

[11]See *New York Times,* 31 July 1967, p. 7. See also ibid., 2 September 1968, p. 11, for the consternation among Chilean Communists when Fidel condemned the similarly conservative Bolivian Communist party.

[12]Paul Sigmund, "Chile, Two Years of 'Popular Unity,'" *Problems of Communism* 21, no. 6 (November-December 1972): 39. Reprinted by permission of *Problems of Communism.* For a description of CIA involvement see *New York Times,* 17 September 1974, p. 2; 20 September 1974, p. 1; and 24 September 1974, p. 22 for President Ford's admission of CIA involvement.

[13]Salvadore Allende Gossens, *El Mercurio,* (November 6, 1970), p. 23; cited in Sigmund, ibid., p. 40. Reprinted by permission of *Problems of Communism.*

[14]A recent in-depth analysis can be found in Jonathan Kandell's article, *New York Times,* 28 January 1974, pp. 1, 10.

[15]Antonio Gramsci, "The Modern Prince," in *Socialist Thought—A Documentary History,* ed. Albert Fried and Ronald Sanders (Garden City: Doubleday Anchor Books, 1964), pp. 522-23.

[16]For a description of the concept of hegemony, see John M. Cammett, *Antonio Gramsci and the Origins of Italian Communism* (Stanford: Stanford University Press, 1967), pp. 204-206.

[17]See, for example, Gramsci's letter to Tania, 2 May 1932, in *Antonio Gramsci— Letters from Prison,* ed. and trans. Lynne Lawner (New York: Harper & Row, 1973), pp. 234-35.

[18]For fuller discussion of these points, see Donald L. M. Blackmer, "Italian Communism: Strategy for the 1970's," *Problems of Communism* 21, no. 3 (May-June 1972): 41-56.

[19]R. N. Berki, "Georg Lukács in Retrospect: Evolution of a Marxist Thinker," *Problems of Communism* 21, no. 6 (November-December 1972): 58. Lukács deserves recognition as a vitalizing force for a moderate and humanistic socialism in Eastern Europe in the last part of his life, even though he identified himself too closely to Stalinism in an earlier period.

PART IV

New Directions for Marxism

11

The United States: The Communist Party and the New Left — a Study in Contrasts

The organized communist movement in the United States was created in 1919 out of the general socialist left, as a specific and positive response to the Bolshevik seizure of power in Russia and the subsequent organization of the Third International. Theoretically, the advanced industrial status of the United States should have given the American Communists a substantial revolutionary edge over many other countries in the world that were far less developed. Practice, however, did not demonstrate the correctness of that theory.[1] The American Communist party was divided from the beginning. Sectarian narrowness; competition among leaders for the dominant positions which soon turned into competition for the shifting sands of Stalin's favor; and an initial weakness compounded by external hostility combined to make the party a long exercise in futility.

There was in the postwar years a considerable *Red Scare* that had its roots in the fear of socialism whether exemplified by **Edward Bellamy**'s novels or by attempts to establish effective unions. The ensuing frustrations of many Socialists made them more radical, more desirous of taking the offensive. This had led in 1905 to the formation of the *Industrial Workers of the World,* a union movement that directly competed with Samuel Gompers' attempts to expand the *American Federation of Labor.* The IWW's organizing attempts, particularly in the American West, were attempts at gaining more than higher wages or better working conditions. In many cases the syndicalism of this more radical union pushed for worker control of the industry concerned, as well as of the local political scene.[2]

An official, federal hostility to the IWW grew more overt during the First World War, a hostility made more justifiable by the IWW's willingness to call strikes during the war. This reached a peak in 1917 when military harassment of union activity culminated in raids on IWW headquarters, as, for example, the army's seizure of the Spokane headquarters in August of 1917. Rumors circulated that German money was financing IWW activity. Increasingly, people made demands on the government to put the IWW out of business. The revolutionary atmosphere from Russia in the summer of 1917 gave a sense of urgency to the matter, an urgency that quickened with the Bolshevik success in November. There was identification of the IWW with the Bolsheviks, and opposition to the radical syndicalism of the union took the form of a crusade against the more readily identifiable devil—communism. Ironically, this identification between the IWW and communism was aided by a prominent Communist, John Reed, who, after returning from Russia, saw the persecuted IWW leaders as similar to the Executive Committee of the Petrograd Soviet of Workers' and Soldiers' Deputies.[3]

The Red Scare culminated in Attorney General A. Mitchell Palmer's raids in 1919 against radical Socialists. In this climate the Communists began to organize in 1919 in response to the call from the Third International. Two parties formed in September of 1919, one calling itself the *Communist Party of America* and the other the *Communist Labor Party of America.* There were further splits yet to come in these weak, ideological groups; both the weakness of the groups and their ideological characters contributed to sectarian narrowness, where insignificant issues took on a life and death significance. There were attempts at unification as well, which eventually culminated in complete Comintern dominance. However, the immediate issue confronting the communist movement was the question of legal, open organization as opposed to a more underground existence. External circumstances to a great extent dictated the answer, at least temporarily.

> The anti-Communist drive culminated two years of official persecution of the entire radical movement. Homes, headquarters, and meetings were broken into, thousands of arrests were made, and aliens were deported en masse. In the end few Communists actually served prison sentences. . . . The raids immediately drove both Communist Parties underground. They adopted conspiratorial methods, and their memberships melted away. By 1920 the two parties were reduced to no more than 10,000 members altogether, and even this figure was cut in half in the next two years.[4]

Clandestine, radicalized activity was therefore encouraged from the beginning. In the more rarified atmosphere of underground activity, ideological purity is always extremely important because the opportunities to pragmatically implement various strategies are prohibited. The lack of theory-diluting experiences preserved and encouraged the all-or-nothing revolutionary goals of the early Communists, making the later Bolshevization of the movement that much simpler.

With underground conditions came an underground mentality. More than ever, American Communists could identify themselves with Russian Bolshevism, which had been nurtured in Czarist conditions of illegality and conspiracy. The romantics and illusionists made a necessity into a virtue by telling themselves that illegality was the natural habitat of a real revolutionary movement.[5]

The issue of whether or not to participate in some form of legal, organized activity was therefore a real problem. Any open participation by Communists in a legal organization required a substantial toning down of revolutionary language. Issues such as the dictatorship of the proletariat or the impending violence of the revolution had to be buried in the less offensive language of reformism. This annoyed more ideologically minded Communists, who saw in this activity a betrayal of principle. However, by 1921, domestic needs in Russia; the failure of revolutionary attempts in other parts of Europe; and Lenin's condemnation of workers' councils and communist separatism resulted in the Comintern demand for a United Front. This movement to the right encouraged cooperative and legal activity and discouraged underground separatism. In addition, the prohibition against factionalism which had begun to characterize the CPSU since 1921 was extended throughout the Comintern—the Moscow line was increasingly a direction that could be disobeyed only by risking expulsion from the movement. As a person did not usually become a Communist lightly, there was a similarity between the threat of expulsion from the party and excommunication from the Church—no "salvation" was imagined possible outside the organization.

As a result American Communists organized a *Workers'* party, operating largely in the open, but controlled by the underground organization. In 1923 the Workers' party was successful in temporarily broadening its base by infiltrating the populist *Farmer-Labor* party at its Chicago convention. The program that the convention endorsed was entirely reformist—calling for a national eight-hour working day; a ban on child labor; compulsory education throughout the country; and a bonus for the soldiers of World War I.[6] However, the victory of the Workers' party in taking over this larger political movement proved to be short-lived, for, as news of the coup reached the less radical members, workers deserted the Farmer-Labor party in droves.

Although it often had a frustrating lack of success, the American Communist party did make many positive contributions to the labor struggle in obtaining a bargaining position with employers. Communists were good organizers in the larger unions even though they did not, except in rare local cases, exercise dominant control. They were disciplined to work long and often dangerous hours in such organizing activity and made substantial contributions in the 1920s and 1930s to the growth of industrial unionism. However, when they placed themselves in competition with the general union movement, such as Samuel Gompers' AFL, the Communists fared badly in the struggle for the allegiance of the laborers. Yet, when they worked within the larger and stronger organization they were often successful. Success crowned their activities when revolutionary goals were subdued; contrariwise, when the revolutionary goals predominated, they courted disaster.

The Comintern shift back to the left in 1924, therefore, was a blow to the hopes of American Communists. For months they had been seeking an alliance with Robert LaFollette's new populist movement, and success seemed close. This alliance would have given them a much broader base. However, in May of 1924 the Comintern abruptly reversed itself and once again forced separatism on international parties, including the American.[7]

Although these shifts can be understood from the Russian point of view, it is difficult to understand why the American party felt compelled to follow. Why did the party not see that their only real potential for success lay in cooperation with other leftist groups, gaining incremental improvements year by year? Ideology was an important factor, but these were not simply true believers in the mindless pursuit of an impossible goal. These were men predisposed to the more revolutionary side of Marxism or they would not have separated from the socialist movement to form the Communist party. Having made that commitment, they found themselves in a domestic context that was antirevolutionary and an international frame of reference that placed them in an inferior position—a status they came to believe themselves.

The Comintern allowed for three levels or organization rankings. The first rank was for those Communists in the Comintern who held power in their nation. At that time it was a rank held only by the Soviet Communist party. A second, lower ranking was for those parties such as the German or the French which had not attained power but had considerable popular or electoral strength. The third and lowest rank was for those parties still in their infancy, which had to rely mainly on propaganda to achieve their goals. American Communists fit into the third category. This conditioned them to take orders rather than to give them, and to take as their model the Soviet experience, however changeable the directions from that experience became.

It is important to realize that the Communists were not the only ones in America who saw Russia as a model in the 1920s. There was an intense feeling among many noncommunist idealist intellectuals that the Soviet Union was the harbinger of a new dawn for humanity. This impression was furthered by the selective perceptions of travelers to Russia who returned to write about their experiences.

> . . . a brief interlude of American relief personnel bringing food to a famine-stricken country in 1921 was followed by an evergrowing procession of social workers, artists, labor leaders, educators, social scientists, businessmen, and representatives of ethnic minorities. The decade closed with more than a thousand American engineers in the Soviet Union building its first great modern industrial plants. For the Soviet Union was, indeed, America's first Point Four project, without the blessing of the State Department, to be sure, but with the support of an influential section of American industry. Thus, like modern Magi, American travelers came seeking a new political hope, and bringing their gifts of technology.[8]

It was scarcely surprising, therefore, that the American party submitted so meekly to what had become Stalin's control of the international movement. The *Model Statutes* of the Comintern in 1925 gave structure both to the implications of the 17th Condition of Membership adopted in 1920,[9] and to Zinoviev's use of the term "bolshevization" at the Fifth Congress of the Comintern in 1924. The Moscow headquarters of the International began to rule by fiat, and any pretense of local autonomy in the American movement was gone. Factional disputes continued, but the winner became the one who gained Stalin's favor, and the loser either recanted completely or was expelled from the organization.

In 1925 the Comintern abruptly moved to the right again, following Stalin's political maneuvering in Russia. The American party again became cooperative with other parts of the left labor movement. Advocating revolutionary goals between 1925 and 1928 was labeled "Trotskyite adventurism." Just one year before the beginnings of the collapse known as the Depression (1928), the Sixth Congress of the Comintern dictated yet another move—to the left, once again following Joseph Vissarionovich. Until 1935, when the Popular Front was adopted with an accompanying shift to the right again, the American party was required to compete with other leftist groups and to organize rival, more ideologically pure unions. These policies in the United States were very unsuccessful—except in creating an enormous amount of anticommunist sentiment in the labor movement; for the fractionalizing of the working class was just the opposite of what the AFL and the CIO were trying to do. In Germany, the new separatism of that Communist party assisted the rise of Hitler—fascism, initially, was not seen as a threat, but the New Deal of President Roosevelt was. However, that position would be reversed very soon. In the meantime, however, the Depression's evident demonstration of the collapse of capitalism's vitality, coupled with the seeming full employment and progress made in the Soviet Union, attracted even more intellectuals to communism.

With the 1935 shift to the Popular Front and the formation of many antifascist front organizations, the party's appeal to the intellectual and the artistic was exceptionally strong. The front organizations grew much more rapidly than the party, however. As Joseph Clark, the foreign editor of the *Daily Worker,* said in his resignation letter in the fall of 1957: "Even during the period of our greatest success [1935-45] we were never a mass party and we were never able to bring socialism into the arena of American political thought and action."[10] The involvement of many prominent American intellectuals and artists in the front groups provided great material for Senator Joseph McCarthy's witch-hunts in the early 1950s, but it accomplished little else.

In 1939 the antifascism suddenly had to become pacifism after the non-aggression treaty between Stalin and Hitler. The front movement collapsed because most of the members of these groups lacked the flexibility of the dedicated American Communist, a maneuverability based on the notion that the only principle was the seeking of revolution. Operationally, that meant following Stalin's directions, no matter how contradictory to previously cherished values. New peace movements were begun, but they were not successful. War quickly erupted in Europe after the September 1939 invasion of Poland by Germany. Pacifism in this context was at best a rearguard battle that sought to maintain American noninvolvement. The new line suddenly changed again in 1941, not in December when the Japanese attacked Pearl Harbor, but half a year earlier. The new line sought direct American involvement in the European war—antifascism again—and Communists in the labor movement began urging a no-strike agreement to assist the war effort. What had happened? Russia had been invaded by Germany in June of 1941.

During the Second World War the American Communist party put aside the revolution for the war effort. After the war it faced the growing anticommunist hostility of the Cold War; the hysteria of the McCarthy era in the early 1950s; and the hardening of American attitudes during the brief Korean conflict, which was believed to be a struggle between democracy and communism. All this was carried over into the Vietnam struggle as a justification for direct American intervention. Within the party factional in-fighting continued, along with following the Soviet lead in international affairs. The events of 1956 that culminated in the Russian invasion of Hungary failed to shake the pro-Soviet stance of many party faithful—but not all. Many more members left the group. The weakened party gradually recovered from the American government's understandable charge that it was in fact an agency of a foreign government, but it remained a broken reed.

This did not mean that the party was entirely without life, for a measure of continued vitality was demonstrated in the early 1970s when allegiance was given to the group by Angela Davis. She is a black intellectual who became involved in the aftermath of the violent 1970 escape attempt of three black prisoners in California. The attractiveness of the American Communist party to Angela Davis may have been the result of its long attempts to secure the support of radical blacks, but it was more likely the party's resurrection of its antifascist position linked to its opposition to American activity in Vietnam. Antiracism fit that frame of reference very well, and the party could also refer to its earlier work against fascism. Angela Davis, writing with Bettina Aptheker, put it in the following words:

> Fascism represents the triumph of the counter-revolution, that is, fascism is the preventive counter-revolution to the socialist transformation of society. With the advent of fascism the exploitation of the working class is infinitely more intense and buttressed by extreme forms of terrorist suppression. . . .
>
> The fascist thrust must be resisted in its incipient stages by the broadest possible coalition, before it has an opportunity to consolidate its power; and the democratic, radical essence of the anti-fascist movement is likewise the prerequisite for the success of the revolutionary movement.[11]

The link between fascism and racism provided a modest increase in membership for the party, but this was a small part of the *Black Liberation* movement. Insistence by blacks on leading their own drive for equality, an independence that peaked in the late 1960s, caused most blacks to ignore the Communist party, even though there was general agreement that the struggle against racism was also a struggle against fascism.

The New Left

The antifascist approach was also utilized by Herbert Marcuse, not as a justification for membership in the Communist party, but as a reason for continued revolutionary activity independent of the party. Monopoly capitalism, Marcuse insisted, had reproduced itself in the consumer society of the present, wherein the satisfaction of material needs for the majority had been accomplished at the expense of even greater exploitation of the working masses. Behind the facade of the consumer society lurked a repression that could easily lead to a fascist counterrevolutionary society.[12] Using even sharper language, Murray Bookchin, reflecting on the necessity of the production of waste in the consumer society, wrote that a century ago scarcity had to be endured, but today it has to be enforced; hence the importance of the state in present-day life, enforcing a scarcity that is no longer necessary.[13] Marcuse is a Marxist Socialist, and Bookchin is an anarchist Socialist. Both critiques of existing society come out of the general Marxist tradition without being a product of the intervening communist parties. They are examples of a larger, but vaguely defined, movement called the New Left which presented a radical new critique of advanced capitalism as an authoritarian (fascist), irrational, and barbaric society. Because the New Left did not base itself on Soviet practice and particularly rejected any identification with Stalinism, the movement represented a new, generally Marxist alternative to Bolshevism.

The American New Left had its origins in the civil rights movement of the 1960s. Black activists seeking equal rights and privileges in the southern United States, frustrated by the lack of progress through the courts, began to sit in at segregated lunch counters and refused to ride buses which separated passengers' seats by the color of a person's skin. This new struggle caught the imagination of students on northern university campuses. Most of these students were simply idealistic; some, however, soon became radicalized by the apparent hopelessness of the struggle for equal rights in the face of organized, closed-minded opposition. Racism as experienced by blacks became in many cases a fascism experienced by whites as well, partially voiding Julius Lester's charge that what blacks felt in their guts whites could only feel in their minds.[14]

This radicalizing activity coincided with demonstrations against American anti-Castro involvement in Cuba, and for a nuclear test ban that would prohibit nuclear testing in the atmosphere. By mid-decade the escalation of American involvement in Vietnam changed the focus of the movement to antiwar demonstrations as a part of the same struggle for equality. The struggle for black rights expanded into a critique of imperialistic government activities abroad—a critique of what was perceived as an authoritarian power structure so perverted that it was blind to the rational and ethical basis of the criticism. The more heated the American involvement in Vietnam became, the more intense was the opposition raised against it. This led to charges that the New Left was part of a communist conspiracy; to vast increases in surveillance by the FBI; and eventually to bullets and death at Jackson State and Kent State universities in 1970.

The hardening opposition of the New Left to American governmental policies led it to seek identification and purpose in the ideology of non-Soviet, anti-American communism, ignoring what did not fit, and often redefining what did. Cuba became a very popular cause, and Che Guevara became a romantic hero—a person who appeared to be putting Marx's and Lenin's ideas into revolutionary practice on behalf of the common people. China in the midst of the cultural revolution was admired by some as another model. This was not so much an ideological agreement as it was an identification with the revolutionary activity in countries by people who were similarly against the foreign policies of the United States. The reductionist formula of "whoever is against what I am against must be on my side" was not seriously analyzed. Admiration of the democratic humanism in Marxism and of revolutionary romanticism combined to make the movement sound more communistic than it really was.

Some students became involved in the New Left for selfish reasons, others for moral reasons, but both groups wished personally to avoid the draft and Vietnam. Once having made the decision that American involvement there was wrong, the decision to avoid the draft became a moral necessity. Sometimes encouraged by faculty too old to make the decision for themselves, and often encouraged by peers, draft resistance mounted. Indeed, so focused did the movement become around the issues of draft and resistance to the war that the strength of the New Left dissipated with the end of military conscription and open American involvement in Vietnam.

Although the movement was short-lived and was concentrated in a few major cities, it was sufficiently widespread both in space and time so that a general idea of its philosophy can be pulled together. However, this is a *general* idea of its philosophy, for the movement was never organized into a single entity, even though its opponents believed this. As an alternative to Bolshevism or to the American Communist party, which occasionally tried to use it, the New Left was not as sharply defined an alternative as it might have been.

A major reason for this lack of coherent organization was the strong anti-authority component in both its methodology and its goal of participatory democracy. The New Leftists felt that advanced capitalist societies were authoritarian to the core, and they reacted against this in at least two ways. Their method of attaining their goals resisted the authoritarianism of Lenin, and partially resisted the authoritarian suggestions of Marcuse. Also, their belief that future goals should be made part of the present as quickly as possible pushed them into attempted implementation of participatory democracy, while still involved in the struggle. This resulted in very long meetings where everyone had a chance to speak and usually did. No one claimed that this was particularly efficient or that progress was always made. However, it was more efficient than it sounds, and progress had a suspicious ring to it—connoting the progress in advanced capitalism—the endless production and pursuit of unnecessary luxuries with which people identified in a twentieth-century version of materialistic alienation. Their goal of participatory democracy for the future was also anti-authority, calling for a system of decentralized, autonomous communities which would be controlled from below rather than from above—communities characterized by equality rather than class relationships. This required an eventual destruction of private property and wage labor, as well as of hierarchical social relationships. The anti-authoritarian side of Marx was emphasized and the authoritarian side was ignored.

Participatory democracy meant openness and spontaneity to the New Left; it meant people in control of their own lives in a real rather than illusory democracy. It meant a willingness to experiment with new life styles and to revise old ways of doing things. Unfortunately this liberalism (often) did not extend to the older generation, which was perceived to be part of the problem rather than part of the solution. Some of this hostility was created by the older generation, more conditioned to the struggle against communism than the young. However, some of it was also created by the younger generation, which was sufficiently ideological to feel that only they knew the truth—an authoritarianism that tolerated no compromise and undercut the potential openness of their participatory democracy.

Standing in the way of these new goals was the entire bourgeois culture. Some felt this could be changed by their protest activities. Others believed that meaningful change was impossible and sought to drop out entirely. Demands for a nonrepressive society took several forms. Immediate implementation of nonrepressiveness resulted in communal living experiments; greater sexual freedom; longer hair; free universities with more relevant courses; freer expressiveness; and the desire to live more natural lives—for example, fewer cosmetics, organic farming, and environmental concerns. These attempts to establish a less repressive society in the present with its own unnoticed conformity of jeans and long hair, coincided with the New Left's attacks on a system they perceived as riddled with hypocrisy.

The older generation, which felt disgust at four letter words in print, seldom appeared to notice the obscenity of glorying in Vietnamese body counts. An alleged struggle for democracy in a far-off country conflicted with the failure to practice democracy at home. The regime for which Americans were dying was viewed as a corrupt dictatorship which denied political freedom to its own opposition, a characterization which some made about the United States' government as well. New Leftists felt that professors were teaching them about objectivity and academic noninvolvement while their own universities were contributing to international racism in distant countries through their secret investment policies. Optimistic discussions about progress and the life beautiful in so-called enlightened and advanced countries were seen as smug hypocrisy, for the school buildings were often located in the middle of appalling slums.[15] Euphemisms about progress in racial integration, while de facto and de jure racism still permeated so much of life for American minority groups, were not acceptable.

The New Left discovered that the university was not an ivory tower untouched by the corruption they discovered elsewhere, but was often in fact engaged in research projects that assisted governmental policies—perpetuating class divisions throughout the world. Soon, the movement included these schools in their indictment. Demands for general freedoms in a more unrepressive society also became demands for an end to university parentalism, uncensored student newspapers, and more relevant academic courses. Occasionally this demand for greater freedom resulted in student attempts to *curtail* the freedom of a professor to teach by disrupting the class. The new freedoms, as with Rousseau, required that others be forced to be just as free—another signal of authoritarianism to which the New Left as well as the old was not immune. Freedom to publish without censorship often degenerated into mere attempts to shock the older generation with the use of street language.

The movement appeared to be national, especially if one lived near one of the major centers of dissent, such as the University of California at Berkeley or Columbia in New York City. It had international components as well. Students in Italy seized the initiative in 1967 and 1968. France nearly had a full-scale revolution when students joined workers in May of 1968. In the same year Belgrade students rioted and seized buildings. It seemed as though authority was being challenged everywhere.

Religious authority was also being attacked in a variety of ways. Religious professionals, Protestant, Jewish, and Catholic, were often found in the forefront of the struggle—much to the dismay of their more conservative superiors. One example of this involvement was that of Father James Groppi, who led a fight for better housing for Milwaukee blacks. His activity on behalf of this cause drew an amazing hostility from opponents. When asked what his parishioners thought about his activities, Father Groppi replied that his parishioners were here—he was with them. "I refuse to remain in the rectory and pray my breviary while my people are hungry, while my people are receiving third-rate educations, while my people are being relegated to secondary status in this racist society."[16] This and other attempts to humanize the churches often conflicted with the more established parishioners' concepts of moral authority. The new activists began to see that practicing the religion often appeared to their church members as of less importance than the maintenance of a moralistic framework for the status quo. Some activists began leaving the religious profession, others remained to continue the struggle against great opposition.

A criticism of the New Left often heard in the 1960s was that while the goals sought might be desirable, the method of seeking those goals—through demonstrations which often resulted in violent confrontations with police and/or angry citizen opponents—was inappropriate, dangerous, and counterproductive. However, the movement felt it had no choice if it was to make its voice heard. Even with demonstrations and protest marches there were few successes, and the search for a more authentically human society was often lost in media concentration on conflicts between police and demonstrators. This became a self-fulfilling prophecy in the sense that it often appeared that the struggle for humanity had become a struggle against police. Nonetheless, the increased bombing of both North and South Vietnam, with the continued promise of peace, created frustrations of enormous magnitude, which led to more confrontations. Because it came to such open conflict so often, the movement and the opposition developed stereotypical models—"pigs" versus "commie freaks." Well-meaning people sat down in front of school buses because they were convinced that within-city busing to achieve equity in education was a communist conspiracy of some sort. Urging people to assert their democratic privileges against government policies in Vietnam was called a communist plot to undermine American unity. Conversely, even traffic policemen were ridiculed as oppressors who enforced a domestic imperialism. Each side encouraged the other either to over-defend authority and unity as the only hope for the future or excessively condemn it as an evil in American life.

Even though radicalized into appearing to have a coherent ideology, the New Left was more a search for a comprehensive theory than the explication of one. Very often when movement representatives were asked by either friendly or hostile questioners what sort of replacement they had in mind for the future, the answers were vague and utopian. If they were to be pulled together from scattered or unconnected sources they would constitute a list like the following:

1) The elimination of a labor which is enforced and determined by the private needs of monopoly capital rather than by the rational social needs of the population. The work process would be automated, the market system abolished, and work would be turned into self-actualizing, socially rewarding endeavors.

2) The creation of a nonrepressive society, converting needs into desires, and transforming genital sexuality to an eroticizing of the whole human personality and its entire social milieu—in short, a freeing of sexuality from repression.[17]

3) The creation of decentralized and fully libertarian communities where people could fully realize themselves through the realization of the social good.

4) The abolition of cultural ethnocentrism and the creation of a worldwide community characterized by love and understanding rather than by economic greed.

5) The transcendence of private property, a collective or social ownership of the means of production and the use of these social economic forces for the peace and harmony of the earth rather than for war and suffering.

6) The erection of new, experimental paradigms for social living—such as the extended family structure used in Tanzania—and communes.[18]

The search for these goals led to a critique of "national interest" as the narrow economic interest of American capitalism, giving a Marxist character to the criticism. The attacks on profits, however, began as a criticism of the use of those profits to finance wars, future wasteful production, and the creation of artificial needs. This improper use of profits was felt to be a result of the monopolistic concentration of capital into corporate giants. Attacks on monopolies and profits, combining with the search for a nonrepressive society, created a revival of the humanistic Marx which the traditional leftist parties had long neglected. Those older groups, isolated and discredited by the Cold War, polarized around issues that arose from the Russian and Chinese revolutions and had little of significance to say about the key issue to the New Left—the quality of life in the United States. The older parties were described as having a ". . . fixation on a frozen Marxism, Leninism, or Trotskyism [which] blinds them to the most current developments of advanced capitalism. Moreover, their organizational structure tends to reduplicate that of the existing order, making them unappealing as an alternative."[19]

The movement had a basis in Marxism, but the New Left ably demonstrated that it was quite prepared to force the Marxian framework to yield new answers to what were perceived as twentieth-century problems. It also questioned some of the older answers. Was the working class still the agent class of the revolution even though hopelessly enmeshed in the bourgeois system? Some felt that it was; others began to think about a proletarianized student class, or blacks and other minority groups. Did the advanced character of American capitalism preclude rather than demand a proletarian type of revolution? Perhaps a revolution would recreate the same patterns of inhumane authority—what then would be gained? This led some to conclude that incremental reforms of the existing, more familiar system were preferable to the polarizing and radicalizing violence of a revolution. The questions continued, and what was being illustrated was that major legacies of the apparently subdued New Left include an openness in the interpretations of Marxism; a willingness to question the Holy Texts of orthodox revolutionary thought; and a willingness to experiment with new solutions and life styles which seeks to bring theory more in tune with a practice based on contemporary analysis. This may yet result in a coherent revolutionary or reformist ideology that builds on the past traditions and struggles, rather than merely an echo of them.

Although a distinctive ideology has not resulted from the New Left, a great deal of reform in the early 1970s emerged out of the movement's diffusion into all aspects of contemporary life. The Women's Liberation movement, with roots in the nineteenth century, received a tremendous impetus when leftist women became dissatisfied with a subordinate role in the New Left movement and pushed out on their own. This movement has broadened into a general appeal for a more humanized society for both sexes. The Black Liberation movement that gave the New Left its beginnings in the 1960s separated from the movement in the latter half of the decade as black consciousness and pride insisted on an independence from all white assistance. Nonetheless there is a considerable overlap between the two movements, and in both a search for new answers to old Marxian questions. Both movements have given encouragement and support to the liberation movements of other minority groups, such as Caesar Chevez's attempts to unionize migrant Chicano laborers and Dennis Bank's AIM Indian movement. Businessmen also seem to be more aware of their social obligations in the 1970s.

The overlap provided by a generalized leftist ideology is, however, insufficient to overcome the fragmentation of the New Left. This frustration has resulted in some underground revolutionary activities that have resorted to the terroristic tactics of political kidnappings and assassinations, both in Latin America and the United States. These tactics gain publicity for the underground revolutionaries as well as funds for continued activity. However, the authoritarian, militaristic style of a group such as the *Simbianese Liberation Army,* the group responsible for the kidnapping of Patricia Hearst in California, is just as likely to be disavowed as admired by the remnants of the New Left. Escalating inflation and a very tight job market, as well as the end to the open American involvement in Vietnam, have made the student leftists of the 1970s much quieter and students in general less willing to participate in demonstrations.

This is only partly due to an increase in student conservatism. It is also because the targets for an antifascist movement are much less visible in the 1970s.[20] American soldiers are not fighting Vietnamese any longer, even though American military and economic aid to South Vietnam continues at a very high level. Regarding China, her recognition and admission to the United Nations removed that particular issue. Maintaining the detente with the Soviet Union appears to reduce the threat of nuclear war, even though the arms race continues. Affirmative Action programs at universities and in American business have given some evidence of alterations in discriminatory hiring practices, blunting the sharp edges of inequality of opportunity. American businessmen learned to publicize their concerns about the environment and energy conservation in such a way as to give them almost a non-profit-seeking motive and a socially concerned image. Less visible targets which required more time and effort to analyze were soon left to the "experts" such as consumer advocate, Ralph Nader, thus dulling the revolutionary edge of the New Left movement.

The United States thus provided an example of a Bolshevized, ineffective Communist party and a disorganized, less ideological alternative struggle from below that became known as the New Left. Does the quiet first half of the 1970s signal an end to Marxist ideology as a vitalizing force for criticism of existing life styles? Are communist societies going to become more capitalistic and the bourgeois societies more socialistic in some sort of "convergence," as many people are beginning to think? Does that potential convergence create an illusion of socialism that will sweep the Marxian dream rather than the capitalist state into the dustbin of history? Answers to these questions are difficult and speculative, but the attempt must be made.

Suggested Readings

Bell, Daniel. *Marxian Socialism in the United States*. Princeton: Princeton University Press, 1952 and 1967.

Califano, Joseph A., Jr. *The Student Revolution*. New York: W. W. Norton, 1970.

Deutscher, Isaac. *Marxism in Our Time*. Berkeley: Ramparts Press, 1971.

Fairfield, Richard. *Communes, USA—A Personal Tour*. Baltimore: Penguin Books, 1972.

Jennes, Linda, ed. *Feminism and Socialism*. New York: Pathfinder Press, 1971.

Marcuse, Herbert. *One-Dimensional Man*. Boston: Beacon Press, 1964.

Sargent, Lyman T. *New Left Thought: An Introduction*. Homewood, Ill.: Dorsey Press, 1972.

Zablocki, Benjamin. *The Joyful Community*. Baltimore: Pelican Books, 1971.

NOTES

[1]This raises the interesting question (anathema to many Marxists) as to whether Marxism is at all applicable where Marx thought it was: in the developed countries. History after Marx has demonstrated the opposite: an applicability to semideveloped countries in the crisis of modernization.

[2]See Melvyn Dubofsky, *We Shall Be All: A History of the Industrial Workers of the World* (Chicago: Quadrangle Books, 1969), for a sympathetic account of the attempts to implement radical syndicalism by the IWW.

[3]Ibid., p. 424.

[4]Theodore Draper, *American Communism and Soviet Russia: The Formative Period* (New York: Viking Press, 1960), p. 20.

[5]Ibid., pp. 20-21.

[6]"Statement of Principles and Organization Rules of the Federated Farmer-Labor Party," *Voice of Labor*, 14 July 1923, p. 6; cited in ibid., p. 48.

[7]Draper has documented the abruptness of the change in tactics. A cablegram from Moscow, published in the American communist newspaper, *Daily Worker*, 16 May 1924, called for vigorous Worker Party activity to bring about the alliance with LaFollette. Just four days later, May 20, an opposite decision was reached in Moscow. See *American Communism and Soviet Russia*, p. 113 and n. 54 (p. 460).

[8]Lewis S. Feuer, *Marx and the Intellectuals: A Set of Post-Ideological Essays* (Garden City: Doubleday Anchor Books, 1969), p. 102. See also pp. 103-104. Reprinted by permission of Doubleday & Company, Inc.

[9]Daniels, *A Documentary History of Communism* 2: 99.

[10]Clark's letter of resignation, *Daily Worker*, 9 September 1957; cited in ibid., p. 253.

[11]From *If They Come In The Morning*, edited by Angela Y. Davis. Copyright © 1971 by the National United Committee to Free Angela Davis, pp. 4-5. Reprinted with permission of The Third Press—Joseph Okpaku Publishing Co., Inc. See pp. 5-6, where this new position is tied to the antifascist statement of Georgi Dimitrov at the Seventh Congress of the Comintern in 1935. This statement is repeated later (p. 35) in reference to the struggle to free political prisoners. This conveniently ignores both previous and subsequent policy shifts by the party.

[12]Herbert Marcuse, *Counter Revolution and Revolt* (Boston: Beacon Press, 1972), pp. 1-24.

[13]Murray Bookchin, "Post-Scarcity Anarchy," in Arthur Lothstein, ed., *"All We Are Saying . . ."—The Philosophy of the New Left* (New York: Capricorn Books, 1970), p. 348.

[14]Julius Lester, *Revolutionary Notes* (New York: Richard W. Baron, 1969), p. 45.

[15]This was partially responsible for Columbia's riots in 1968, and it was definitely the ignition for the Paris revolts of May 1968, when the new section of Paris University was opened in the industrial slum called Petit Nanterre, a section of Nanterre, France.

[16]James E. Groppi, "The Place of a Priest," in *The Age of Protest,* ed. Walt Anderson (Pacific Palisades, Cal.: Goodyear 1969), p. 217. This is a reprint of Groppi's "Open Housing: The Fight in the Streets," *Humanist* (July-August, 1968).

[17]This resembled very much the thinking of an earlier, nearly unremembered Marxist-Freudian named Wilhelm Reich, who felt that sexual repression was a basic barrier to human development. For an interesting description, see Eustace Chesser, *Salvation Through Sex, The Life and Work of Wilhelm Reich* (New York: William Morrow, 1973).

[18]The six points are drawn, with only modest changes, from a list prepared by Arthur Lothstein in his Introduction to *"All We Are Saying,"* p. 21. The utopian goals constitute a partial list of seven descriptive points about the New Left in his sympathetic analysis. Reprinted by permission of the publisher.

[19]Ronald Aronson and John C. Cowley, "The New Left in the United States," in Lothstein, ed., *"All We Are Saying,"* p. 36. Copyright © The Merlin Press, Ltd., 1967. Reprinted by permission of Monthly Review Press.

[20]As students of revolution realize, this device is a most effective neutralizer of revolutionary attitudes—bringing great credit to the reformer without solving the basic problem.

12

Toward the Twenty-First Century: Marxism in the Future

An analysis of the past that ends with the present is incomplete. The future is neither as impenetrable nor as inevitable as it sometimes appears. It demands probing, so as to sense present trends and potential human conduct in order to guide development into the right channels. The scope of potential disagreement about what those channels ought to be is less wide than one might think. The increasing global interdependence of people of all races and areas, as well as between humans and their environment, suggests that the last quarter of the twentieth century might well see the end of past divisions and the beginning of a new age of cooperation.

This has already begun in that the relations between the countries formerly involved in the Cold War have improved sharply. Russia and the United States are trading with each other much more than in the past, and the leaders of each country are beginning to visit each other's capital on a regular basis. Countries in Eastern and Western Europe, as well as Japan and the United States are increasingly involved with each other in trade agreements. China and Japan are expanding their trade relations, and China and America have established diplomatic relations whose underlying purpose is trade as well as increasing both countries' maneuverability in relation to the Soviet Union. Cuba is becoming less isolated from the United States and from the other Latin American countries. A complete normalization of American-Cuban relations appears probable, in keeping with American detente relations with China and Russia. The long years of Cold War ideological separatism between communist and noncommunist areas—artificially vitalized by external military operations such as Vietnam and Czechoslovakia—are steadily phasing into a period of detente which is only occasionally ruffled by rivalries in the Middle East.

This has prompted some to speak of convergence, a word suggesting that Socialism is becoming more capitalistic and that Capitalism is becoming more socialistic or that both kinds of societies are evolving toward a similar goal. This is apparently supported by the easing of Cold War tensions; an apparently greater consumer orientation in the Soviet economy; and an apparently more viable concern for social welfare in the American. The concepts of convergence, however, unless great care is taken with their explication, perpetuate loose understandings of both socialism and capitalism.[1] In several senses the two systems have always been similar to each other, especially when comparing practice rather than theory. Those who speak of convergence often possess an uncritical optimism about that merger, as though it will undoubtedly mean something positive. This is not necessarily so. If radical charges of fascism in American policy making are correct, or in the next few years this style of government is created, the convergence of an authoritarian America with a similar Soviet Union would hardly be a positive step. Rather, it would be a situation to be devoutly avoided. If convergence lies in the future, it is vital to ask *what kind?*

What sort of world *should* be created in the next twenty-five years? This question implies that people have options—that they have some power over what is going to happen. This is an assumption with which Marxism agrees.

> Marxist humanism starts from the real individual and real society, and its doctrine is based on the assumption that man, in the course of *transforming* objective reality, *creates* his own world and indirectly influences his own development. Hence this humanism is consistently *autonomous* in the sense of interpreting the human world as a result of the play of its own forces, without resorting to any ultra-humanism and thus heteronomous forces.[2]

This also implies that Marxism is not an outmoded set of ideas. Although heavily tarnished by adaptations and interpretations, the promise of Marxism and communism remains to be realized. The potential implementation of that humanism, however, requires significant alterations in the way that Marxism and communism are understood.

The history of Marxist communism during the past century has clearly revealed that the ideas which Karl Marx felt to be clear, scientific, and pragmatic were only partially so. This has resulted in interpretations and applications of his ideas that were widely varied. The confusion and ambiguity implicit in Marxism did not help—an ambiguity which was amplified by developments after Marx's death. His ideas served as the basis for both reform and revolutionary movements, neither of which attained his goals of a communal-humanist society. The reform movements remain a part of the same old society where the private extraction of profit still depletes social wealth to the disadvantage of the majority. Revolutionary movements created allegedly new societies, but at the expense of a vast increase in the power of their state apparatus over the lives of their citizens. In other places, as in Eastern Europe, Marxism-Leninism was imposed by force from the outside as an authoritarian system of control by a more powerful neighboring nation. The reform movements differ from each other considerably, as well as from the revolutionary ones. The latter also differ from each other, with exceptional vehemence at times. Clearly, not all of Marx's ideas were correct.

These problems of interpretation and adaption that have already occurred would not have arisen if Marx had been correct in his predictive assumptions. Historical materialism, he felt, demonstrated that the height of human alienation had been reached in his own day, and that the representative of that materially alienated humanity was the newly emerging class in the capitalist relations of production—the proletariat. The working class symbolized material alienation just as religion symbolized alienation in the mental sphere. Marx concluded that the giant contradiction between the great wealth controlled by the few and the vast, miserable poverty of the productive majority would be exacerbated by technological advances until the consciousness of its unnecessary servitude would impel the proletariat to create a new human society on the ashes of the old. This new society would produce collective products for use rather than for exchange. Following a rational world plan, social production would provide the wealth or abundance that would undergird the freedom and peaceful unity between peoples and between humans and nature.

Although conceding that there would be a necessity for the use of state power after the revolution, Marx believed that this would be temporary. As soon as the classlessness of the new society made itself felt in the social milieu in which people developed their characters, the new human-social life style would fully emerge. Social wealth, previously drained by the private extraction of profit and hampered by the chaos of capitalist production, would then be able to grow unhindered. The new society was for humans and was to be run by them—democratically. Alienation would phase into human fulfillment.

This promise has never been fulfilled. The revolution that Marx envisaged never occurred. The longer the imagined revolution took to come, the more necessary it became to explain why it was so long delayed, yet why it must still come. The Marxist movement gradually became the province of those who could explain the delay in international revolution and at the same time suggest Marxist-sounding strategies for the intervening period. What had begun as a scientific attempt to explain the past, so as to be able to chart the direction of the future, became an institutionalized ideology as those predictions failed to materialize. What Marx was often willing to change, such as the necessity of violence in the coming revolution, could no longer be altered so easily. What Marx had not changed, tended to freeze into position.

In a sense this resembled the early Christian church's development of the set of ideas called Christianity. The early Christians hoped for an imminent return of Jesus to earth. When this failed to materialize, the delay had to be explained in such a way as not to challenge the basic presuppositions of agreement that had begun the movement. The general agreement had to become belief based on faith. One belief led to another, and before long an immense edifice of theology had been constructed. Although a great deal of what Jesus was reported to have said was in reference to local conditions and circumstances, these words had to be universalized both geographically and temporally as the ideas were taught in different areas and the centuries passed. The result for many Christians was the creation of a petrified forest of ideas—eternally immobile—and subsequent questioning became heresy.

Something similar happened to Marxism and to many Marxists. It was particularly visible in the Third International's repeated genuflections to the Soviet "official line." Although those days are past and there appears to be a great deal more openness in the thinking of Marxists, much of the ideological-institutionalized character remains. Whereever this is true, Marxism is an ideology or false consciousness which inhibits the cardinal principle of praxis—criticism of one's own ideas in the light of new data. To the extent that Marxism is this kind of ideology it is a movement in which pious practitioners lead the unthinking faithful in irrelevant homage to outmoded ideas, reifying its own principles by treating its abstractions—such as the dialectic or the revolutionary proletariat—as more real than the empirical reality from which the abstractions were first drawn. What is more important —the humanism that motivated Karl Marx to become a revolutionary theorist or the correctness of historical materialism?

Consider the working class. This group symbolized human alienation because its relation to the means of production was one of servitude. However, *all* positions relative to the means of production were alienated, not only the proletariat. Capitalists were also alienated.[3] Certainly, if the extent of alienation were the test of proletarianness, minority groups in the last half of the twentieth century would better fit that category. The continued preoccupation of Marxists with the proletariat, as the best example of human estrangement in times long after Marx's day, ignores the great changes that have taken place in the conditions of that class. It has organized for the most part into strong unions which give it great economic strength, and it has formed a fairly cohesive political force in contemporary politics, precisely where Marx thought it would be most revolutionary. Workers are much better educated than previously, more technically oriented, higher paid, and working in improved conditions. Are they still the symbol of alienated humanity? In the sense of their relation to the means of production as nonowners they are still such a symbol, but not nearly as obviously as during Marx's day. Other groups such as blacks, Chicanos, American Indians on reservations, or women, constitute more obvious examples of alienation and servitude than do workers. To the extent that Marxist literature continues to force these other groups into a proletarian mold, or is preoccupied exclusively with working-class concerns, the movement has reified the proletarian concept. This inhibits a Marxist's ability to sense the more generalized alienation, that Herbert Marcuse has described, and the potential worsening of that alienation on a worldwide scale in the future.[4]

Such a rigid understanding of Marxism is simplistic and dogmatic. Louis Althusser, a contemporary French Communist, is an example of a Marxist who believes rather than analyzes. However, he covers this with a skillful use of words to actually reverse Marx's humanism, which he characterizes as coming from the early "Hegelian" period. The older Marx, in the view of Althusser, expressed a philosophical antihumanism. The modern movement to socialist humanism, he concludes, is the taking of the need for a theory for the theory itself; the rejection of the "older" Marx of *Capital* berefts the Marxist of his proper theory, leaving only the need for theory which humanism fills.

> The philosophical humanism which might easily become a threat to us and which shelters behind the unprecedented achievements of socialism itself, is this complement which, in default of theory, is destined to give certain Marxist ideologues the *feeling* of the theory that they lack; a feeling that cannot lay claim to that most precious of all the things Marx gave us—the possibility of scientific knowledge.[5]

The scientific knowledge that Althusser values is not a contemporary analysis so much as it is the extension into the present of the nineteenth-century model that Marx used: the class analysis of society with its divisions into workers and owners. The imperfections of the fit between model and reality can be ignored because the model is an object of belief rather than a result of scientific knowledge. Science is equivalent to Marxism-Leninism for Althusser, and communism is the Soviet version. The communist society, to which the Russians claimed to aspire at the end of the twenty-year program beginning in 1961, is little more than an attempt to pass production levels achieved in the United States years ago.[6] Thus, the party would remain in a dominant position in the society. Yet Louis Althusser can describe this in glowing terms.

> The communism to which the Soviet Union is committed is a world without economic exploitation, without violence, without discrimination—a world opening up before the Soviets the infinite vistas of progress, of science, of culture, of bread and freedom, of free development. . . .[7]

Even in the future society of socialism-communism, Althusser insists, human adaptation to its condition cannot be left to spontaneity. It must be constantly dominated and controlled.[8] The class division of society is no longer the abstraction describing the real, but the real itself, justifying divisive social conflict which terminates in a still manipulated society. Humanism, on the other hand, does not have to fit the ideological, non-scientific mold that Althusser created for it. Marx constructed his scientific theories *out of his humanism*. He did not later ignore it—he built on it. The same possibility exists today.

A second French Communist, André Gorz, bridges the gap between institutionalized ideology and scientific theory. He defines socialism as the subordination of the purpose and methods of production to human needs and development.[9] Although still speaking in the jargon of traditional Marxist class divisions, Gorz adds a significant amount of humanism and shows a greater ability to distinguish changes in the working class. His strategy for the achievement of socialism is mass political and labor organization and activity which he feels will bring about a common consciousness of shared needs among people both at work and at home. The demonstrations and strikes will challenge the basic model and mechanics of capitalist accumulation in the name of a socialism based on public service, and operate according to a democratic plan which reflects human needs and priorities rather than the expansion of monopolies.[10] The new strategy will have to develop a distinctive anticapitalist alternative with strategically scaled and economically coherent objectives, including the demand for self-management. This will increase the attractiveness of the socialist alternative to the more technically oriented working people who resist being ordered about in their work and who now work for capitalism because they have no other outlet for their talents. Gorz thus hopes to make the road to socialism more realistic and more in keeping with the anti-authority attitudes characteristic of today's better-educated working class.[11]

Gorz's socialist goal is also democratic. He writes that the goals of Marxism cannot be achieved

> ... unless the power of decision passes out of the hands of capital into those of workers. This goal will not be reached merely through nationalization (which risks turning into no more than bureaucratic governmentalization) of the centers of accumulation of capital and credit: it also requires the multiplication of centers of democratic decision making and their autonomy; that is to say, a complex and coordinated network of regional and local autonomous bodies.[12]

First a request for a more scientific theory from Althusser's statements, and now demands by Gorz for a society humanized both by its goals and by its methods of local and regional decision centers. A Marxism applicable to the future is beginning to emerge.

Another contributer to this development is a third French Communist, Roger Garaudy, expelled from the French Central Committee in February of 1970. The medium through which Garaudy seeks to update Marxism is the dialectic. He does not reify the concept. The dialectic, Garaudy writes, is not merely a vehicle for critical explanations of the past and a device to obscure the present, as with Stalin. The dialectic is as much the art of forming questions as it is the method of finding answers to them. Dialectical thinking is reasoning that continues to grow because it is in constant touch with reality, and the real is not an immutable datum but a world in constant genesis. A reasoning process that seeks to form realistic models must challenge itself to continual reforming of the problems in correspondence to new situations. One ought not to give successive answers to the same question, but must completely recast the very formulation of the question that one is asking.[13]

Dialectical thinking, therefore, must be open-ended. Its purpose is the construction of an order.

> To say that there is a dialectic of nature, is to say that the structure and the movement of reality are such that only a dialectical thought can make phenomena intelligible and allow us to handle them. . . .
>
> At the current stage of the development of the sciences, the representation of the real which emerges from the sum total of confirmed knowledge, is that of an organic whole in constant process not only of development but also of auto-creation. It is this structure that we call "dialectical" as opposed to the mechanistic, metaphysical, concepts which would look on the world as an accumulation of isolated, abstract, elements whose form and movement are external to the matter to which they apply, and in which nothing new appears apart from a new arrangement of the preexisting elements.[14]

This notion of the dialectic places one of the key concepts in traditional Marxism in a different light. Instead of seeing the concept as a device for highlighting divisions in the society, the dialectic becomes the device by which resolution of conflict is sought. The dialectic seeks order and finds that order in the organic wholeness of the universe in a constant process of self-creation. This led Garaudy to appreciate **cybernetics** and information theory as *confirmations* of Marx's dialectical materialism.[15] It also led to the conclusion that cybernetic ordering provided a stimulus to the development of a new humanism—a humanism which Marx pioneered, "integrating all that was won by Graeco-Roman humanism and Judaeo-Christian humanism, and going beyond both in a new synthesis of nature and man, of the external world and subjectivity, of necessary law and liberty.[16]

Is it possible that a new Marxism, a revitalized humanism, can be created? Scientific in the modern sense of a very low tolerance for error? Speaking to modern and potential problems? Maintaining its humanist base through democratic self-management and participatory democracy? Helping to construct an order in society that includes all this and openness to future changes as well? It is possible, but only if it is agreed that Marx's original conceptual categories do not necessarily describe and analyze every social phenomenon that might occur. Adaptations which do not distort the spirit are necessary, even though they alter the letter of original Marxism. The result would be a more open-ended, less ideological Marxism that has at its core the humanist promise. This would make Marx seem less like a union organizer using obscure language and more like an ethical pragmatist; less revolutionary in the old, violent divisive sense, but more revolutionary in the sense of offering solutions that resolve and heal divisions and differences among humans. The net result would be a radical humanism, or better still, using Adam Schaff's phrase, a militant humanism with a categorical imperative to overthrow all conditions in which people are degraded, enslaved, neglected, contemptible beings. This would include all people—not merely a working class which allegedly represents them—but everyone. This militant humanism would seek a resolution of present chaos and conflict, a resolution of abject poverty in the midst of great wealth, and a resolution that has as its goal human fulfillment.

This approach to Marxism asks the questions: what are the contemporary problems that the future decision makers will have to solve? What appear to be the main contradictions in the immediate future that this old-new Marxism can help resolve in a humanist direction? Once the problem is isolated, solutions are possible since humans do not really think of questions until the answers are at hand.

The problem in the contemporary world that overshadows all the rest is a problem of faulty perception. It is a failure to see—and to act appropriately in the light of that knowledge—the evolving global system of interrelations. The consequences of that faulty perception and behavior have created imbalances between population and resources; between highly productive and less productive areas of the world; and between highly developed technology and low levels of social organization no longer adequate to their task. Unless this problem is faced and solutions implemented, the imbalances threaten to become crises and create a spectre far more fearful than the spectre of communism to the Europe of Marx's day. Furthermore, unless the situation is resolved in a humanist direction, to which a modern Marxist (and a modern Christian as well) can make an important contribution, the alternatives are anarchy or **totalitarianism.**

The imbalance resulting from faulty perceptions of global interdependence can be expressed in a variety of ways. Over 80 percent of the world's production is achieved by one-third of the world's population. This one-third of the total world population lives in an energy-wasting lifestyle where the production of obsolescence seems to be a necessary way of life. This capitalism, whether state or private, apparently has to continue expanding or it loses its dynamism, but this expansion is at the expense of depleted world resources. Over two-thirds of the world's population live in the less productive areas, producing only one-sixth of the world's goods. Here another dimension of the same problem exists, for this area produces something that is equally energy consumptive: excessive populations in relation to available resources. If the industrial countries' growth rates do not strip the world of available resources and foul it with industrial pollution, it seems evident that the rest of the world will soon accomplish the same end as a result of far too many people.

This situation is not particularly amenable to reform-type suggestions. Demands for slower population growth in the less developed areas that are made by industrial countries appear to have racial overtones, in the sense that white dominance of the world is threatened by such population growth. This is true. What is often forgotten, however, is that the large populations will inherit heavy problems. Accusations from less developed areas that the rate of economic growth of industrialized nations is too rapid and consuming too many resources, and the activities designed to secure a bigger share in world wealth through nationalization of foreign operations appear to the developed countries as attempts to rob them of their legitimate wealth. This is also true, but what the developed countries neglect to remember is the global interdependence of their economies. Selfishness may have short-run gratifications, but it will have long-run consequences that will be extremely unpleasant.

The edges of an immense problem that will face human societies in the next few years are already visible in an area where existence has always been marginal—India. Food riots took place in 1974 that were unified protests involving housewives, students, shopkeepers, and farmers protesting the staggering rise in food prices and governmental corruption. The prices of essential commodities such as wheat, rice, and oil have more than doubled in the 1973-74 time period and continue to increase in 1974.[17] The food riots alone accounted for over a hundred deaths, but the prospect for millions of other Indians is very precarious—not because of rioting, but because of acute food shortages. The reasons for the shortages are not local. It is a worldwide imbalance that has not been adequately faced. The visibility of the crisis in India is an indication of the problem facing, first, the entire Asian area, next the Latin American and African areas, and finally the industrialized nations of both the communist and noncommunist nations.[18] It is a global crisis in the making. Creating the ability to perceive the global system of interdependence is, moreover, a prerequisite to imagining solutions to serious imbalances before they turn into full crises.

World food supplies are dependent on annual yields in a way that was not true before. Traditionally, for example, the United States maintained large stocks of reserves which it could use in influencing international food prices or in its aid programs to areas hit by temporary shortages. Those stocks are gone, and so is almost all of the aid program. In America it was formerly the case that large amounts of land were kept out of food production by means of welfare subsidies to farmers. This kept price-depressing surpluses down, and reduced the cost of storing reserves. By 1974 this program had ended as well. Land reserves, unless voluntary and unremunerated, no longer exist. The world is particularly dependent on annual yields from rich agricultural areas such as the United States and Canada. Possible adverse climatic conditions, previously more of a local threat, have now become a global one.

This food situation is exacerbated in a variety of ways by the oil crisis. Worldwide shortages and monopolistic control of petroleum products at the well or pump forced international prices to rise dramatically. Oil companies' large profits, while pleasing to stockholders, are a short-term satisfaction with long-term disastrous potentials. These high prices have so raised the cost of fertilizers that considerably less fertilizer will be used by the poorer countries such as India and other Asian nations. The impact of using less fertilizer is very serious. A million tons of fertilizer is roughly equivalent to 9 to 10 million tons of food grains. A slowdown in fertilizer use, therefore, has staggering geometric implications for the world food supply. Another aspect of the problem is that irrigation systems are often dependent on fuel for the operation of water pumps. Less available fuel, whether through shortages or excessively high prices, means less irrigation, which means less food. This is not an abstract problem in an economics handbook—these are real people faced with a real problem that in India is compounded by an estimated daily population increase of thirty-seven thousand.

The situation is further compounded by the differences in eating habits between the developed countries, especially the United States, and the less developed areas. In a country such as India, people consume an average of approximately 400 pounds of cereal grain per person each year. In the United States the average intake per person is in the neighborhood of 1,850 pounds per year. Making the situation worse is the fact that in a country such as America the food grains are often converted into beef at a tremendous loss in energy that is not compensated for by a corresponding level of protein. It is a tasty habit, but very wasteful. The low income nations might be said to have a labor-intensive agricultural economy, but the high income nations have developed an energy-intensive economy that depletes world resources at a tremendous rate with minimal nutritional gains. As a matter of fact, ". . .the billion people in the rich nations, with Cadillac tastes for livestock products, use practically as much cereal as feed for livestock as the two billion people in the low-income nations use directly as food."[19]

Other dimensions of the interrelated global problem are the monetary flows to the oil-rich nations; great uncertainty about international prices and currencies; potentially critical fluctuations in trade balances; and rising prices that create inflationary spirals in the face of declining energy resources.

This international situation will make the last quarter of this century quite different from the 1960s and early 1970s. Things are no longer viewed in the same way. During the third quarter of the century, for example, the United States became heavily involved in the Vietnam conflict. The ostensible reason was the containment of communism. Preventing the "evil" from taking place took an enormous sacrifice of money, equipment, and lives. Some fifty thousand Americans and over a million Vietnamese were killed. One would think, therefore, that this area was vital to American interests since it was thought that if Vietnam fell to communism, other nations would also fall like dominoes. However, as the dimensions of the new problem have become clearer, this thinking is beginning to change. Discussing the impact of the energy crisis on developing nations, Gerald A. Pollack, one of the Senior Economic Advisers at the Exxon Corporation, recently wrote:

> Thus, the eastern half of the Dark Continent will become darker still and the nations of the subcontinent of Asia will no longer merit the adjective "emerging." These latter countries represent those very dominoes to which the United States has paid such profound attention during the cold war. It seems unlikely that the industrial nations or the oil-rich Arab states will be willing to provide financial support on the scale that could well be necessary to avoid political violence and anarchy in these countries.[20]

The old issues are no longer important. As in the case of the Soviet Union in the period 1918-21, the struggle for socialism (or against socialism) has·

become the struggle for survival. As in Chile during late 1973 and early 1974, the question of civil rights paled next to the question of bread.

Can solutions be found that maintain both bread and freedom? Survival and socialism? If modernized Marxism is to have any impact, the solutions resolving present and future global imbalances and crises must create an order based on the satisfaction of all human needs, consistent with continued survival on the planet earth. For these new requirements, the older, institutionalized Marxism is irrelevant. Of course, the problems of the future that are beginning to become visible can be viewed pessimistically. Dire prophecies of doom are tempting, and probably wrong. However, it is equally incorrect to naïvely believe that new technology will always solve the problems that humans create for themselves. Nonetheless, the problems facing the people of tomorrow are just as much a challenge as danger signals. It is possible that the new crises dialectically create the very possibility for the realization of Marx's vision of socialist humanism. Adam Schaff puts it rather well.

> The technical revolution, which is disintegrating the old world, also holds out the possibility of creating a new world. For the first time in history there is a real chance of making mankind's most ancient dream—a happy life *for all men*—come true. Can this dream be *fully* realized? The future will show: personally I am sceptical. But there is certainly the possibility of a *better, happier* life; this is already a great deal, and more can surely be expected.[21]

These words were written in the mid-1960s. What appeared to Adam Schaff as a possibility now seems a necessity, for the alternative is either chaos or authoritarian protectionism of elite interests. It does not matter which institutionalized ideology provides the authoritarianism, for a humanized society is just as impossible when the secret police call themselves proletarian guardians as when they are obviously protecting capitalist interests. The problem is more than the old traditional Marxist variants can handle. Even if countries such as India are considered the "proletariat" in the worldwide situation, does anyone imagine that a poor-nation overthrow of the industrialized nations would be the harbinger of a new humanist social order? Yet international class war is a possibility that traditional Marxism ought to welcome. Is that not what Marx predicted? However, such an international conflict would kill millions of people, destroy the world's wealth for decades, and result in the nadir—not the height—of civilization's evolution. Physicians used to bleed people to alleviate high blood pressure, but not any more. Virgins were sacrificed to propitiate the gods, but no longer. Marx, both proximate to and enamored of the French Revolution, called for divisive violence to gain human ends, but not any more. Another, more modern solution to world problems can, and must, similarly be found.

General system theory provides a framework for such a solution. More specifically, a general theory of systems applied to the global scale has some promise of a scientific answer, one that seeks resolution rather than disruptive conflict. It is open-ended so that unforeseen situations can be anticipated, and it is a solution compatible with the satisfaction of human needs. A general theory of systems places humanism in a larger, global frame of reference that is an extension of the cybernetics and information theory that intrigued Roger Garaudy at the end of the 1960s.

The word "systems" in a general theory of systems refers to a set of interrelated elements that act together in such a way as to maintain the whole through energy consumption and by adaptation as new information warrants it. What defines a system is its organizational stability over time, interacting within itself and between itself and its external environment. The human body is such a system, containing within the body several subsystems, such as the respiratory system, interacting with each other to maintain the body. The human is also a subset of a series of larger systems. In other words, a man or a woman is already living in a hierarchy of more extensive systems such as the political or the economic system on the larger scale and the local community on a smaller scale. The human is a system itself containing subsystems and is itself a subsystem of larger systems surrounding it and with which it interacts.

A system can be natural or contrived. A frog is a natural system. The temperature in a person's house is controlled normally by a contrived system, an artificial system regulated by the thermostat on the wall in order to control the amount of heat produced in the winter or the amount of cooling in the summer. A contrived system functions because it resembles a natural system—the interrelating set of parts are organized in such a fashion as to maintain the whole. Both kinds of systems can range in a hierarchy from the very simple to the very complex. The organizing principle will be the same even though the very complex system will require much more energy and more information to maintain itself. System maintainance, therefore, is a result of the organization of subunits for survival over time.

The problem that faces humans in the last quarter of the twentieth century is not the construction of such a global system, but the failure to realize that we already live in such a relation of global interdependence. This world-wide system requires conscious efforts by aware individuals in order to function without severe imbalances which could lead to disastrous crises such as a lack of food, or a lack of drinkable water. We live in and are a part of a hierarchy of systems. The apex is the world-wide system that operates in much the same way that any natural system does.[22]

The fact of human global systemness has not always been so obvious. Over time, human societies have gradually become more interdependent as the space between them has been deleted. Societies evolved from wandering hunters to agricultural communities, then to towns mixed with rural life, and to more extensive regional organizations. Next, these developed into national entities which by now are grouped into supranational regional organizations of which the multinational corporation, or Yugoslavs working in West Germany, are components. There is no doubt that humans now live in a global, interdependent system. However, there is also little doubt that what is still needed is a far greater amount of information so that the system can operate to avoid crises, and a vital second ingredient is a personal, individual awareness of the world-wide community.

First, a global information structure could be the apex of a complex hierarchically arranged set of information subsystems (the populations of nations or regions) that could take over the social steering if the international system were somehow to fail. Not a world government, but an information network which would feed data to the subsystems, down to the local level, and which could then receive information from the local level on up to the top. The international order would require large amounts of information. Statistical indices of resource availability and use as well as commodity distribution would be needed. This is human information or information relative to human survival over time. At the base of the complex structure would be local meetings or town meetings where information could be dispersed and gathered. Modern technology could easily transform these local meetings into efficient information-gathering devices. Higher groups in the pyramidal structure might consist of delegates chosen at the lower levels with easy recall procedures built into the system. These higher groups would gradually become fewer until the top of the structure was reached, staffed by humans chosen for their competence and reliability and by computers programmed for human needs. The world in balance could be the goal of the information organization and this would be consistent with the humanist promise of Marxism.[23]

Second, an understanding and awareness of the global system and the necessity of adequate information flows must be developed, for none of the solutions makes any sense unless people are educated to understand and approve. In other words, what needs developing is an educated personal and individual sense of community—a community that is local, regional, national, and global—the community of human beings. Until a person is aware that what happens in Kuwait or Tanzania or the Yukon is of vital significance to him or to her, these solutions will be meaningless. To impose them by coercion in the name of humanism would be paternalistic hypocracy.

The sense of the human community, moreover, is not unique to Marxism. Many philosophies and religions have taught a similar message along with other ideas, just like Marxism. Part of global interdependence may well be a new convergence of ideas and idea systems, previously thought to be mutually exclusive, in a grand confluence of humanism that not only knows where it is going but seeks the best way to get there.

Accomplishing a global information mechanism and a personal sense of community in individuals does not mean that everyone has to live or think alike. Nor would individualism or freedom be curtailed except in the sense of prohibiting people from exploiting the human and ecological resources of the world to their private advantage. Differences between peoples could easily remain and even be encouraged as adding to the richness of life. Many if not most of the old traditions could remain untouched—except for the notion that the stronger deserves the greater share or that some are more equal than others.

> To be more specific, it is necessary *to bind together everyone's lot;* to render the lot of each member of the association independent of chance, and of happy or unfavorable circumstance; *to assure to every man and to his posterity, no matter how numerous that may be, as much as they need, but no more than they need;* and to shut off from everybody all the possible paths by which they might obtain some part of the products of nature and of work that is more than their individual due.
>
> The sole means of arriving at this is to establish a *common administration;* to suppress private property; to place every man of talent in the line of work he knows best; to oblige him to deposit the fruit of his work in the common store, to establish a simple *administration of needs,* which, keeping a record of all individuals and all the things that are available to them, will distribute these available goods with the most scrupulous equality, and will see to it that they make their way into the home of every citizen.[24]

These stirring words of Babeuf were spoken nearly two hundred years ago, when he was on trial for his life because of his participation in the abortive coup against the Directory in 1796. His daughter had died of malnutrition while rich Frenchmen had developed gout. What did Babeuf mean in 1796? What might these words mean now? We *are* all bound together, we *can* establish a common administration of needs, we *can* distribute the available goods of world production with an eye to equality.

Although Babeuf's words can still move the reader's emotions, it is not necessary to seek an implementation of primitive egalitarianism in the future. One meaning of a more scientific humanism is the forsaking of panaceas. A global and humanized community will not necessarily mean the ending of crime or mental illness, for example. Nor need it be based on absolute egalitarianism in order to be humanistic. Indeed, Svetozar Stojanović may be correct in maintaining that such a distribution of social wealth provides no reconciliation between personal and social interests and that a combination of distribution according to one's labor as well as one's need might be more satisfying to the full range of human needs.[25]

The promise of a humanized global system is not for a heaven on earth, but a means of realizing the formerly tarnished promise of communism—that people would bring the forces surrounding their existence under their social control in a manner consistent with freedom and dignity for every living human.

Suggested Readings

Aronowitz, Stanley. *False Promises—The Shaping of American Working Class Consciousness.* New York: McGraw-Hill, 1973.

Bell, Daniel. *The Coming of Post-Industrial Society—A Venture in Social Forecasting.* New York: Basic Books, 1973.

Bennelo, C. George and Roussopoulos, Dimitrios, eds. *The Case for Participatory Democracy.* New York: Viking Press, 1971.

Ellul, Jacques. *The Political Illusion.* New York: Random House Vintage Books, 1967.

Kolakowski, Leszek. *Toward a Marxist Humanism—Essays on the Left Today.* Translated by Jane Zielonko Peel. New York: Grove Press, 1968.

Megill, Kenneth A. *The New Democratic Theory.* New York: Free Press, 1970.

The People Left Behind, A Report by the President's National Advisory Commission on Rural Poverty. Washington, D.C.: U.S. Government Printing Office, 1967.

Reischauer, Edwin O. *Toward the 21st Century: Education for a Changing World.* New York: Knopf, 1973.

Weisbrod, Burton A., ed. *The Economics of Poverty: An American Paradox.* Englewood Cliffs: Prentice-Hall Spectrum Books, 1965.

NOTES

[1]An example of a careful study of convergence is Alfred G. Meyer, "Theories of Convergence," in *Change in Communist Systems,* ed. Chalmers Johnson (Stanford: Stanford University Press, 1970) pp. 313-41.

[2]Adam Schaff, *Marxism and the Human Individual,* ed. Robert Cohen, trans. Olgierd Wojtasiewicz (New York: McGraw-Hill, 1970), pp. 169-70.

[3]See Bertell Ollman, *Alienation: Marx's Conception of Man in Capitalist Society* (Cambridge: University Press, 1971), esp. pp. 154-57.

[4]Herbert Marcuse, *One Dimensional Man* (Boston: Beacon Press, 1964).

[5]Louis Althusser, *For Marx,* trans. Ben Brewster (New York: Random House Pantheon Books, 1969), p. 241. Reprinted by permission of Pantheon Books, a Division of Random House, Inc.

[6]This is the Third Party Program, adopted for domestic and international political reasons, at the height of Khrushchev's optimism about Soviet achievements in 1961. It has been mentioned very infrequently in Russia since Khrushchev's ouster.

[7]Althusser, *For Marx*, p. 238. Reprinted by permission of Pantheon Books, a Division of Random House, Inc.

[8]Ibid., p. 235. Also see Maurice Cranston, "The Ideology of Althusser," *Problems of Communism* 22, no. 2 (March-April 1973): 53-60.

[9]André Gorz, *Strategy for Labor, A Radical Proposal*, trans. Martin Nicolaus and Victoria Ortiz (Boston: Beacon Press, 1967), p. 96.

[10]Ibid., pp. 96-97.

[11]Ibid., see esp. pp. 124 and 126.

[12]Ibid., p. 105. Reprinted by permission of Beacon Press.

[13]Roger Garaudy, *Marxism in the Twentieth Century*, trans. René Hague (New York: Charles Scribner's Sons, 1970), p. 57.

[14]Ibid., p. 61. Reprinted by permission of Charles Scribner's Sons.

[15]Ibid., p. 70; see also p. 73.

[16]Ibid., p. 75. Reprinted by permission of Charles Scribner's Sons.

[17]For a description of events in Gujarat, India, see *New York Times*, 22 April 1974, p. 2. See also ibid., 5 November 1974, p. 5; and 7 November 1974, p. 12, for example.

[18]In 1974 drought caused immense human suffering in Mauritania, Mali, Niger, Chad, Upper Volta, and Ethiopia. See James Reston, "Impeaching at Turtle Bay," *New York Times*, 24 April 1974, p. 37; and ibid., 16 November 1974, p. 8.

[19]Lyle P. Schertz, "World Food: Prices and the Poor," *Foreign Affairs* 52, no. 3 (April 1974): 513. Schertz's entire article, pp. 511-37, deserves mention as providing a great deal of information about the problem, some of which has been utilized in the previous paragraphs.

[20]Gerald A. Pollack, "The Economic Consequences of the Energy Crisis," ibid., p. 471. Copyright by the Council on Foreign Relations, Inc. Reprinted by permission of *Foreign Affairs*.

[21]Schaff, *Marxism and the Human Individual*, p. 176. The quotation is taken slightly out of context, but the contexts are similar and should elicit the same response.

[22]Ervin Laszlo, *A Strategy for the Future: The Systems Approach to World Order* (New York: George Braziller, 1974), p. 18. Distinctions made above between natural and contrived systems are adapted from Laszlo's distinction between natural and artificial systems.

[23]A great deal more information is available in Laszlo's remarkable book. The references to Marxism and the Marxist promise are my own additions to his systems model, but references to a broad, appealing humanism are his own. They constitute a *vital* part of his model. See also the suggestions in *New York Times*, 10 August 1974, p. 31; and 11 November 1974, p. 1. Also see V.G. Afanasyev, *The Scientific Management of Society*, (Moscow: Progress Publishers, 1971) particularly p. 125, for an example of how systems theory can be parochial: the scientific management of society is based on the leadership of the CPSU.

[24]"Babeuf's Defense—From the Trial at Vendôme, February-May 1797," in *Socialist Thought: A Documentary History*, ed. Albert Fried and Ronald Sanders (Garden City: Doubleday Anchor Books, 1964), pp. 67-68. Reprinted by permission of Doubleday & Company, Inc.

[25]Svetozar Stojanović, *Between Ideals and Reality*, trans. Gerson S. Sher (New York: Oxford University Press, 1973) p. 215.

Glossary

1. *Alienation.* An old word that has had a variety of meanings in its long history. The old Latin version referred to the legal transfer of property or, in a medical sense, a mental disorder. However, alienation in the modern context was first used in philosophy, specifically German Idealism, in the sense of an unnatural separation—a separation that ought not to be. In particular this referred to an externalization of self or reason that is treated as something distinct from oneself. Hegel used the concept to describe the unnecessary gap between the created world of cultural institutions and the self which was not aware of that world as self-creation surrounding the human. Hegel's entire philosophy is based on this notion of historical alienation and return. Ludwig Feuerbach placed alienation in a religious context by teaching that the divine entity was in fact an externalization of human essence, whose perceived distance from the human constituted alienation. The human, in other words, is separated from itself unnaturally, and can only overcome this loss by pulling that essence back to itself.

Marx took this Feuerbachian use of the term and expanded it to also include secular elements. For the religious principle, the unnatural externalization of self, occurred in many other areas as well, including political and economic life. Alienation was found particularly in human labor and was symbolized by the proletariat. In this most important area of human activity the creative force of a person's life stood apart from that person as an external, alien object, not expressive of human essence, but confronting humans as an other, as nonhuman. One of the major accomplishments of the projected proletarian revolution would be the overcoming of this alienation, and resulting history would therefore be truly *human* history because of that transcendence.

In the past few decades the term has been generalized to refer to our inability to control the complex phenomena that surround us, or, simply, our not feeling at home in our environment. In general the more humanistic interpreters of Marx stress the centrality of alienation in Marx's thought, and the less humanistic interpreters attempt to isolate the importance of the concept to Marx's early period but not to his writings after 1848. In addition, the stressing of the importance of the concept of alienation by both Communists and non-Communists is often a critique of the organization of contemporary communist systems as having departed from Marxian ideals.

2. *Anarchism.* Translating the word loosely from the Greek, it is the denial of the *arché* or overriding principle of organization. At the end of the eighteenth century and particularly in the nineteenth century anarchism came to be understood *positively* as a demand for a natural form of human organization as opposed to unnatural forms such as states or political organizations requiring coercion for their continued existence. As such, anarchism states emphatically that no liberty,

equality, or fraternity is possible so long as the state exists. The natural form of organization to which anarchism sought a return varied with individual anarchists, but because anarchism sought a return to a previous ideal of human life, and because it often counselled revolution as a means of bringing anarchism about, the anarchists formed a part of the socialist movement in the nineteenth century. However, this was an uneasy association that periodically broke apart.

Some anarchists stressed individualism very strongly. For example, William Godwin (1756-1836), Pierre Joseph Proudhon (1809-1865), and Max Stirner (1806-1856). Others were known more for their collectivist variants of anarchism, such as Mikhail Bakunin (1814-1876) and Peter Kropotkin (1842-1921). However, the distinction should not be taken too seriously. Proudhon advocated a mutualism of economic interchange that was not too distinct from the mutualism of Kropotkin. Also, some counselled violence as the means of attaining the natural state, while others urged a nonviolent approach. Bakunin advocated a society of free agricultural and industrial associations that was achievable only through violent action. On this point of the necessity of violent insurrection the Bakunists and the Marxists could apparently agree. Other anarchists, such as Godwin, Shelley (1792-1822), and Leo Tolstoy (1829-1910), stressed a nonviolent, ethical variant.

Marx was unable to long tolerate cooperation with the anarchists. He quickly turned on Proudhon maintaining that Proudhon did not understand Hegel or see things in their proper historical light. This can be viewed either as an ideological argument or as a pragmatic competition for the adherence of the French working class. Marx's later struggle with the Bakunists in the First International can be viewed simply as competition between two rival groups. The ideological dimension in which the struggle took place revealed fundamental differences over the desirability of the dictatorship of the proletariat subsequent to the proletarian revolution. The Bakunists argued against even this much state, however temporary Marx felt that it would be. This struggle was partially responsible for the death of the First International.

Anarchism stressed individual liberties so much that it had an impossible task in attempting to form any sort of unified movement for any length of time. In at least two senses it had enduring significance. First, particularly in Italy and Spain, and to some extent in France as well, anarcho-syndicalism blended the anti-state attitudes of anarchism with the notion of labor union dominance of society. Second, when the frustrations of some segments of the anarchist movement became overwhelming, policies of political assassination began to be adopted. A partially true stereotype quickly arose, depicting anarchists as being potential assassins.

3. *Babeuf, François Noël* (1760-1797). One of the leaders of the Conspiracy of Equals in its abortive coup in France in 1796. Babeuf, who was executed in May 1797, stood for a primitive communism that sought a solution for the problem of rich versus poor in the abolition of private property rather than its equalization. Calling Babeuf the father of European communism, however, might well be an overstatement, for in 1796 private property meant agricultural property, not industrial. Nonetheless, Babeuvism introduced the separation between the vaguer ideals of equality in the French democratic movement and the feeling that equality of consumption could only occur if regulated by the community as a whole. This

would require a temporary dictatorship in order to bring about a primitive equalitarianism—a reflection of the French revolutionary heritage. After Babeuf's death his ideas were transmitted to the French radicals of the nineteenth century by Philippe Michel Buonarroti (1761-1837), an Italian-born, naturalized French citizen who was a follower of Babeuf. Buonarroti provided a link between Babeuf and Louis-Auguste Blanqui, who is often credited with the notion of the dictatorship of the proletariat, merely a later version of the Babeuvist dictatorship of the people which in turn has roots in the Jacobin movement and in radical interpretations of Jean-Jacques Rousseau.

4. *Bellamy, Edward* (1850-1898), an American author who is chiefly known for his novels *Looking Backward* (1888) and a less successful sequel *Equality* (1897). These were socialist and utopian novels that stimulated the development of Bellamy clubs for a time. The novels revealed the nineteenth-century optimism about science eventually being able to replace all undesirable labor, and sought to answer every conceivable question that might be raised about a socialist society. If one likes old-fashioned romances, they make interesting reading. More significantly, Bellamy stands in the tradition of **Etienne Cabet** or the Utopian Socialists. Marx distinguished himself from this tradition by refusing as much as possible to articulate details of the future. This attitude, however, created other problems, as Edward Bernstein later pointed out.

5. *Blanqui, Louis-Auguste* (1805-1881) was a French radical in the Babeuvist tradition in the nineteenth century. He was very influential on the French left and spent nearly half his life in prison because of his revolutionary activities. He is often credited with the origins of the idea of the dictatorship of the proletariat. There is some doubt as to the accuracy of this claim, but there is also ambiguity in Blanqui's concept of what the proletariat was. In some cases he equated the term with toiler, which would include French peasants, thus constituting a majority of the French population. At other times he spoke of the necessity of first gaining the dictatorship and then appealing to the more conservative French peasant, leading interpreters to conclude that he advocated a minority dictatorship in the name of the majority. Whether deserved or not, this latter position is usually attributed to him. Blanquism in that sense is normally a pejorative term, standing for the alleged Jacobin-Babeuvist-Blanquist tradition of armed seizure of power by a minority, a position to which Lenin's name would later be added. Blanqui's influence was very strong in the Paris Commune of 1871.

6. *Bourgeoisie.* A term used by Marxists to denote the ruling class in a capitalist mode of production. It is, however, a fairly loose term which is sometimes used as a synonym for the middle class. The bourgeoisie was the agent class of the revolution alleged to have broken feudalistic modes of production, thus opening the way for the capitalistic mode. This class was, therefore, the driving force behind the industrial revolution, and the owner of the means of production in the capitalistic society. As such, the industrial bourgeoisie presupposes the existence of the proletariat, or the laboring force, which provides by its exploited labor the wealth of the bourgeoisie. The ideology of the bourgeoisie is classical liberalism. However, Marxists generally add quickly that this capitalist ideology will be discarded at the

slightest threat to bourgeois power. In other words, bourgeois society can be progressive by eliminating the privileges of an aristocracy, but it can also be reactionary. To the extent that the entrepreneurial function has been replaced in modern times by a managerial elite, Marx's concept of the bourgeoisie is less than satisfying. Similarly, the actual owners of the means of production may be small stockholders who themselves work for a living.

7. *Bukharin, Nikolai Ivanovich* (1888-1928) was a Russian Bolshevik of considerable reputation and influence. Born in Moscow, Bukharin became a Bolshevik in 1906, and after several arrests and exiles, during which he participated in radical socialist groups in other parts of Europe, he emigrated to the United States in 1916. In New York, Bukharin and Trotsky edited the socialist newspaper *Novyi mir.* Although both men returned to Russia in 1917, their work in the United States had an impact on the later development of the American Communist party. In Russia in 1917 Bukharin declared himself in favor of Lenin's position (April Theses) and led the Moscow Bolshevik uprising. In late 1917 and 1918 Bukharin led the left-wing faction of the Bolsheviks, opposing Lenin on such issues as the developing "worker's opposition" and the nationalities question. In 1921 he fully supported the New Economic Policy, and began to shift from the left to the right. His advocacy of socialism in one country in the mid 1920s eased Stalin's move to the right in 1925 and helped to seal Trotsky's fate. A full member of the Politburo after 1924, Bukharin enjoyed great popularity and possessed great authority because of his many official responsibilities (such as head of the Comintern after 1926), but also because of his intellectual abilities.

Differing from Stalin in 1928 over the abandonment of the NEP, he quickly lost favor and spent the last years of his life in relative obscurity. Arrested in 1937, he was charged with very serious crimes. In 1938 he was executed, a prominent victim of the purge. His place in Bolshevik history is an important one, for many of Lenin's theoretical positions were based on Bukharin's original analyses.

8. *Cabet, Etienne* (1788-1856) was one of the early utopian Socialist-Communists. He is perhaps best known for his utopian book *Voyage en Icarie* (1840), written while he was in England in exile from his native France because of his radical views. Icaria was an island, organized along communist lines. The novel described life where there was no inheritance; a progressive income tax; wages regulated by the state; eugenics applied to marriage; public education; and information disseminated by a state-controlled newspaper. The novel became very influential among the French working class, and a considerable Icarian movement developed. In the late 1840s the Icarians determined to move to America where they could set up such a society. Swindled by American land developers, they ended up in the middle of a wilderness where nearly everyone contracted malaria. Subsequently they attempted to organize a communal settlement at Nauvoo, Illinois, but they were never very successful. One of the reasons was that Cabet did not permit his settlers tobacco or whiskey and interfered with their private affairs in other ways. Cabet was one of the principal utopian Socialists, perhaps a major factor in Marx's attempt to distinguish himself from the utopians.

9. *Cadres.* A cadre is a framework or organization principle that was used in the 1790s by the French revolutionary government when it needed to incorporate many new and raw recruits into its military, without the old aristocracy, to form an officer corps. The new recruits were placed in a framework that included commissioned and noncommissioned officers, called cadres; in other words, the concept refers to a notion of military leadership of relatively inexperienced members by skilled individuals. The concept lay ready, therefore, for later use by the Bolsheviks, particularly in the context of administering Russia after 1917 with a minority party. This is a civilian or nonmilitary usage, but it refers basically to the same phenomenon, although occasionally it simply means leadership, or groups of leaders. Thus the term may refer to personnel qualified for leadership within a definite area. Since this is normally decided by agencies of the party or government in countries such as Russia, a cadres policy is simply a policy of determining that positions of responsibility are staffed by qualified and/or approved individuals. The higher the position, the higher the agency responsible for selecting the qualified individual. This overall system of leader selection is often referred to as the *nomenklatura* system wherein positions are listed according to which agency of the party must be consulted prior to a person's appointment. Most party members are cadres, and most cadres are party members because of party practice of co-opting non-party leaders into the party, but this can vary from country to country.

10. *Class.* This began to become an important word in the late eighteenth and early nineteenth centuries when it was used to denote role in the production process after the industrial revolution. Saint-Simon, Babeuf, and Lorenz von Stein described nineteenth-century society as basically a two-class milieu, and Marx was one of several Socialists who added the notion of *conflict* between the two classes (owners and nonowners of the means of production), a conflict that for Marx permeated society and history *dynamically.* Class antagonisms provided the push of historical movement both in the past and in the present. Marx was aware that there were classes other than the two basic ones which polarized the society. Examples would be the **petite bourgeoisie** (small businessmen) or lumpenproletariat (the dregs of the working class).

11. *Class consciousness.* An awareness of class position in one's society plus a desire in the oppressed class to end its class existence. Class consciousness thus connoted revolutionary readiness. Marx, with only a few exceptions, wrote as though he believed the proletariat capable of developing it. Lenin on the other hand came to believe that the workers would never develop more than spontaneity—a state far short of revolutionary consciousness. Hence, particularly for Lenin, there was the necessity of the party which contained the class consciousness *on behalf of the working class.*

12. *Collectivization of agriculture.* Marx felt that agriculture in the communism period would be operated in much the same way as the factory in the industrial sector, i.e., by collective, coordinated labor. In actual practice, however, Marxism came to be implemented in societies where socialism had to be constructed in the

industrial area. During that construction process it seemed inconsistent to allow private ownership of land to exist side by side with the social ownership of industry. Additionally, private control of land, crops, harvests, and so forth made it more difficult to extract exportable surpluses to finance rapid industrialization. Hence collectivization of agriculture refers to the process by which private farms are combined into collectives. The collectives were often given heavy delivery quotas which depressed incentives for collective farm laborers. A collective in Russia is a communal farm made up of former private farms, whereas a state farm is a communal farm carved out of new territory. On the former, the farmers are the people or families who live there, plus experts sent out from the center. On the latter, workers are brought in and work basically for wages as in a factory.

13. *Cominform* is a shorthand way of writing Communist Information Bureau. This organization was founded in September 1947 in Poland as a regional international group composed of delegates from Russia, Yugoslavia, Hungary, Poland, Czechoslovakia, Bulgaria, Rumania, as well as from the Italian and French Communist parties. It was formally dissolved in April 1956. Its headquarters in the beginning were in Belgrade, Yugoslavia, a reflection of Tito's domination of the Cominform in its early period. Two delegates from each Central Committee of the member countries comprised the Information Bureau which was set up to exchange information between countries and to maintain contacts. The journal of the Cominform, sent to the various countries, became a means by which the Moscow official line could be transmitted in the absence of the Comintern organization. In 1948 the conflict between Stalin and Tito emerged within the Cominform and the headquarters were moved to Bucharest, Rumania. The dissolution of the Cominform in 1956 coincided with the post-Stalin leadership's interests in international detente and peaceful coexistence.

14. *Commodity production.* The word commodity in Marxian parlance refers to a product of human labor that embodies a particular social relation, depending on the mode of production of that specific stage of human history. A commodity can be produced for use or for exchange. Since early human history, however, commodity production for exchange has led to an increasing gap between producer and thing produced, making commodity production (particularly in capitalism) synonymous with alienation. The embodiment of human labor (the product) confronts people as an alien object. The term is used most frequently with reference to capitalism and is often used pejoratively to express alienating relations of property.

15. *Cooperatives.* A cooperative is a voluntary, and sometimes involuntary, association of persons for the sake of jointly conducting some business so as to accomplish greater gains than could be realized individually. This may be as small as a car pool or as large as a farmer's grain cooperative. It can be an organization of producers or consumers, or a group set up to fight fires in the local area. Cooperatives are very widespread and almost impossible to count because no reliable statistics on their number exist. Marx felt that co-ops were a way to partially alleviate capitalist exploitation, but insisted that the cooperative principle was insufficient to overcome capitalism. In authoritarian systems membership is often

coerced, and in free market systems membership is usually voluntary even though a Marxist would point to the hidden coercion of economic relations in the allegedly free system that makes membership less than voluntary.

16. *Council for Mutual Economic Assistance* (Comecon) is an international economic organization established in 1949 that includes the following countries: Russia, Poland, Czechoslovakia, Rumania, Hungary, and Bulgaria. Albania and the German Democratic Republic joined in the following year. In 1962 Mongolia joined, and other countries such as Cuba function as observers at the meetings. Yugoslavia cooperates without being a member or an official observer. Comecon was the Soviet response to the U.S.-sponsored Marshall Plan, and it sought to redirect capital flow to Russia rather than to the West and to create a socialist world market that could compete favorably with the Western market. Part of the idea was economic specialization by different countries and a reduction of competition, but this was not simple to accomplish. Some countries such as Rumania resented being relegated to the status of agricultural supplier and proceeded with industrialization anyway. Poorer countries are supposed to be helped by richer ones, but this does not work particularly well. Comecon's headquarters are in Moscow, and attempts are made to coordinate rationally the economic plans of the member countries and to realize the benefits of economy of scale. In 1963 a Bank for International Economic Cooperation was formed to coordinate loans, credits, foreign exchange, and so on. Comecon has not been especially successful to date.

17. *Counterrevolution* is a term that developed during the French Revolution. It was used by Marx as well as by many others later to describe the efforts of allegedly bourgeois forces to prevent the proletarian revolution or to reverse it after it had captured power. Counterrevolution simply means antirevolution, and therefore often stands for right-wing or reactionary positions. In non-Marxist thought the word carries no particular pejorative connotation but merely describes activity designed to prevent a revolution.

18. *Cybernetics* refers to the science of control procedures. The word literally means "helmsman." Generally speaking, cybernetics refers to a controlled system in which information flow is a vital ingredient in the control and steering of the system seeking to maintain itself over time. One generally relies on engineering language to express cybernetic principles, but the ideas have applicability both to machines and to people. Cybernetic concepts are now normally referred to as systems theory, and the broadest concept (global) is a general theory of systems.

19. *Democratic centralism* is a principle of organization applied to all Communist parties modeled after Lenin's Bolsheviks. The term seeks to combine freedom and order, but is more centralistic than democratic. Under Lenin's leadership the Bolshevik party was infused with near military discipline. Democratic centralism was opposed by Rosa Luxemburg and initially by Trotsky even though he became an ardent democratic centralist later. By 1921 the centralism had conclusively triumphed over democracy in the party. In theory the phrase refers to the election of the higher body by the lower; the binding nature of the higher decisions

on the lower; an authoritarian center; and the permissibility of democratic debate on as yet undecided issues. In practice the notion of democratic centralism is a facade for authoritarian manipulation of the party by its leaders.

20. *Determinism* is the philosophic position that human decisions are definitely fixed by forces lying beyond the individual will. Its opposite in philosophy would be the unequivocal expression of free will. This enters into Marxism in the sense that natural and social phenomena as well as human consciousness—in their broad outlines—are said to be determined by material causes. Human history is determined by its material foundations, whose periodic alterations constitute historical materialism. Marxism is often described as economic determinism in that the mode of production fundamentally conditions everything else in the society. This can be understood as either a quite rigid sort of determinism or a more general sort. In the former case, everything else in the society is a result of the dominant mode of production or economic base in a straightforward cause-and-effect relationship; in the latter case, the situation described is not so simple, for the elements of the superstructure also act upon the material base even though in the final analysis the economic basis of the society dominates. Philosophical and humanistic Marxism lies in the latter category of determinism.

21. *Dialectic.* The dialectic began as a device by which a philosopher could lead another in the search for truth by pointing out that things were very often the opposite of what they appeared to be in experience. Truth was therefore discovered through the mediation or the balancing of opposites. The truth for Plato was the universal and eternal world of the forms, and seeking the truth was seeking the universal in the particular. In Aristotle the concept became formalized, and by the time of the Stoics the dialectic was a question and answer format of logic. However, when logic was hypostatized—universalized into the unifying principle of the cosmos, as with Hegel—the dialectic became the manner in which the universe developed, i.e., through the resolution of simultaneously contradictory elements. All this took place fundamentally in the mind (consciousness) or in thought. However, when Marx materialized Hegelianism the dialectic became the manner in which material history progressed (historical materialism) through the resolution of conflicts between antagonistic classes in the society. In Engel's mature years this was expanded with only limited assistance from Marx into the much larger principle of dialectical materialism.

22. *Dialectical materialism* is the name given to Engel's expansion of the notion of the dialectic into the world of nature and science as an objective law of evolutionary development, not just for history but for nature as well. In the world of nature the human is not surrounded by "things" so much as by "processes," and those processes develop dialectically through the resolution of conflicts into higher forms continually and inevitably. This expanded inevitability affected historical materialism as well, in the sense of reducing the human activity component in order to play up the inevitable progress of the dialectical process. This made socialism a *scientific* socialism with a comforting sense of inevitable triumph that inhibited voluntarism, and made socialist scientists force empirical data into the dialectical framework. Dialectical materialism is not accepted as correct by all Marxists.

23. *Economism* was a strain of Russian revisionism in the late nineteenth and early twentieth centuries. The term as used by Lenin was pejorative, and it applied to a group which felt that the proletariat ought to leave the bourgeois revolution (minimum program) in the hands of the bourgeoisie and concentrate on trade unionism and economic issues. Because the group avoided political action and emphasized action for economic gains only, its ideology was called economism. Indirectly, as with the Legal Marxists in Russia, this attitude helped to create the more moderate Menshevik position later.

24. *Finance capital* is a phrase useful in the description of the mechanics of imperialism as Lenin developed his ideas around 1916. Finance capital refers to that part of the expansion of capitalism toward monopolist state capitalism where the banks begin to play a very important role in financing capitalist expansion and in coordinating the formerly loose (anarchic) character of capitalist production.

25. *Fourier, François Marie Charles* (1772-1837). Charles Fourier was an eccentric pioneer of French utopian socialism. He combined a deep sense of sympathy for others with a desire to organize the minutiae of his proposed communities. The mixed industrial and agricultural associations (phalansteries) were voluntary communities that could be financed by private capital sold in shares. Work on the phalanstery would be done in common, and housing would also be common even though privacy was available for those desiring it.

Fourier did not propose strict equality—incomes would differ. The distribution of income was not left to chance, for capitalists would receive four-twelfths, laborers five-twelfths, and talent three-twelfths of the total. Disagreeable work would be paid at a higher rate, as would labor that was considered necessary as opposed to labor which produced luxuries.

Antedating later work concerning the dangers of repressing instincts, Fourier insisted that people should follow their passions or desires in their work and daily life. This meant that the work performed should never be boring but in line with a person's own interests. These interests, he believed, varied sufficiently so that all of the community work could be done without compromising the "follow the passions" principle. Dirty work would, of course, be done by those who liked to get dirty—the small children.

In daily life the following of the passions in these 1,600-1,800 member communities might often result in a weakening of marriage ties and an encouragement of free love. Fourier was very strong for female equality and had little sympathy for the institution of marriage (he was a bachelor). Children, nonetheless, were to be reared with great kindness and respect. The goal of his proposed communities was harmony—life without conflict.

26. *Guerrilla warfare* is an old concept that was used very effectively by Mao Tse-tung in his struggle against the Nationalists in China during the long period from 1927 until 1949 when he was finally successful. The concept implies that one's forces are numerically (or in some other way) weaker than the opposing force, so that the straightforward confrontation of forces probably would be disastrous. Because of this fact the war must be fought in a different way. One's army must not be too visible and for near invisibility the very active support of the indigenous population is vital. A successful guerrilla army is a popularly supported army. Its

near invisibility allows it to concentrate its forces at enemy weak points so that numerical or military superiority is on the side of the guerrillas. Guerrilla warfare is a commitment to long warfare wherein conclusive battles are normally avoided because of the very real danger of losing. Retreat—often thought of in traditional military terms as the last thing to do—becomes in guerrilla warfare a tactic of great importance. Attack at the opponent's weak point, inflict as much damage as possible, withdraw immediately before the enemy has time to muster his forces, and attack again at another weak point, periodically fading into the population until the danger of retaliation is lessened. It is a war of economic, political, and moral attrition rather than a decisive military confrontation, until the very end of the struggle.

27. *Humanism* may have reference to the revival of classical Greek and Roman studies that formed a part of the Renaissance and now underlies the meaning of "humanities" in the average university catalogue. Another related meaning of the word, however, refers to an emphasis in one's thinking on human conditions and the solution to human problems. Humanism need not be atheistic. A Christian humanist, for example, may seek to demonstrate divine love through activities which aim at bettering the human condition.

To Feuerbach and Marx, however, humanism meant atheism, for the affirmation of the human required the denial of everything that stood in the way of complete human fulfillment. Religion had to be negated but so also did private property. The human essence was understood as both natural and social. The attainment of harmonious unity between people and nature as well as between humans in their social life was the goal of Marx's revolutionary activities, and his humanism was his basic motivation. Marxian humanism, in seeking the fulfillment of the human essence, thus meant socialism; and socialism did not mean governmental ownership of production but people as species-humans controlling their own lives and destinies.

28. *Idealism.* A philosophic position with a very long history that seeks to locate basic reality in idea rather than in matter. Idealism understands the world of things as an approximation of an idea or as a particular manifestation of a universal or collection of universals which can be apprehended only in the mind. Idealism should be distinguished from a popular use of the term referring to an individual's high, sometimes utopian, goals. Philosophical idealism is a statement about where basic reality is located—in spirit or idea rather than in matter. Prominent idealists were Plato and Hegel.

29. *Ideology.* A systematic set of ideas that purports to explain reality, or a set of ideas that creates the parameters of individual consciousness in the sense of allowing the individual to feel that the perceived world is comprehensible and that his or her place in that world is also understandable. In the beginning the term was pejorative, and Marx normally used it in a negative manner. Since then, however, the term is more generally used. Marxism is an ideology, or can be. Christianity can be an ideological system. However, to Marx the term connoted false consciousness, as in the phrase "bourgeois ideology."

30. *Internationals.* There were four altogether. The first International Work-ingmen's Association began in 1864 and lasted into the 1870s. It was composed mainly of delegates from European countries, but other countries were repre-sented as well. From 1868-72 Marx was a dominant voice in The First Inter-national. Its demise was foreshadowed both by the Paris Commune of 1871 for which the International was unjustly blamed, and Marx's dispute with the Bak-unists which precipitated the moving of its headquarters to the United States to prevent a Bakunist takeover. It expired shortly thereafter. The Second Inter-national, from 1889 to 1914, did not fare much better. It was an effective coor-dinator of working-class socialist policy and dominated by the German group, but it was itself riddled with the problems of internal cohesion faced by the individual European parties. World War I, which demonstrated a victóry of nationalism over socialism in the Second International, effectively brought about its demise, even though attempts were made to revive it after the war.

The Third International was the Communist International or Comintern, be-gun by Lenin and the Bolsheviks in 1919 and dissolved by Stalin in 1943 as a con-cession to his wartime allies. The Comintern effectively split the labor movement into Communists and Socialists and quickly became a foreign instrument of So-viet domestic policy, often contradicting the Soviet desire for normal diplomatic relations with other governments. As a source of funds and political advice it func-tioned fairly effectively, but the advice usually made more sense in Moscow than in the country where it was to be applied.

The Fourth International is an anti-Stalinist international formed by Trotsky and his disciples in September 1938. This organization was crippled almost imme-diately by the emergence of World War II and the murder of Trotsky in 1940. Al-though still alive the Fourth International is politically and numerically in-significant.

31. *Iskra.* The Russian word for "spark," and the name of the newspaper that Le-nin and other émigré members of the Russian Social Democratic Labor Party in Swiss exile began in the early twentieth century. It was Lenin's initial belief that such a newspaper would centralize activity and thinking within Russia; fight revi-sionism or economism; and be a vehicle for bringing about the minimum and sub-sequently the maximum program. Difficulties emerged, however, for the members of the editorial board often spent much time debating with each other. Attempts to resolve the editorial board problem lay behind the 1903 split between the Bol-sheviks and Mensheviks at the Second Congress of the Russian Social Demo-cratic Labor Party.

32. *Marxism-Leninism* refers to the combination of Marx's and Lenin's ideas, or more precisely Marxism as understood by Lenin and its application to Russia in 1917 and subsequent years. The success of the Bolsheviks in winning power in Russia and in maintaining themselves over the years has given Marxism-Leninism a patina of correctness, making it apparently worthy of study and emulation. The term refers to the applicability of Marxism to semideveloped societies, particu-larly under conditions of imperialism, and to the dialectics of backwardness and theories of minimum and maximum programs. The chief impact of Marxism-

Leninism has been, therefore, the encouragement of revolutionary activity in the name of Marxism in underdeveloped societies. Marxism-Leninism also stands for a concept of revolution led by a party in the name of the proletariat, and a clear choice of the violent, insurrectionary path to socialism as opposed to the reformist, piecemeal approach. There have been attempts to continue the hyphenation, as in Marxism-Leninism-Stalinism, or Marxism-Leninism-Trotskyism, or Marxism-Leninism-Maoism, which have met with only limited acceptance. Marxism-Leninism continues to be the official ideology of the Soviet Union, however, not as motive for action so much as a post hoc rationalization in ideological terms of decisions made for more pragmatic reasons.

33. *Materialism* is a philosophical position which locates basic reality in physical matter rather than in idea or spirit. A materialist in this sense is not necessarily a person who seeks and finds his own identity and worth in the quantity of material goods he or she has acquired, but one who believes that ideas emanate from a material cause rather than the other way around. There are many kinds of materialists and what links them is the locating of basic reality in material things. In Marx's case, his materialism distinguished him from Hegel, and his "materialization" of idealistic Hegelianism (with the initial assistance of Feuerbach's transformational critique) constitutes the general frame of reference for Marxism. Locating basic reality in material things "concretized" Marx's philosophy so that he felt he was describing real people in real-life situations—the most important of which were their economic interrelations.

34. *Means of production* refers to the productive forces of any society. Laborers and instruments of production, such as simple or complex machinery and tools, constitute the means by which a society accomplishes that extremely vital function of producing. Obviously, owning the means of production gives great power to the owning class.

35. *Mode of production* is the way in which the means of production are organized in any given historical period. The mode of production describes the relationships within the production process. The components of the relationship are labor, workers, products, tools, technique, and ownership. A given mode of production expresses a definite relation between and among these elements. A product, for example, may be collectively owned or privately owned, produced by individual artisans or by collective labor in a factory system, and produced for exchange or for the satisfaction of needs without the intervening market. The organization of the productive forces of society has been characterized since very early history by a basic division of labor—separating the owners and nonowners of the means of production into two basic antagonistic classes. The mode of production periodically undergoes transformation through changes in commodity exchange and technology, laying the basis for social revolution.

36. *Monopoly capitalism* refers to that stage in capitalism's historical development where ruthless competition has reduced the number of capitalists and concentrated capital in the hands of the few who own most of the productive forces. When finance capitalism is added, monopoly capitalism becomes a major component of late capitalism in its imperialist phase—so characterizing the entire

economy that the developed nation stands over the undeveloped nation as the bourgeoisie does to the proletariat. In the absence of imperialism, or as a result of the breakdown of imperialism, monopoly capitalism is part of the death throes of that mode of production. Its efficient economy of scale has increasingly made human labor superfluous, thus decreasing the rate of profit, increasing both the size of the industrial reserve army and the potential gravity of inevitable crises because unemployed workers make very poor consumers.

37. *National Front* refers in particular to a subset of the Popular Front in those countries where conditions have created an opportunity for the Communist party to create a government of national unity which it controls in the name of a national coalition. The word "front" means "alliance" or "coalition." Similarly, a liberation front is a coalition of various groups unified by a desire to free a country or area from oppression. Neither a liberation front nor a national front need necessarily be undesirable. Obviously if one views all communist control as evil, a communist front is evil, and vice-versa. It needs remembering that not all Communists are alike—not all are Bolsheviks or Bolshevized—and that the radicalness of a particular front can be caused by its opposition.

38. *Negation (of the Negation)* is a philosophical concept older than Hegel but used particularly by Hegel to mean the denying of the denier, or negating the negator, *plus* a return to the beginning of the process. The term is used by Marx with reference to the abolition of private property in the proletarian revolution, or expropriating the expropriator. Private property in this sense is negating human life by artificially separating it—a consequence of earlier alienation. Abolishing private property thus denies the negator. Since Marx derived the concept from Hegel it is fair to ask whether Marx also intended the negation of the negation to represent a return to the beginning. There is a sense of reluctance in Marxism to admit this, but historical materialism does seem to *suggest* that all of history represents a departure and return to primitive communalism *plus* the technological achievements of the intervening years. Later, Engels extended the concept in dialectical materialism to the world of nature and science. Lenin and recent Russian philosophers have continued this attempt.

39. *Paris Commune* was an 1871 revolutionary organization of authority in Paris that sought to extend federations of autonomous communities throughout France. Some interpreted it as the final outcome of the French Revolution of 1789; others saw it as a precursor of proletarian revolutionary activity that culminated in the October Revolution in Russia in 1917. However it was interpreted, its ideological impact on socialism was profound for generations. It began in March 1871 as the Franco-Prussian War drew to a Prussian-dominated close. Paris was far less willing to surrender than the provinces; radical sentiments had been exacerbated by food shortages; and patriotism was stimulated by the evident weakness of Adolphe Thiers and the National Assembly. Dominated by Jacobin and Blanquist influences, the Parisian population gave strong support to the Commune, at least initially. In fact, part of the fascinating story of the Commune is the internal struggle between socialist radical democracy and centralist Jacobinism, with the latter eventually triumphing. The reassertion of control by the central French

government at Versailles in May 1871 cost the lives of some twenty-thousand men, women and children. The bloody suppression of the Paris Commune gave it additional ideological life. Marxism was not a major influence in the Commune. Besides Jacobinism and Blanquism, the ideas of Proudhon and Saint Simon were probably more in evidence than those of Marx. Some of the radicals, however, were members of or delegates to the First International—a body in which Marx was a major figure. Many of the Communards were not even working class.

40. *Personality cult* is a Russian reference to the way Stalin ruled the Soviet Union. In its more generalized form the expression stands for dictatorship, and adulation of the dictator in particular, which violate the principle of collegiality within the party. Hence collegial rule is generally counterposed to the cult of the personality with the former being viewed positively and the latter negatively. The cult of the personality came to be synonymous with Stalinism, particularly after Khrushchev's anti-Stalin speech in February 1956. The principle of collegiality in this context does not prevent a centralization of political authority in one person so long as that individual rules by and for the party. When hero-worship is encouraged, however, allowing the person to rule without the party, it is condemned as a personality cult.

41. *Petite bourgeoisie* was an expression that referred to the class of small businessmen and small shopkeepers, as opposed to large industrialists. This was one instance of Marx's class analysis of society evidencing more than the two polarities of bourgeoisie and proletariat. It was also a recognition that the small capitalist differed from the large, even though the ruthless competition of expanding capitalism would eventually force the petite bourgeoisie out of business and into the ranks of the proletariat.

42. *Popular Front* was both a tactic of the Comintern and a way of describing the activities of the indigenous communist parties. Begun in France in 1934, the Popular Front became an operational policy of the Comintern in 1935, particularly because of the perceived dangers of fascism or German militarism and the need for more cooperation, at least temporarily, with the nations of the West. Thus the move to the right, or the playing down of the revolutionary struggle in domestic European politics so as to reduce tensions between Russia and the West. As for the individual parties, the Popular Front (as in earlier moves to the right) allowed them to cooperate with socialist and other liberal parties in broad coalitions or fronts. The Chilean coalition of Salvadore Allende (1970-71) was also called the Popular Front (*Unidad Popular*). In Eastern Europe immediately after the end of World War II, the Popular Fronts became national fronts, and the various communist parties initially disguised their actual control by means of the facade of a coalition allegedly representative of the whole country.

43. *Pravda* is the Bolshevik newspaper begun in 1912 which, subsequent to the Bolshevik success in 1917, became the official organ of the Central Committee of the Communist party of the Soviet Union. The word means "truth." The other major Russian newspaper is called *Izvestia,* and is an organ of the Council of Ministers of the Soviet government. *Izvestia* means "news."

44. *Private property* in the Marxist sense is property that separates people from the natural social essence as humans. Private property is the consequence of already existing alienation, and once introduced it becomes a profound exacerbator of that alienation, resulting in an externalization of human essence in material commodities. Life becomes a race to acquire commodities; the number and worth of the possessed commodities determine the value of the human compared to that of other people. Private property thus is a fundamental separator of persons and a massive contributor to alienation. This is why communism could be defined as the abolition of private property or the abolition of artificial separators so that the social essence of humans could be regained. The fact that private property is particularly visible in the productive process means that it fundamentally affects all of life, hence the importance of the socialization of the means of production.

45. *Proletariat* referred particularly to the working class. In Marx's analysis, however, that working class or proletariat stood for much more than simply a word describing a class of people in the society. It stood for the nonowners of the means of production in the capitalist division of labor, and was often used as a synonym for oppression. The proletariat thus came to mean alienation in the special sense of representing the age-old human separation from human essence. To end its class oppression the proletariat must end its class existence, thereby ending alienation on a broader scale for all humanity. In other words, the term "proletariat" stands for a great deal in Marxist thought besides the empirical description of the industrial working class.

46. *Saint Simon* (1760-1825) was a Frenchman of enormous influence through his writings, his pupils, and his disciples. He urged the development of a science based on positivist empirical study (a line followed by his pupil, Auguste Comte) and encouraged an influential utopian socialism through the activities of his disciples Enfantin, Bazard, and Leroux. Saint Simon was not a socialist, but one who believed that the industrial revolution anticipated a new, third stage in human development—the technocratic—and that this would be the golden age of humanity. Thus Saint Simon could be said to favor both the capitalists *and* the workers, but his followers altered this into a variant of early socialism that was very influential in France and in the Rhineland area of Germany. Some of Marx's teachers were Saint Simonians; Marx's father-in-law may have been influenced by this type of socialism, and some of the backers of the *Rheinische Zeitung* were certainly Saint Simonians. The utopian side of Saint Simonian socialism would cause Marx later to reject it, but in addition Saint Simonism was turned into a mystical religious kind of movement as well, which gave Marx further reason for opposing it.

47. *State capitalism* can refer to a capitalist society in which the government plays an important role in the economy. However, the term is normally pejorative and applied (especially by Trotskyites) to the efforts to construct socialism and communism in the Soviet Union, where the means of production are owned by the state, and the function of the economy is what Marx imagined the historic role of capitalism to be—providing the wealth for socialism and communism. The socialism of Marx—i.e., the socialization of the means of production and the

dictatorship of the proletariat—should not result in state capitalism. The under-developed areas to which the Marxian concepts were applied, however, made state capitalism a perceived necessity. Although state capitalism, or a command economy stressing heavy industry, appears in many people's minds as synonymous with communism, there is no necessary correlation—unless by communism one means the Bolshevik variant.

48. *Superstructure* in Marxian terms refers to the forms of society that are constructed on and are a result of the dominant economic foundation of the society. In this view, the institutions of any society such as law, religion, morality, marriage, property, and so forth, are a reflection of the economic basis of the period. Even the consciousness of humans is a reflection of this base. Some have interpreted Marx in a fairly rigid fashion, insisting that what he meant was a thoroughgoing economic determinism that made everything in the superstructure a result of the economic cause. The causation arrows would then go only one way. However, Engels insisted that both he and Marx did not mean it to be so interpreted—that elements in the superstructure reacted on and caused alterations in the economic base, but that in the final analysis it would be clear that the principal element was in fact the economic one. Changes in the economic base necessitated alterations in the superstructure (historical materialism). The primary impact of the economic foundation in the society of the future accounts for much of Marx's expectations of the new and different character of people and institutions in socialism.

49. *Surplus value* was an important part of Marx's analysis of capitalism. According to the labor theory of value, the monetary value of any article was a reflection of the amount of socially necessary labor time expended in its manufacture. Supply and demand fluctuations were understood as departures from an average value over time. If, for example, a vase was valued at two dollars, this meant that the same amount of labor time was used to manufacture the vase as was spent in extracting two dollars worth of gold. Value was a direct reflection of human labor time. If this is granted, the market price of a commodity ought to reflect the labor time costs to the manufacturer. These costs were both fixed and variable. The fixed costs referred to raw materials and machinery, both of which contained congealed human labor time that had created their value and subsequent cost per unit in the manufacturing process. The variable costs were wages paid to workers. The average market price accurately reflected human labor time *but not human labor time costs,* for the manufacturer had not remunerated the workers for all of the commodities they had produced.

The wage paid to the worker did not reflect the value he or she had created. By prolonging or intensifying the working day, the manufacturer could increase the surplus value. The extra value made the market price higher than labor time costs derived from the exploitation of the work force by the capitalist. This was a deplorable necessity so that capitalism could perform its historic role. Surplus value may be loosely understood as profit, but the two terms are not identical.

50. *Totalitarianism* is a term popularized by Carl Friedrich and Zbigniew Brzezinski in their book, *Totalitarian Dictatorship & Autocracy,* first published by

Harvard University Press in 1956. A second edition appeared in 1965. A Praeger paperback was published in 1961, and again in 1966 for the second edition. Totalitarianism purported to be a model of communist and fascist societies. These societies, the authors felt, where characterized by the following elements: 1) an officially adopted, elaborate ideology that focused on a perfected future; 2) a single mass party consisting of a small minority of the population and led by a dictator; 3) a technologically modern system of terroristic rule through party and secret police; 4) a near complete control of all forms of mass communication; 5) a near complete monopoly of effective weapons of armed combat; and 6) a bureaucratically organized and centrally controlled economy. In addition, the authors felt that totalitarian societies were historically novel.

Subsequent scholarship has questioned the applicability of the model to fascist societies, and has suggested that the model really fits only the Stalin period of Bolshevik rule in Russia or selected periods in other countries. The model is therefore historically limited unless one uses the word "totalitarian" to refer pejoratively to any authoritarian dictatorship without specific reference to the model's components. Such a loose use of the term makes it a descriptive adjective that has no necessary relation to the original model. Clearer descriptive words are available and should be used.

51. *Trotsky,* or Lev Davidovitch Bronstein (1879-1940), was one of the very influential figures in Russian communism. Already an active revolutionary at the time of the split between the Bolsheviks and the Mensheviks, Trotsky at first sided with the Mensheviks and then attempted to occupy a center position to facilitate the reconciliation between the two factions. He did not become an active Bolshevik until mid-1917, and his previous anti-Lenin writings and attitudes as well as the high position Lenin created for him in the party developed a widespread resentment among other Bolsheviks. An eloquent orator and a fervent revolutionary, Trotsky was invaluable in the Bolshevik seizure of power in 1917, and his leadership of the newly formed Red Army during the civil war period was a prominent factor in the Bolshevik victory. In the early twenties, however, he was curiously unwilling to assume a status that might well have placed him in line for the leadership when Lenin died, and he was absent from Moscow at the time of Lenin's death. His arrogance alienated many Bolsheviks besides Stalin, but that arrogance was subordinate to his strong sense of party unity, especially after the formal prohibition of factionalism in 1921. Trotsky was the chief reason for and victim of Stalin's political maneuvering in the 1920s, and he was eventually forced into exile where he became a rallying point for pro-Leninist but anti-Stalinist communists. Trotsky was murdered in Mexico in 1940, allegedly by a trusted individual who was an agent of Stalin. An entire wing of the socialist-communist movement has grown up around his name.

52. *Utopian socialism* was a variant of socialism which Marx greatly disliked. Two elements in particular characterized utopian socialism. First, a desire to describe socialism in precise detail, seeking to answer every conceivable question that a person might have about the future society, which had the effect of locking that society into the image of the futurist. Second, utopians failed to set socialism

into an empirical base, advocating socialism because it would be desirable and not because it necessarily flowed from historical development. Utopian socialism was therefore a socialism of the imagination rather than the socialism of the real world, and it bore no necessary relation to historical possibility. Nonetheless, the capacity of utopian socialists in firing the imaginations and desires of the proletariat was profound.

53. *Vanguard* refers to the group on the leading edge of a movement, the leading subset of the larger movement. In the *Manifesto* the Communist League was thought to be such a vanguard, alone knowing the line of march for the proletariat. In Lenin's thinking, the party was the vanguard that bore the revolutionary consciousness which the proletariat by itself was unable to develop. As such, the vanguard party stood for the proletariat and performed its historical role in the name of the working class.

54. *War communism* was evident in the 1918-21 period in Russia during which the introduction of socialist measures through decrees established a necessary emphasis on control of society in order to fight the civil war. War communism, therefore, refered to a narrowing of the concept of revolution or a widening of the concept of counterrevolution; a retreat from such innovations as worker control of industry; the introduction of former capitalists to manage some industries; the forced requisition of grain from the countryside; and the creation of the Red Army along traditional military lines (nondemocratic) and with ranks clearly distinguished. War communism was replaced in 1921 by the New Economic Policy.

55. *Warsaw Pact* or the Warsaw Treaty Organization refers to the 1955 formation of a military bloc of Russia and East European countries that replaced the unilateral defense treaties Russia had developed with individual satellite countries. The Warsaw Pact, a mutual defense organization, was not so much a response to NATO which formed in 1949, but to the American decision to rearm the Federal Republic of Germany in 1954, making it part of the NATO or anti-Soviet alliance. Of particular danger, from the Russian point of view, was Eisenhower's and Dulles' evident intention of giving the Germans nuclear weapons. The Warsaw Pact military force was ostensibly the occupier of Czechoslovakia in 1968.

Index

Absolute general law of capitalist accumulation, 43-44
Abundance, 42, 44, 56-57, 59, 106-7
Action Program (Czechoslovakia), 141
African socialism, 171, 207
Agitation, On (1894 pamphlet), 92-93
Agriculture and survival 221-24
AIM movement. *See* Bank, Dennis
Albania, 130, 132
Alexander II (Tsar), 87, 90
Alienation, 14-15, 23, 25-31, 39, 42, 47, 51, 54, 165-66, 203, 215, 217, 231
Allocation of resources under communism, 58-60, 105, 227-28
Althusser, Louis 217-18
American Communist party, 195-201
Anarchism, 52, 55, 231
Anarcho-syndicalism, 69
Antithesis. *See* Triad
April Theses (Lenin), 98
Asiatic Society, 38
Association (Communist), 55-61, 105-6
Atheism, 22, 23, 25, 28, 29, 51, 90, 240
Atomic bomb, atomic arms, 125, 134, 137, 161, 248
Authoritarianism. *See* Elitism
Authority, in Marx's future communism, 52-56

Babeuf, François Noël, 9, 232
Backward countries, socialism in, 97, 98-99, 104-5, 106-7
Backwardness, dialectics of, 97
Bakunin, Mikhail, 24, 52, 232, 241
Bank, Dennis (AIM movement), 208
Batista, Fulgencio, 177, 178
Bauer, Bruno, 22, 23
Bay of Pigs, invasion of, 179
Bazard, Saint-Amand, 245

Bebel, August, 66, 73, 75, 76
Bellamy, Edward, 195, 233
Berlin blockade, 129
Bernstein, Eduard, 74-75, 88, 186
Bismarck, Prince Otto von, 66, 67
Black Liberation movement, 201, 202, 208
Blacks, American, 201, 202, 205, 207, 208
Blanqui, Louis-Auguste, 68, 70, 233, 244
"Bloody Sunday," Russia, 95
Bolshevik revolution, 98-99
Bolsheviks, 94, 95, 96, 98, 99, 104, 106-9, 111, 114, 115, 116
Borodin, Michael, 155
Bourgeoisie, 10, 29, 40, 42-46, 89, 233
Bourgeois revolution, 40, 89, 95, 96, 155
Boxer Rebellion, 152
Brest-Litovsk, Treaty of, 107, 116
Brezhnev, Leonid I., 141
Brousse, Paul, 68-69
Bukharin, Nikolai, 114, 234
Bulgaria, 125, 133, 141
Buonarroti, Philippe M., 9, 233

Cabet, Etienne, 233, 234
Cadet party. *See* Constitutional Democrats
Cadres, 163, 235
Canton regime (China), 155
Capitalism, 1, 31, 37, 40-44, 68, 86, 203
Castro, Fidel, 178-82, 202
Chartism, 4
Cheka, 108-9
Chen Tu-hsiu, 156
Chiang Kai-shek, 155-57
Chicano, 217
Chile, 171, 182-86
Chinese Communist party, 154, 156-63
Christianity, 15, 16, 22, 26, 68, 83, 106, 149, 151, 205, 216
Chu Teh, 156

Civil war: Russia, 106-11; China, 155-58
Class, 23, 27, 30, 39, 46, 51, 75, 207,
  217, 235; conflict, 30, 38, 44, 46, 47, 51,
  93; consciousness, 40, 92, 94, 154, 235
Classless society, 51-61, 105-6, 207
Coexistence, peaceful, 134, 161
Cold war, 125-34, 159, 171, 207, 213
Collectivization (agriculture), 117, 131,
  159, 160-61, 235-36
Cologne Gazette. See *Rheinische Zeitung*
Comecon. *See* Council for Mutual
  Economic Assistance
Comintern Program (1928), 117
Commodity production, 42, 236
Communism, primitive, 37, 38, 60, 243
Communist front, 117, 127, 243
Communist Information Bureau
  (Cominform), 130, 136, 236
Communist International (Comintern),
  104, 115-18, 154, 155, 156, 157, 241
Communist League, 31, 103-4
Communist Manifesto, 31, 103, 156
Communist party of the Soviet Union
  (CPSU), 104, 161
Comte, Auguste, 245
Concentration, of labor camps, 118, 119,
  129
Confucianism, 149-50, 166
Conspiracy of the Equals, 9, 24, 232
Constitutional Democrats, 94, 108
Constitution, Soviet (1936), 119
Containment policy, 128, 133
Contradictions, Mao's Theory of, 158,
  159, 162, 166
Convergence, Theory of, 209, 214
Cooperatives, 75, 236-37
Corn Laws, 2
Cottage industry, 1
Council for Mutual Economic Assistance
  (Comecon), 129, 237
Counterrevolution, 52, 109, 237
Crimean War, 86
Crises, economic, 44, 45
Critique of the Gotha Programme, 32, 67
Croce, Benedetto, 186
Cuba, 177-82
Cuban missile crisis, 179-80
Cultural Revolution (China), 163, 164
Cybernetics, 220, 237
Czechoslovakia, 128-29, 132, 141-42

Daily Worker, 200
Davis, Angela, 201
Decembrists, 85
De Leon, Daniel, 77
Democracy, 23, 31, 47, 54, 55, 105, 108,
  218, 219

Democratic centralism, 94, 237-38
Democratic Centralists, The, 112
De-Stalinization, 135, 137, 138, 139, 140,
  160
Determinism, 36, 238; economic, 36-37, 46
Dialectic, 13, 14, 24, 35, 36, 37, 38, 39, 40,
  42, 43, 44, 154, 219, 220
Dialectical materialism, 165, 238
Dictatorship of the proletariat, 52, 53, 54,
  109, 162
Division of labor, 30, 39, 40, 55
Djilas, Milovan, 175
Doctors' Club. *See* Young Hegelians
Draft resistance (American), 203, 208
Dubcek, Alexander, 141-42
Dulles, John Foster, 134, 137, 139
Duma, 96, 98
Dzerzhinsky, Felix E., 72

East Germany (German Democratic
  Republic), 133, 134, 141
Economism, 93, 239
Education, in communism (multi-
  dimensional), 57, 105-6
Egalitarianism, in communist future, 9,
  58-60, 105-6, 224, 227-28
Eisenachers, 46, 66
Elitism, 46, 70, 94, 106, 154, 156, 198, 224,
  233
Emancipation of Labor Group, 88
Enfantin, Barthélemy-Prosper, 245
Engels, Freidrich, 4, 24, 32, 36, 45, 46, 47,
  56, 57, 60-61, 66, 70, 74, 238
English socialism, 4, 70-71, 77-78
Equality. *See* Egalitarianism
Erfurt Program, 67, 68
Escalante, Anibel, 179
Essence of Christianity, 22, 24-25
Estates (French classes), 5-6
Estonia, 107, 123

Fabian Society, 70, 74
Factionalism, prohibition of (CPSU),
  112-13
Factory Acts, 3
Famine (Russia), 91, 113
Farmer Labor party (America), 197
Fascism, 117, 118
February Revolution in Russia, 97-98
Federal Republic of Germany. *See* West
  Germany
Feudalism, 37, 39-40
Feuerbach, Ludwig, 22, 24-25
Finance capitalism. *See* Imperialism
Finland, 107, 108, 171
Five Year Plans, 117, 118, 130, 160
Food supplies, 221-24
Fourier, François-Marie-Charles, 24, 239

Franco-Prussian War, 67, 243
"Freemen." *See* Young Hegelians
French Revolution, 1, 5-10, 16, 30, 45, 224

Gans, Eduard, 21
Gapon, Father Georgi, 95
Garaudy, Roger, 219-20
General strike, 69-70, 73, 134
General Theory of Systems, A, 225-28
"Gens" period. *See* Historical materialism
German Democratic Republic. *See* East
    Germany
German Idealism. *See* Hegelianism
German Social Democratic party, 46,
    66-68, 73-76
Germany, 4-5, 31, 47, 65, 66-68, 73-76,
    106, 115, 117, 123, 124, 125, 126
Global interdependence, 225-28
Gomulka, Wladyslaw, 132, 138, 140
Gorz, André, 218-19
Gotha Program, 67, 68
Gramsci, Antonio, 186-87
Grand National Consolidated Trades
    Union (1834), 4
Great Leap Forward, 160-62
Great Proletarian Cultural Revolution,
    163, 164
Great Purge, 118
Greece, 125, 128, 133
Griffuelhes, Victor, 70
Groppi, Father James, 205
Grundrisse, 31
Guerrilla warfare, 156, 239-40
Guesde, Jules, 68, 69, 73, 77
Guevara, Ernesto Che, 180, 202
Guild socialism, 77

Hegelianism, 1, 11-16, 20, 21, 25, 28, 35,
    36, 66, 150
Hess, Moses, 23-24
Historical materialism, 30, 35-49, 165, 216
"Historic Bloc" (Italian Communist
    party), 187
Hobson, John A., 96
Ho Chi Minh, 127-28
Humanism, 28, 29, 51-52, 138, 178, 182,
    214, 216, 217, 218, 220, 224, 226, 227,
    228, 240
Human nature, under communism, 53-54,
    105, 166
Hundred Flowers campaign, 160
Hungary, 125, 128, 132, 139-40, 160
Hyndman, H. M., 70

Idea, absolute. *See* Hegelianism
Idealism, 11, 13, 23, 240. *See also*
    Hegelianism
Ideology, 9, 45, 153, 165, 216, 240

Imperialism, 96-97, 106, 154, 179, 239, 242
Incentives for work, economic or material,
    58-59, 165, 227-28
Independent Labour party, 69, 71, 77
Independent Socialist party, 76, 78
Industrial reserve army, 43
Industrial revolution, 1-5, 10, 16
Industrial Workers of the World (IWW),
    195-96
Internationals: First, 32, 46-47, 241;
    Second, 65, 68, 69, 72, 76, 79, 104, 241;
    Third. *See* Communist International;
    Fourth, 241
Intervention, Allied (Russian Civil War),
    107
Iskra, 93, 114, 241
Isvestia, 244
Italian Communist party, 172, 186-89

Jacobins, 8, 233
Japan, 124, 127, 152, 153, 213
Jaures, Jean, 76
Journey to Icaria, 232
Judaism, 19, 26, 85, 92, 205

Kant, Immanuel, 11-12
Karakhan Proposal, 154
Kautsky, Karl, 73, 74, 75, 76, 88
Kennedy, John F., 179
Khrushchev, Nikita S., 113, 135, 137, 138
    139, 140, 141, 160, 161, 162, 179
Korea, 125, 127, 128, 133, 152, 159
Kosygin, Aleksei, 141
Kremer, Alexander, 92
Kronstadt rebellion, 111, 112
Kulaks, 119
Kuomintang (KMT), 117, 152, 155, 156

Labor, 28, 29, 30, 41, 42, 43, 57; discipline
    of, 56, 57, 58, 105, 227; Theory of Value,
    41; unions, 4, 66, 68, 69, 70, 71, 76, 77,
    87, 94, 108, 111, 185, 188, 195, 198, 199,
    217
Lasalle, Ferdinand, 66, 67
Latin America, 172, 177, 180, 181
Latvia, 107, 123
League of German Workers' Educational
    Societies, 66
Left socialist revolutionaries, 94, 108
Leisure time, in communism, 60
Lenin, Vladimir Ilyich, 70, 72, 74, 78,
    89-99, 103-6, 108-14, 142, 154, 186, 202,
    203, 233, 234, 235, 237, 239
Liebknecht, Karl, 78
Liebknecht, Wilhelm, 66, 67, 68, 73, 75
Life of Jesus, 21
Li Ta-chao, 156
Lithuania, 92, 107, 123

Long March, 157
Lopez, Luis Corvalan, 182
Lublin committee, 126, 127
Lukács, George, 188-89
Luxemburg, Rosa, 72, 75, 76, 78

Macarthur, General Douglas, 153, 169
    (n. 10)
McCarthy, Joseph, 133
Mao Tse-tung, 137, 149, 151, 156-60,
    162-67, 180, 239
Marcuse, Herbert, 201, 202, 203
Marshall Plan, 129
Martov, Y. O., 89, 92, 93
Marxism, 1-79, 88-89, 118, 153, 165, 176,
    177, 183, 189, 203, 207, 214, 215-221,
    226
Marxism-Leninism, 136, 154, 156, 207,
    215, 218, 241-42
Materialism, 11, 36, 242
Maximum and Minimum Programs, 89,
    95, 96, 99
May Day, 69, 72, 114
May Fourth movement, 154
Means of production, 52, 53, 54, 58, 242
Mir, 86, 88
Missionaries, in China, 151, 152
Mode of production, 52, 242
Monopoly capitalism. See Imperialism
Morris, William, 70

Nagy, Imre, 139-40
Napoleon, 9
Narodniki. See Populists
NATO, 133
National Front, 127, 243
Naturalism, 28
Nature, 13, 14, 28, 54, 61
Nazi-Soviet Nonagression Pact, 123
Negation (of the negation), 44, 243
Neue Rheinische Zeitung, 31
Neue Zeit, 73
New Economic Policy (NEP), 113, 115,
    117
New Left, 201-9
Nicholas II, 97, 98
Nixon, Richard M., 134
Nomenklatura, 235
Northern Union of Workers, 87
Novotny, Antonin, 141

October Revolution, 98-99
Offshore Islands, Quemoy and Matsu, 161
Oil crisis, 222-23
Open Door policy, 152
Opium War, 151

Óriental despotism. See Asiatic society
Overpopulation, 221
Overproduction, 44
Owen, Robert, 4, 71

Palmer, A. Mitchell, 196
Paris Commune, 55, 67, 68, 106, 246
Peasantry, 46, 66, 68-69, 84, 85, 86, 87, 88,
    91, 98, 107, 111, 113, 149, 152, 156, 157,
    159, 164
Pelloutier, Fernand, 70
Permanent revolution, 95, 115
Personality Cult, 135, 244
Peter the Great, 83
Petite bourgeoisie 235, 244
Planning: economic, 56, 57, 58, 59, 60, 117,
    118, 130, 226-28; in communism, 56-58
Plekhanov, Georgi, 71, 72, 88, 89, 91
Poland, 8, 65, 71-72, 75-76, 78, 107, 117,
    123, 126-27, 128, 137-39, 140, 141, 160,
    200
Popular Front, 117, 118, 182, 244
Population control, 221
Populists, 86, 88, 92, 129, 197
Possibilists, 69
Potresov, A. N., 89, 93
Pravda, 96, 135, 136, 244
Praxis, 21, 22, 23, 216
Praxis (Zagreb journal), 176
Predictions, Marxist, 45-46, 215-16
Private Property, 26, 29, 30, 51, 53, 54
Production, 30, 35, 36, 37, 38, 41, 42, 43,
    44, 54, 57
Products of Labor opposing Laborer,
    28-29
Proletariat, 24, 27, 29, 30, 46, 51, 73, 87,
    89, 93, 95, 96, 99, 154, 158; increasing
    misery of, 43-45, 46, 51; revolution of,
    44-45, 51, 73-75, 89, 94
Promise of Communism, 26, 28-29, 51-61,
    215, 228
Proudhon, Pierre J., 232
Provisional Government (Russia), 98
Purges. See Great Purges

Quod Apostilici Muneris, 67

Radek, Karl, 115
Rakosi, Matyas, 139
Reason, 10, 12, 14
Red Army, The, 106, 107, 108, 124, 126,
    130, 140, 142, 171
Red Guards, The, 163
Red Scare, The, 195-96
Reform, rather than revolution, 47, 65, 67,
    70, 71, 73, 74, 78, 154, 183, 188
Reification, 24-25, 26, 28, 29, 216, 219

Reign of Terror, 8
Relations of production, 36, 37, 38, 40, 41,
    42, 44, 53, 61
Religion, 10, 16, 21-29, 51, 205, 226
Revisionism: Bernsteinian, 74-75;
    Khrushchevian, 162
Revolution: of 1848 (Europe), 31; of 1911
    (China), 152; of 1905 (Russia), 95-96;
    of 1917 (Russia), 97-98, 153, 196
Rhee, Syngman, 127
Rheinische Zeitung, 23-24
Rhineland, 10, 19, 21, 23
Robespierre, Maximilien, 8
Romanov Dynasty, 98
Romantic Revolution, 10-11
Roosevelt, Franklin D., 124, 199
Rousseau, Jean Jacques, 6
Ruge, Arnold, 22, 27
Rumania 125, 141, 237
Russian Social Democratic Labor party,
    93, 94
Rykov, Alexii, 114

Saint Simon, 11, 21, 245
Schaff, Adam, 220, 224
Self-estrangement. See Alienation
Serbia, 175
Serfs, 39, 84, 85, 86
Siberia, 89, 93
Simbirsk, 89
Sino-Soviet conflict, 137, 155-56, 160-62
Slave society, 38-39
Smith, Adam, 43, 156
Socialism 21, 23, 24, 44, 66, 67, 68, 70, 74,
    77, 103, 104, 105, 106, 110; Ricardian,
    4; scientific, 53, 238; utopian, 31, 55,
    247-48
Socialism/Communism, French, 68-70,
    76-77, 115, 171
"Socialism in One Country," 115, 116
Socialist Revolutionary party, 94, 108
Sorel, Georges, 69
South Russian Union of Workers, 87
Soviet of Workers and Soldiers Deputies,
    98
Spark, Theory of the, 95, 116
Spartacus League, 78
Species Human, 25-26, 28-29
Spirit. See Idealism
Spontaneity, 94, 235
Stalinism, 109, 132, 137, 141, 172, 181,
    202
Stalinists, 138, 139, 141
Stalin, Joseph V., 113-19, 123-35, 140, 142,
    154, 157, 160, 162, 172, 178, 199, 200,
    244, 247
State, 15, 16, 22, 23, 26, 44, 52-53, 54, 175

State capitalism, 119, 245-46
Stein, Lorenz von, 24
Strauss, David F., 21
Strikes, 71, 72, 76, 77, 87, 92, 93, 94, 95,
    97, 134, 137, 185, 188
Subbotniks, 110
Suffrage, universal, 26, 27
Sun Yat Sen, 152, 155
Superstructure, 37, 246
Surplus value, 41-42, 73
Switzerland, 67, 88
Syndicalism, 69, 70, 76, 77
Synthesis. See Triad, Hegelian

Taiping Rebellion, 151-52
Taoist, 154, 166
Telescoping Revolutions, blurring
    minimum-maximum programs, 95, 96,
    99, 104
Third International. See Communist
    International
Tito, Joseph Broz, 129-30, 131, 132, 133,
    134, 138, 140, 176, 236
Tolstoy, Count Leo N., 232
Tomsky, Mikhail P., 114
Totalitarianism, 221, 246
Triad, Hegelian, 12-15
Trotsky, Leon, 89, 95, 96, 98, 107, 111,
    112, 114, 115, 118, 207, 234, 237, 241,
    247
Truman Doctrine, 128, 129, 133
Truman, Harry S., 125-26, 128
Twenty-one Conditions, for Comintern
    Membership, 104, 116, 199
Twenty-Sixth of July movement, 178, 179

Ukraine, 107
Ulbricht, Walter, 141
Ulyanov, Alexander Ilyich, 90
Ulyanov, Vladimir. See Lenin
Underconsumption, 43, 44
Unemployment compensation, in
    communism, 58
Uneven development. See Imperialism
Union of the Public Good, 85
United Nations, 127

Value. See Labor, Theory of
Vanguard, 93, 248
Vietminh, 127-28, 133
Vietnam, 127-28, 133, 201, 202, 203, 204,
    206, 208, 223
Vilna Organization, 92-93
Violence, revolutionary, 46-47, 73, 74-75
Voyage en Icarie, 232

War communism, 108, 248
Warinski, Ludwig, 71
Warlords (China), 151, 155
Warsaw Pact, 140, 142, 248
Weakest link. *See* Imperialism
Weimar Republic, 78
Westernizers (in Russia), 86
West Germany, 133, 134, 248
Withering away of the State, 52-53
Women, in communism, 57-58
Women's liberation, 208
Workers' control of industry, 69-70, 98,
    108, 172, 218-19
Workers' Councils, 173-74, 175

Workers' Opposition, 111-12, 113
Working Class. *See* Proletariat

Yalta Conference, and Agreement, 124,
    126, 127
Yenan, 157, 162
Yin-yang, 154, 158, 166
Young Hegelians, 16, 20, 21, 22, 23, 32
Yugoslavia, 128, 129-32, 135, 160, 171,
    172-77

Zinoviev, Grigori, 114
Zollverein, 5